WORDS
of
WISDOM

MORE GOOD ADVICE

Compiled and Edited by

WILLIAM SAFIRE
and
LEONARD SAFIR

A FIRESIDE BOOK
PUBLISHED BY SIMON & SCHUSTER INC.

New York · *London* · *Toronto* · *Sydney* · *Tokyo*

FIRESIDE

Simon & Schuster Building
Rockefeller Center
1230 Avenue of the Americas
New York, New York 10020

First Fireside Edition, 1990

FIRESIDE and colophon are registered trademarks
of Simon & Schuster Inc.

Designed by Irving Perkins Associates, Inc.
Manufactured in the United States of America

10 9 8 7 6 5 4 3 2 1

10 9 8 7 6 5 4 3 2 1 Pbk.

Library of Congress Cataloging in Publication Data

Words of wisdom: more good advice/compiled and edited by William
Safire and Leonard Safir.
p.   cm.
Includes index.
1. Conduct of life—Quotations, maxims, etc.   2. Quotations,
English.   I. Safire, William, 1929–   .   II. Safir, Leonard.

PN6084.C556W66   1989   88-31336
082—dc 19   CIP

ISBN 0-671-67535-4

ISBN 0-671-69587-8 Pbk.

To
John Reagan ("Tex") McCrary
who gave us our start

Ask counsel of the Ancients, what is best; but of the Moderns, what is fittest.
—Thomas Fuller

Learn . . . learn the motions of the mind,
Why you are made, for what you are design'd,
And the great moral end of human kind.
Study thyself, what rank, or what degree
The wise Creator has ordain'd for thee:
And all the offices of that estate
Perform, and with thy prudence guide thy fate.
—Author unknown

CONTENTS

PREFACE

"Sit down to write what you have thought," advised William Cobbett, "and not to think about what you shall write."

Those words hit home to all writers, professional and otherwise. When we sit before a blank page, or black screen, motivated only by the need to fill it up—thereby making our deadline and keeping our job—the result is usually hackwork. But on those happy occasions when we are fired up with an idea, writing becomes less a chore than a mode of presentation; the way we spill out our notion can even be a pleasure.

It's good advice, that line of Cobbett's. He was a vituperative cuss, joyfully heaping his invective on politicians in the early nineteenth century, and made history by being the only man chased out of both England and America for libeling the high and mighty. One of his best books was *Advice to Young Men and, Incidentally, To Young Women*, which is cited herein.

In phrasing that counsel, the phrasemaker obviously set out to construct an aphorism. The easiest way to build a memorable phrase is to use *antithesis*, using words of opposite meaning to balance each other. "Art is long; life is short" wrote Hippocrates, even before taking his Oath; another example, more pointedly from the advice dodge, can be found in the works of Roger Sherman, one of the Constitution's framers: "When you are in a minority, talk; when you are in a majority, vote."

Phrasemakers—that's what aphorists now call themselves, and can charge more for it—have another trick to make their words memorable, which Mr. Cobbett's advice exemplifies. They take advantage of what the Greek rhetoricians called *antimetabole*, "turning about in the other direction"; in this device, words are repeated in reverse grammatical order. Here's Francis Bacon: "If we begin with certainties, we will end

9

in doubts; but if we begin with doubts, and are patient with them, we shall end in certainties."

John F. Kennedy liked that technique of transposing words, and is remembered for both "Let us never negotiate out of fear, but let us never fear to negotiate" and "Ask not what your country can do for you—ask what you can do for your country." The antimetabolic technique can be trivialized, as it was in facetious advice to panicked stockbrokers—"Always close the door before you leave, but never leave after you have opened the window"—but it is a surefire method of making advice memorable.

In creating memorable advice, anybody can play. Advice to dreamers: Don't wonder about what you do; do what you wonder about. Advice to advisers: If you cannot advise your friend to change, change your friend to advise. See? Nothin' to it. It's especially easy with words that are both nouns and verbs. Don't judge a quotation by its author; author your own quotation with good judgment.

Keeping in mind Cobbett's antimetabolic dictum, I have sat down to write what I have long been thinking about on the subject of advice. No sooner did "how-to" become a compound adjective than it became a dirty word.

The creeping commercialization of counsel has led to a sonic boom within the advice industry. If the advice explosion continues, we will become a nation of sheeplike advisees, hooked on direction by consultants, traumatized by the admonitions of moralizers, cowed by the expertise of specialists, bulldozed by the authority of pundits, inundated by the wave of detailed instructions pounded in by the vast how-to hierarchy.

I roll out of bed in the morning to the sound of my own voice on a wake-up machine warning me against touching the snooze alarm, suggesting the only way to make it to the office is to get to the bathroom sink immediately; that's the first and last time I advise myself all day.

On the can of shave cream is advice on how to shave better, by not rinsing the soap off my face before applying the lather. My toothpaste tube, now expensively standing upright, suggests I see my dentist more often, a tradeoff for some dental association plug for its fluoride.

Then the live cavalcade of counsel starts on the talk shows. Before breakfast, some exercise enthusiast tells me why my abused body is going to pot, a doctor explains why I take too many pills and also advises an aspirin a day just to be safe, and a grimly cheery weather announcer who insists on billing herself as a meteorologist tells me whether or not to wear a raincoat, which she characterizes as "foul-weather gear." A nutritionist tells me why my breakfast is not giving me the proper start because it doesn't contain enough moral fiber. The dog-training consultant comes by to train me, not the dog, because the dog and I are both alpha males thinking constantly of biting each other. My daughter, a self-styled fashion consultant, snatches my tie off my neck and hands me one that supposedly goes with my shirt.

On the way to work, a traffic announcer waves me away from my favorite route, which he says is afflicted by rubberneckers, whatever they are. The Surgeon General gets in his licks on the news, warning me off tobacco, away from taking stairs at a bound, and against partaking of shellfish from a remote archipelago. A bumper sticker on the car in front of me advises me that if I'm close enough to read the message, I'm guilty of tailgating, and a radio talk show host interviews a nice lady who tells me that my participation in the kinkiest of sex practices should leave me feeling guilty of nothing. Three hundred bytes of advice are laid on me before the day has officially begun.

At the office, a flashing light on the phone is telling me how many messages are waiting, and I know most of them will subtly hint at what I should be doing that day. Feature columnists read my horoscope and freely counsel new ways to handle the affairs of what used to be called the lovelorn. An investment adviser calls to suggest when to panic. I have lunch with a political consultant who advises me not to listen to what he has been advising his clients, the leaders of the nation, because they have been listening to the geopolitical security advisers. My computerized spelling adviser blinks out the correct way to spell *horoscope* because it doesn't understand a play on words.

There is hardly time left in the day to speak to a party planner— have those invitations gone out yet?—or a marriage counselor, because the interior decorator is coming and I'll have to get her out in time for a session in the backyard with the cleanup kid who calls himself a landscape architect. At this point, I would be tempted to go to the gym for a steambath and a massage, but I just don't want to listen to the patter of a physical culturist conversing with an aerobics adviser. Instead I turn to my word processor, which has tied itself in knots, and I am forced to consult my computer consultant, who at least comes free, because I never hit the delete button on his allowance when he was a kid.

This incessant barrage of advice—whether sought-after opinion, or unsolicited kibbitzing—is enough to drive reasonably other-directed people to a psychologist, or a yogi, or a tarot-card reader. This universal state is especially disconcerting to me, a political columnist and language guru, because the dispensation of advice has become my stock in trade.

That's what I do—give advice, asked for or not. When the President is about to hold a news conference, I get into print first telling him what to expect to be asked and what he should answer. When the Pope issues an encyclical, I write him back. When people all over the world can't decide if it's "to the manner born" or "to the manor born," I give 'em the word (manner) and when distinguished usagists wonder if "news conference" is to be preferred to "press conference," I lay down the line. (It was "press conference" until Richard Nixon wanted it known that the conference was his, in which to make news, and not the damned press's, to harass him. That's when the White House started referring to "news conferences," and the electronic media thought it was a put-down to the newspaper types and went along. Nobody ever caught us on that one.)

What is a professional advice-dispenser to do, surrounded by legions of old pros with literary agents who want to get into the act, not to mention the competition from amateurs? Join the cacophony, or get out of the advice dodge before the wave breaks?

My advice to myself was: Become selective. Do not let the advice-on-anything explosion obliterate the good advice that is readily available. Spread all the advice out on a table, pick at it magpie-style, and see what you like best. More important, pick out the advice that best suits your problem and your character.

In taking this extraordinarily sensible approach, I have had the good fortune to be associated with my brother Len, one of the outstanding advice mavens of our time. He was largely responsible for the first volume in this series, *Good Advice*, in which Napoleon's phrase "If you start to take Vienna—take Vienna" became part of the American matrix of heroic advice, cited widely by Presidents and pitchmen.

In almost every category herein, the reader will find some slightly contradictory advice; that tradition dates back to the English proverbians who matched "Look before you leap" with "He who hesitates is lost." Under "Discretion," for example, you will find the highminded "Perish discretion when it interferes with duty," which may suit you under many circumstances; now and then, as circumstances change, you may find more profound wisdom about discretion, that better part of valor, in "Never say 'oops' in the operating room."

Or under "Gambling," you will be instructed that "The best throw of the dice is to throw them away"; right, that's good advice. But in the next breath, be advised: "If you must play, decide upon three things at the start: the rules of the game, the stakes, and the quitting time." If neither of those counsels may fit your needs, consider Damon Runyon's wisdom on the subject of losing a bet when it seems you have a sure thing: " 'Son,' the old man said, 'as you go around and about in this world, some day you will come upon a man who will lay down in front of you a new deck of cards with the seal unbroken and offer to bet he can make the jack of spades jump out of the deck and squirt cider in your ear. Son,' the old man continued, 'do not bet him because as sure as you do, you are going to get an earful of cider.' "

I am addicted to good political advice, and we have come up with a few doozies (from the snazzy automobile the Deusenberg, perhaps influenced by "daisy"). "Sometimes in politics one must duel with skunks," said Speaker Joe Cannon, "but no one should be fool enough to allow the skunks to choose the weapons." That's for a campaign in which your opponent is cutting you up; but that advice won't help in a spot when you may be your own worst enemy. For such a circumstance, try the First Law of Holes, described by Dennis Healey: "If you are in one, stop digging."

Selectivity is the key, which is up to the advisee; all we can offer is the treasure house. Take the topic of Humility. ("If I only had a little humility," said Ted Turner, "I'd be perfect." That quotation is not in here, because it is mere observation, not hard advice; we specialize in the imperative mood, with direction explicit.) "Place yourself in the background," ordered E. B. White, about writing but also about living. "Write in a way that draws the reader's attention to the sense and substance of the writing, rather than to the mood and temper of the author." I sometimes feel that way, and can sometimes work a bit of subtlety into writing, and living, while in that deferential frame of mind.

More often than not, however—and especially in advice about what advice books to read, I find myself drawn to the not-so-humble William Cobbett: "When I am asked what books a young man or young woman ought to read, I always answer, Let him or her read all the books that I have written."

A

Ability

Give sail to ability.
—Japanese proverb

Don't learn the tricks of the trade. Learn the trade.
—Anonymous

Let him who knows how ring the bells.
—Spanish proverb

Neglect not the gift that is in thee.
—New Testament
I Timothy 4:14

Never assume that habitual silence means ability in reserve.
—Geoffrey Madan

(See *Ancestry, Favor, Merit, Privilege, Proficiency*)

Acting/Actors

Remember, there are no small parts, only small actors.
—Konstantin Stanislavski

15

Don't use your conscious past. Use your creative imagination to create a past that belongs to your characters.
                    —Stella Adler

How to prepare for a part: Dig, dig, dig, dig. Find out more and more about the character. . . . You add more and more, and then you rub out what you don't need. That happens quietly in the rehearsal process, which involves routine and a good deal of boredom. But if you want to paint or draw, you've got to go through the hell of a school of anatomy. So with acting; you've got a lot of boring digging, a lot of preparation and hard work—and that way you try to penetrate to the essence.
                    —Sir Ralph Richardson

Play *to* the lines, *through* the lines, but never *between* the lines. There simply isn't time for it.
                    —George Bernard Shaw advising Ellen Terry
                      on how to perform Shakespeare

If you really do want to be an actor who can satisfy himself and his audience, you need to be vulnerable. To do this, it is imperative that you reach the emotional and intellectual level of ability where you can go out stark naked, emotionally, in front of an audience, and expose yourself. . . . [Rosalind Russell] once said, "You have to be able to expose yourself totally—to stand in front of an audience nude . . . and turn around . . . very slowly."
                    —Jack Lemmon

Do everything. One thing may turn out right.
                    —Humphrey Bogart
                      quoted by Geraldine Fitzgerald

The only thing in acting is the truth; you have to be truthful to the situation, whether it's comedy or drama, whether you're in a three-ring circus or slitting your throat. If you go beyond truth, if what you are doing becomes unreal, you get into ham very quickly. I'll explain what I mean with an anecdote. There was a French actor who was famous for his Cyrano de Bergerac. One day he allowed himself the

luxury of a tear; he made himself cry instead of the audience. After-
wards, he called the whole company on stage and apologized publicly.
The point is that we have to move an audience, not ourselves.
—Rex Harrison

Be on time, know your words and hit the chalk mark. Just react. Acting
to me has always been reacting. Listen like hell all the time.

I'm an actor—it's a job, a trade. And what you do is, too—or ought
to be. Don't start thinking of yourself as some kind of la-di-da member
of the elite or you'll wind up on your ass.
—Spencer Tracy

We were brought up in the school that teaches: You do what the script
tells you. Deliver the goods without comment. Live it—do it—or shut
up. After all, the writer is what's important. If the script is good and
you don't get in its way, it will come off o.k. I never discussed a script
with Spence; we just did it. The same with Hank in *On Golden Pond*.
Naturally and unconsciously, we joined into what I call a musical
necessity—the chemistry that brings out the essence of the characters
and the work.
—Katharine Hepburn

(See *Applause, Movie Acting, Show Business*)

Adaptation

Bloom where you are planted.
—Nancy Reader Campion's
Aunt Grace

When we cannot act as we wish, we must act as we can.
—Terence

The art of life lies in a constant readjustment to our surroundings.
—Kakuzo Okakura

If you live in the river you should make friends with the crocodile.
        —Indian proverb (Punjabi)

Stretch your legs according to your coverlet.
        —English proverb

You must shift your sail with the wind.
        —Italian proverb

If the wind will not serve, take to the oars.
        —Latin proverb

Adversity

When things go wrong—don't go with them.
        —Anonymous

The way I see it, if you want the rainbow, you gotta put up with the rain.
        —Dolly Parton

Compare your griefs with those of other men and they will seem less.
        —Spanish proverb

If I were asked to give what I consider the single most useful bit of advice for all humanity, it would be this: Expect trouble as an inevitable part of life, and when it comes, hold your head high, look it squarely in the eye and say, "I will be bigger than you. You cannot defeat me." Then repeat to yourself the most comforting of all words, "This too shall pass." Maintaining self-respect in the face of a devastating experience is of prime importance.
        —Ann Landers

Discover someone to help shoulder your misfortunes. Then you will never be alone . . . neither fate, nor the crowd, so readily attacks two.
        —Baltasar Gracián

First ask yourself: What is the worst that can happen? Then prepare to accept it. Then proceed to improve on the worst.
—Dale Carnegie

(See *Courage, Despair, Disappointment, Discouragement, Fortitude, Misfortune*)

Advice

Give your ears, hear the sayings,
Give your heart to understand them;
It profits to put them in your heart.
—Amenemope
11th century B.C.

Write down the advice of him who loves you, though you like it not at present.
—English proverb

Know when to speak, for many times it brings
Danger to give the best advice to kings.
—Robert Herrick

Be wary of the man who urges an action in which he himself incurs no risk.
—Joaquin Setanti

Neither cast ye your pearls before swine.
—New Testament
Matthew 7:6

If your strength is small, don't carry heavy burdens. If your words are worthless, don't give advice.
—Chinese proverb

Seek advice from those only whom you deem competent to give it, and then you need not hesitate to follow it. Receive good advice gracefully, asked or unasked.
            —Charles Simmons

Don't give cherries to a pig; don't give advice to a fool.
            —Irish proverb

Don't assume you're always going to be understood. I wrote in a column that one should put a cup of liquid in the cavity of a turkey when roasting it. Someone wrote me that "the turkey tasted great, but the plastic cup melted." So now I say: "Pour a cup. . . ."
            —Heloise

(See *Bad Advice, Counsel, Facetious Advice, Questionable Advice*)

Affectation

Take heed how you disguise yourself and copy others. Stick to nature if you desire to please, for whatever is fictitious and affected, is always insipid and distasteful.
            —Charles Palmer

> Never pretend to skill, nor wish to seem
> Deep-learn'd, to court a popular esteem;
> But if admir'd by men, you pass for wise,
> And draw their list'ning ears, and gazing eyes;
> Rather mistrust, and doubt yourself from thence:
> They're often fond of folly more than sense.
>   —Author unknown

Avoid all affectation and singularity. What is according to nature is best and what is contrary to it is always distasteful. Nothing is graceful that is not our own.
            —Jeremy Collier

Don't *attitudinize*.
—Samuel Johnson

(See *Honesty, Hypocrisy, Sincerity*)

Affection

One must not be mean with the affections; what is spent of the fund is renewed in the spending itself.
—Sigmund Freud

Be not in haste to marry, nor to engage your affections, where there is no probability of a return. Do not fancy every woman you see the heroine of a romance. . . . Avoid this error as you would shrink back from a precipice. All your fine sentiments and romantic notions will (of themselves) make no more impression on one of these delicate creatures, than on a piece of marble. Their soft bosoms are steel to your amorous refinements, if you have no other pretensions. It is not what you think of them that determines their choice, but what they think of you.
—William Hazlitt

In nine cases out of ten, a woman had better show more affection than she feels.
—Jane Austen

Don't expect others to take as much interest in you as you do yourself. . . . No person should be expected to distort the main lines of his life for the sake of another individual. On occasion there may exist such a strong affection that even the greatest sacrifices become natural, but if they are not natural they should not be made, and no person should be held blameworthy for not making them.
—Bertrand Russell

Do not save your loving speeches
For your friends till they are dead;

Do not write them on their tombstones,
Speak them rather now instead.
—Anna Cummins

(See *Love*)

Aging

On the aging process: The problem for some can involve how you maintain your humanity in the face of bitterness . . . about yourself and your perceived failures, or your wish that the world were a better place for yourself and your children to live in. One compensation is to integrate and to broaden one's perspective. A new vital connection can be made with the grandchildren, for example, or in passing on one's knowledge to the next generation. There are very few things you can do to defy the aging process. Keeping your hopes alive is definitely one of them.
—Dr. Stanley H. Cath

Be aware that young people have to be able to make their own mistakes and that times change.
—Gina Shapira

Love, while you are able to love.
—A. Frieligrath

Rebuke not an elder, but intreat him as a father.
—New Testament
I Timothy 5:1

Hearken unto thy father that begat thee, and despise not thy mother when she is old.
—Old Testament
Proverbs 23:22

(See *Maturity, Mid-Life*)

Aim

Pursue worthy aims.
> —Solon

Thomas Carlyle was once talking to a young friend, and asked him what his aim in life was. The young man replied that he had none. "Get one, then, and get it *quick*," said Carlyle, sharply. "Make something your specialty. Life is a very uncertain affair. Knowing a little about five hundred things won't do us much good. We must be able to do something well, that our work will be needed and valuable."
> —Kate L. Gates

> Pitch thy behavior low, thy projects high,
>> So shall thou humble and magnanimous be.
> Sink not in spirit; who aimeth at the sky
>> Shoots higher much than he that means a tree.
>> —George Herbert

In the long run men hit only what they aim at. Therefore, though they should fail immediately, they had better aim at something high.
> —Henry David Thoreau

(See *Ambition, Aspiration, Purpose*)

Allure

Be mysterious.
> —John Bouvier's advice to his daughter
> Jacqueline [Onassis]

Play to allure the gods.
> —Advice given to Alma Maria Schindler (wife
> of Gustav Mahler) by her father

The best way to apply fragrance . . . is to spray it into the air . . . and walk into it.
                    —Estée Lauder

"Where should one use perfume?" a young woman asked. "Wherever one wants to be kissed," I said.
                    —Gabrielle ("Coco") Chanel

Be careful what you show—and what you don't show.
                    —Marlene Dietrich

If your point of view is right, your allure will take care of itself. . . . Leave yourself alone as much as possible. Don't worry—I never do, I'm too busy to remember things.
                    —Paulette Goddard

(See *Appearance, Beauty, Deportment, Dress, Fashion, Grooming, Image*)

Ambition

Know ye not that they which run in a race run all, but one receiveth the prize? So run, that ye may obtain.
                    —New Testament
                    I Corinthians 9:24

Be ambitious to merit the favour of your prince; but do not choose to be his favorite.

Since advancement is dangerous, take heed of being too ambitious, and think yourself high enough, if you can but stand upright.
                    —George Shelley

            Hew not too high,
            Lest the chips fall in thine eye.
            —14th-century proverb

Don't be afraid to give up the good to go for the great.
—Kenny Rogers

(See *Aim, Aspiration, Purpose*)

Ancestry

What thou hast inherited from thy fathers,
Acquire it to make it thine.
—Johann Wolfgang von Goethe
quoted by Sigmund Freud

Rejoice, O Sancho, in the humility of thy lineage and scorn not to say, thou camest of labouring men, for when thou art not ashamed thyself, no body will seek to make thee so. . . . If you follow virtue for your mean, and strive to do virtuous deeds, you need not envy those that are born of Princes and great men, for blood is inherited, but virtue is achieved.
—Don Quixote to Sancho Panza in
Miguel de Cervantes' *Don Quixote*

Pride thyself on what virtue thou hast, and not on thy parentage.
—Saadi

Beware of men who flourish with hereditary honors.
—Latin proverb

Do well and you will have no need for ancestors.
—Voltaire

(See *Ability, Favor, Merit, Proficiency*)

Anger

Life is but short; no time can be afforded but for the indulgence of real sorrow, or contests upon questions seriously momentous. Let us not throw away any of our days upon useless resentment, or contend who shall hold out longest in stubborn malignity. It is best not to be angry; and best, in the next place, to be quickly reconciled.
          —Samuel Johnson

When you are very angry, don't go to law; when you are very hungry, don't make verses.
          —Chinese proverb

> Reprove not, in their wrath, excited men;
> Good counsel comes all out of season then:
> But when their fury is appeased and past,
> They will perceive their faults, and mend at last.
>   —John Randolph

We are told "Let not the sun go down on your wrath," but I would add, never act or write till it has done so. This rule has saved me from many an act of folly. It is wonderful what a different view we take of the same event four-and-twenty hours after it has happened.
          —Sydney Smith

"Don't let them push your button." The one trying to get you angry wants to control you. If you meet a negative approach positively, you are not letting the climate get out of your hands.
          —Gerard I. Nierenberg

Name calling, putdowns and personal attacks can turn anger into hate . . . Learning how to fight constructively involves understanding a few simple guidelines:
    State your needs. (What you want, what you need and, eventually, what you'll settle for.)
    Don't attack the other person.
    Don't bring up old wounds.
          —Deirdre S. Laiken and Alan J. Schneider

To obtain a man's opinion of you, make him mad.
—Oliver Wendell Holmes

Anxiety

Eat not thy heart; which forbids to afflict our souls, and waste them with vexatious cares.
—Plutarch

Life is eating us up. We shall be fables presently. Keep cool: it will be all one a hundred years hence.
—Ralph Waldo Emerson

In my younger days I heard someone, I forget who, remark, "Sell to the sleeping point." That is a gem of wisdom of the purest ray serene. When we are worried it is because our subconscious mind is trying to telegraph us some message of warning. The wisest course is to sell to the point where one stops worrying.
—Bernard M. Baruch

Do not . . . hope wholly to reason away your troubles; do not feed them with attention, and they will die imperceptibly away. Fix your thoughts upon your business, fill your intervals with company, and sunshine will again break in upon your mind.
—Samuel Johnson

The only thing to know is how to use your neuroses.
—Arthur Adamov

Better to be despised for too anxious apprehensions, than be ruined by too confident a security.
—Edmund Burke

(See *Depression, Despair, Melancholy/Blues, Peace of Mind, Stress, Worry*)

Appearance

Never suffer your courage to exert itself in fierceness, your resolution in obstinacy, your wisdom in cunning, nor your patience in sullenness and despair.
—Charles Palmer

Keep up appearances; there lies the test;
The world will give thee credit for the rest.
—Charles Churchill

Be not deceived with the first appearance of things, for show is not substance.
—English proverb

Never despise any one for any thing that he cannot help—least of all, for his poverty. I would wish you to keep up appearances yourself as a defence against the idle sneers of the world, but I would not have you value yourself upon them. . . . Instead of saying above—"Never despise any one for any thing that he cannot help"—I might have said, "Never despise any one at all"; for contempt implies a triumph over and pleasure in the ill of another.
—William Hazlitt

Beware of a gaudy exterior. The wise will infer a lean interior.
—Charles Simmons

You know those snooty little pillows that sit on so many sofas? One of them says: "You can't be too rich or too thin." Fiddle to that. Too rich you can't be, but too thin is cadaverous and men don't like it any more than they like fatties. Five soft pounds more on the morning scale keeps the phone ringing ten years longer.
—Nancy Holmes

Don't judge a man's wealth—or his piety—by his appearance on Sunday.
—Benjamin Franklin

(See *Allure, Beauty, Deportment, Fashion, Grooming, Image*)

Applause

If you achieve success, you will get applause, and if you get applause, you will hear it. My advice to you concerning applause is this: Enjoy it but never quite believe it.
—Robert Montgomery

Do not trust to the cheering, for those persons would shout as much if you and I were going to be hanged.
—Oliver Cromwell

Advice on audiences: Listen to them when they are reacting as a mass— never listen to an individual reaction.
—Richard Rodgers

(See *Fame, Greatness, Praise, Reputation*)

Appraisal

Whenever you start measuring somebody, measure him right, child, measure him right. Make sure you done taken into account what hills and valleys he came through before he got to wherever he is.
—Mama, in the play A *Raisin in the Sun*
by Lorraine Hansberry

Let us take men as they are, not as they ought to be.
—Franz Schubert

Measure men round the heart.
—English proverb

View the whole world, and with impartial eyes,
Consider and examine all that rise;
Weigh well their actions, and their treach'rous ends,

How greatness grows, and by what steps ascends;
What murders, treasons, perjuries, deceit,
How many fall, to make one monster great.
　　　—Author unknown

If you want to judge a man, take a look at his enemies.
　　　—Harry Golden

Be not swept off your feet by the vividness of the impression, but say, "Impression, wait for me a little. Let me see what you are and what you represent. Let me try you."
　　　—Epictetus

Take the advice of light when you're looking at linen and jewels;
Looking at faces and forms, take the advice of the day.
　　　—Ovid

It's no use trying to sum people up. One must follow hints, not exactly what is said, nor yet entirely what is done.
　　　—Virginia Woolf

(See *Discernment*)

Argument

Venture not to defend what your judgment doubts of.
　　　—English saying

Why, Sir, you must provide yourself with a good deal of extraneous matter, which you are to produce occasionally, so as to fill up the time; for you must consider, that they do not listen much. If you begin with the strength of your case, it may be lost before they begin to listen.
　　　—Samuel Johnson

Affect not little shifts and subterfuges to avoid the force of an argument.
　　　—Isaac Watts

If your arguments be rational, offer them in as moving a manner as the nature of the subject will admit, but beware of letting the pathetic past swallow up the rational.
—Jonathan Swift

Be not too fond of argument. . . . Rather suggest what remarks may have occurred to you on a subject than aim at dictating your opinions to others or at defending yourself on all points. You will learn more by agreeing in the main with others and entering into their trains of thinking, than by contradicting and urging them to extremities.
—William Hazlitt

(See *Persuasion*)

Arrogance

Disdain not your inferior, though poor, since he may be your superior in wisdom, and the noble endowments of mind.
—George Shelley

Do thou restrain the haughty spirit in thy breast, for better far is gentle courtesy.
—Homer

Never yield to that temptation, which to most young men, is very strong, of exploring other people's weaknesses and infirmities, or of showing your own superiority. You may get the laugh on your side by it, for the present; but you will make enemies by it for ever; and even those who laugh with you then, will, upon reflection, fear, and consequently hate you: besides that, it is ill-natured, and that a good heart desires rather to conceal, than expose, other people's weaknesses or misfortunes. If you have wit, use it to please, and not to hurt. You may shine, like the sun in temperate zones, without scorching.
—Lord Chesterfield

Do not imagine that you will make people friends by showing your superiority over them; it is what they will neither admit nor forgive, unless you have a high and acknowledged reputation beforehand, which renders this petty vanity more inexcusable. Seek to gain the good-will of others rather than to extort their applause.
—William Hazlitt

Suffer not any beloved study to prejudice your mind so far in favour of it as to despise all other learning. This is a fault of some little souls who have got a smattering of astronomy, chemistry, metaphysics, history &c. and for want of due acquaintance with other sciences, make a scoff at them all in comparison of their favorite science.
—Isaac Watts

Always hold your head up, but be careful to keep your nose at a friendly level.
—Max L. Forman

(See *Humility, Pride*)

Art/Artists

Let the arts inform you and guide you toward excellence. Whether you choose a career in the arts or not, keep the arts at the center of your consciousness, because beyond all else the arts will best inform you of the nature of human excellence.
—Bryan Lindsay

There's only one way to know about art: through exposure. Don't read too much. If you look enough, your brain cells absorb it, and that's your expertise. It's a painless process. . . . Pick one or two artists that you really like. Look at originals and reproductions of their work for 15 minutes a day for three months. After a month you'll feel you're a minor expert; after three months you'll feel like a major expert. You won't be, but you'll know so much more than most.
—Jean Sutherland Boggs

An artist should be judged by his best, just as an athlete is. Pick out my one or two best things and say, "That's what he did: all the rest was rehearsal."
—Artie Shaw

No one should drive a hard bargain with an artist.
—Ludwig van Beethoven

Try to keep the rebel artist alive in you, no matter how attractive or exhausting the temptation.
—Norman Mailer

Treat a work of art like a prince. Let it speak to you first.
—Arthur Schopenhauer

Art is not what the public considers essential, so you have to be prepared for a long, hard fight.
—Lee Krasner

You must not think that feeling is everything. . . . Art is nothing without form.

The artist must raise everything to a higher level. He is like a pump; he has inside him a great pipe that reaches down into the entrails of things, the deepest layers. He sucks up what was lying there below, dim and unnoticed, and brings it in great jets to the sunlight.
—Gustave Flaubert

The artist must employ the symbols in use in his day and nation to convey his enlarged sense to his fellowmen.
—Ralph Waldo Emerson

You mustn't ever settle for gimmick art or trendy "gallery art." Don't settle for a concept too quickly, too soon. . . . Whatever it is you're doing—writing, painting or performing—art should not be precious or obscure. Art is communication. You're communicating your feelings and vision.
—Elizabeth Murray

On being successful as an artist: You have to have your work shown in a good gallery for the same reason that Dior never sold his originals from a counter in Woolworth's.
—Andy Warhol

In art, truth and reality begin when one no longer understands what one is doing or what one knows, and when there remains an energy that is all the stronger for being constrained, controlled and compressed. It is therefore necessary to present oneself with the greatest humility: white, pure, and candid with a mind as if empty, in a spiritual state analogous to that of a communicant approaching the Lord's Table. Obviously it is necessary to have all of one's experience behind one, but to preserve the freshness of one's instincts.
—Henri Matisse

In the pure realm of art, illuminate your subject with one single ray of light, starting from one point.
—Joseph Joubert

There is no abstract art. You must always start with something. Afterward you can remove all traces of reality.
—Pablo Picasso

Copy nature and you infringe on the work of our Lord. Interpret nature and you are an artist.
—Jacques Lipchitz

If you practice an art, be proud of it and make it proud of you. . . . It may break your heart, but it will fill your heart before it breaks it: it will make you a person in your own right.
—Maxwell Anderson

(See *Music, Painting, Sculpture*)

Artfulness

Keep to yourself the final touches of your art.
—Baltasar Gracián

In a courtroom where smoking was permitted, the great trial lawyer, Clarence Darrow, sometimes lit a cigar when the prosecution began its argument and sat, leaning forward in rapt attention, while the cigar ash grew longer, longer. Soon the jury's attention became so fixed upon that ash, awaiting its fall, that the prosecution argument went largely unheeded. Some claimed that Darrow had cigars especially made, with a wire running through them to hold up the ash—and his intimates knew him to be capable of that.
—Kenneth Davis

Aspiration

If you would attain to what you are not yet, you must always be displeased by what you are. For where you were pleased with yourself there you have remained. But once you have said, "It is enough," you are lost. Keep adding, keep walking, keep advancing; do not stop, do not turn back, do not turn from the straight road.
—St. Augustine

Let's climb up to the top of our ivory tower, right up to the last step, close to the heavens!
—Gustave Flaubert

Attempt the impossible in order to improve your work.
—Bette Davis

Becoming a star may not be your destiny, but being the best that you can be is a goal that you can set for yourselves.
—Bryan Lindsay

(See *Aim, Ambition, Purpose*)

Assertiveness

Advice to youth: Bite your tongue. Get a cinder in your eye. When you feel good, you feel nothing.
　　　　　　　　—R. Buckminster Fuller

Take care to get what you like or you will be forced to like what you get. Where there is no ventilation fresh air is declared unwholesome. Where there is no religion hypocrisy becomes good taste. Where there is no knowledge, ignorance calls itself science.
　　　　　　　　—George Bernard Shaw

Promote yourself but do not demote another.
　　　　　　　　—Israel Salanter

I sometimes say that success just happens. That's not true. You have to make it happen. When I make up my mind to do something, I make sure it happens. You can't wait for the phone to ring. You have to ring them.
　　　　　　　　—Lord (Lew) Grade

Hide not your light under a bushel.
　　　　　　　　—American proverb

If you can't say just what you mean, in words and all other efforts at precise meaning, then sing it. If you can't bawl it, yell it; if you can't yell it, howl it; if you can't howl it, scream it; if you can't scream it, try whispering it; if that does not do, then whine and sob it.
　　　　　　　　—Bernard Berenson

If you want *action*, let people know what is expected of them. For example, there's the story of the museum guide who was just finishing the tour, saying: "And here, ladies and gentlemen, at the close, this splendid Greek statue. Note the noble way in which the neck supports the head, the splendid curve of the shoulders, and, ladies and gentlemen, note the natural way in which the open hand is stretched out, as if to emphasize: 'Don't forget a tip for the guide.' "
　　　　　　　　—Maxwell Droke

Authorship

Ye who write, choose a subject suited to your abilities.
—Horace

Give me a condor's quill! Give me Vesuvius's crater for an ink-stand. . . . To produce a mighty book you must choose a mighty theme. No great and enduring volume can ever be written on a flea, though many there be that have tried it.
—Herman Melville

He who purposes to be an author, should first be a student.
—John Dryden

An author ought to write for the youth of his generation, the critics of the next, and the schoolmasters of ever afterwards.
—F. Scott Fitzgerald

A writer should concern himself with whatever absorbs his fancy, stirs his heart, and unlimbers his typewriter . . . a writer has the duty to be good, not lousy; true, not false; lively, not dull; accurate, not full of error. He should tend to lift people up, not lower them down.
—E. B. White

No matter how piercing and appalling his insights, the desolation creeping over his outer world, the lurid lights and shadows of his inner world, the writer must live with hope, work in faith.
—J. B. Priestley

Once you feel the urge and the need to write, you must put whatever comes to your lips or your pen straight down without hesitating or selecting. You must refrain from all self-criticism when you first write something down, because, otherwise, when one is young, one often loses one's finest inspiration, the richest flowerings of the imagination, which no amount of reflection and critical scrutiny can restore.
—Johann Wolfgang von Goethe

The author in his work should be like God in the Universe—everywhere present, nowhere visible.
                              —Gustave Flaubert

Have faith. May you surround yourself with parents, editors, mates, and children as tolerant and supportive as mine have been. But the essential support and encouragement of course come from within, arising out of the mad notion that your society needs to know what only you can tell it.
                              —John Updike

Don't you be a writer. Writing is an escape from something. You be a scientist.
                              —Sinclair Lewis
                              to his small son

(See *Books, Language/Writing, Literary Composition, Reading, Words, Writing*)

B

Bad Advice

Shoot first; ask questions later.
　　　　　—Old American frontier axiom

It is infinitely better to take the side of the wicked who prosper than
of the righteous who fail.
　　　　　—Donatien-Alphonse-François Comte de Sade
　　　　　(commonly called Marquis)

Love well, whip well.
　　　　　—Benjamin Franklin

If you want to enjoy peace, first square the magistrate.
　　　　　—Chinese proverb

If you want to get on in this world, make many promises, but don't
keep them.
　　　　　—Napoleon I

Live in danger. Build your cities on the slopes of Vesuvius.
　　　　　—Friedrich Nietzsche

Do as we say, and not as we do.
　　　　　—Giovanni Boccaccio

. . . Take note, take note, O world,
To be direct and honest is not safe. . . .
I should be wise, for honesty's a fool
and loses what it works for.
—Iago in Shakespeare's *Othello*

Don't fear to pledge. By winds the perjuries of love
Are blown, null and void, across the land and farthest seas.
—Tibullus

Don't get it right; get it written!
—Journalistic dictum

Beat a woman with a hammer and you'll make gold.
—Russian proverb

Never argue. In society nothing must be discussed; give only results.
—Benjamin Disraeli

Live fast, die young, have a beautiful corpse.
—Motto of James Dean

In love, a sure way to be loved is hardly to love at all.
—Duc de La Rochefoucauld

One should always play fairly when one has the winning cards.
—Oscar Wilde

Don't say it—spray it!
—Graffiti slogan
quoted by Bay Rigby

It's not whether you win or lose, but how you place the blame.
—Anonymous

We should always forgive those of our enemies we cannot whip.
—English proverb

Above all things, never let your son touch a novel or romance. How
delusive, how destructive are those pictures of consummate bliss! They

teach the youthful to sigh after beauty and happiness that never existed . . . such books teach us very little of the world.
—Oliver Goldsmith

I do not believe a man can ever leave his business. He ought to think of it by day and dream of it by night.
—Henry Ford

"If you have a good dog, don't bark yourself" is a good proverb, and in Ernest Bevin I had an exceptionally good dog.
—Clement Attlee

Never set forth evil maxims, however well expressed, to catch the attention and memory of mankind.
—Joseph Joubert

Balance

Make a painting in which every part of the painting is of equal importance.
—Chuck Close

Beauty

If you foolishly ignore beauty, you'll soon find yourself without it. Your life will be impoverished. But if you wisely invest in beauty, it will remain with you all the days of your life.
—Frank Lloyd Wright

Affect not to despise beauty; no one is freed from its dominion.
But regard it not as a pearl of great price; it is fleeting as the bow in the clouds.
—Martin Farquhar Tupper

Gaze not on beauty too much, lest it blast thee; nor too long lest it blind thee; nor too near, lest it burn thee . . . if thou lust after it, it destroys thee; if virtue accompany it, it is the heart's paradise; if vice associate it, it is the soul's purgatory: it is the wise man's bonfire, and the fool's furnace.
> —Francis Quarles

Outward beauty is not enough, and the woman who would appear fair must not be content with any common manner. Words, wit, play, sweet talk and laughter, surpass the work of too simple nature. Naked loveliness is wasted all in vain, if it have not the will to please.
> —Pliny the Elder

Advice for a teenage daughter—five inexpensive beauty hints:
> For attractive lips, speak words of kindness;
> For lovely eyes, seek out the good in people;
> For a slim figure, share your food with the hungry;
> For beautiful hair, let a child run his fingers through it once a day.
> And, for poise, walk with the knowledge that you will never walk alone.
> —Sam Levenson

(See *Allure, Appearance, Deportment, Dress, Fashion, Grooming, Image*)

Beginnings

Begin to weave and God will give the thread.
> —German proverb

If you wish to learn the highest truths, begin with the alphabet.
> —Japanese proverb

Beware of undertaking too much at the start. Be content with quite a little. Allow for accidents. Allow for human nature, especially your own.
> —Arnold Bennett

Begin somewhere; you cannot build a reputation on what you intend
to do.
—Liz Smith

Make voyages! Attempt them . . . there's nothing else.
—Tennessee Williams

(See *Doing, Enterprise, Initiative*)

Behavior

Think of these things, whence you came, where you are going, and
to whom you must account.
—Benjamin Franklin

Vain man! Mind your own business! Do no wrong! Do all the good
you can! Eat your canvas-back ducks! drink your Burgundy! Sleep your
siesta, when necessary, and trust in God.
—John Adams, in letter to Thomas Jefferson

Beware of fainting fits . . . though at the time they may be refreshing
and agreeable yet believe me they will in the end, if too often repeated
and at improper seasons, prove destructive to your Constitution.
—Jane Austen

"So live as if you were living already for the second time and as if you
had acted the first time as wrongly as you are about to act now!" It
seems to me that there is nothing that would stimulate a man's sense
of responsibleness more than this maxim, which invites him to imagine
first that the present is past and, second, that the past may yet be
changed and amended. Such a precept confronts him with life's *fi-
niteness* as well as the *finality* of what he makes out of both his life
and himself.
—Victor E. Frankl

Do not seek to distinguish yourself by being ridiculous; nor entertain
that miserable ambition to be the sport and butt of the company. By

aiming at a certain standard of behaviour or intellect, you will at least show your taste and value for what is excellent.
—William Hazlitt

Eye nature's walks, shoot folly as it flies,
And catch the manners, living as they rise;
Laugh where we must, be candid where we can;
But vindicate the ways of God to man.
—Alexander Pope

I don't say we all ought to misbehave, but we ought to look as if we could.
—Orson Welles

(See *Conduct of Life*)

Beliefs

We like winning. We've tried both and winning is better. But don't believe that winning is really everything. It's more important to stand for something. If you don't stand for something, what do you win?
—Lane Kirkland

Every man who is truly a man must learn to be alone in the midst of all others, and if need be against all others.
—Romain Rolland

Why abandon a belief merely because it ceases to be true? Cling to it long enough, and . . . it will turn true again, for so it goes. Most of the change we think we see in life is due to truths being in and out of favor.
—Robert Frost

Believe nothing on the faith of traditions, even though they have been held in honour for many generations, and in divers places. Do not believe a thing because many speak of it. Do not believe on the faith of the sages of the past. Do not believe what you have imagined, persuading yourself that a god inspires you. Believe nothing on the sole authority of your masters or priests. After examination, believe

what you yourself have tested and found to be reasonable, and conform your conduct thereto.
——Gautama Buddha

Do not believe hastily: what harm quick belief can do.
——Ovid

(See *Dreams, Ideals, Principles, Vision*)

Boasting

Before you tell someone how good you are, you must tell him how bad you used to be.
——Semon Emil Knudson

You have to do a little bragging on yourself even to your relations——man doesn't get anywhere without advertising.
——John Nance Garner

He that tooteth not his own horn, the same shall not be tooted.
——John L. Lewis
to his children

Get someone else to blow your horn and the sound will carry twice as far.
——Will Rogers

Neither crow nor croak.
——English proverb

First do it, then say it.
——Russian proverb quoted by
Sergei Bubka, Russian pole-vaulter

If you would have your hen lay, you must bear the cackling.
——Edward J. Clode

(See *Over-Confidence*)

Books

Make thy books thy companions. Let thy cases and shelves be thy pleasure grounds and gardens.
          —Judah ibn-Tibbon
          12th century

Read the best books first, or you may not have a chance to read them at all.
          —Henry David Thoreau

Judge the goodness of a book by the energy of the punches it has given you. . . . I believe that the greatest characteristic of genius, is, above all, force.
          —Gustave Flaubert

Where a book raises your spirit, and inspires you with noble and courageous feelings, seek for no other rule to judge the event by; it is good and made by a good workman.
          —Jean de la Bruyère

Beware of the man of one book.
          —Latin proverb

It is the vice of scholars to suppose that there is no knowledge in the world but that of books. Do you avoid it, I conjure you; and thereby save yourself the pain and mortification that must otherwise ensue from finding out your mistake continually!
          —William Hazlitt

Choose an author as you would a friend.
          —Wentworth Dillon

Read for ideas, not for authors.
          —Oliver Wendell Holmes, Jr.

(See *Authorship, Literary Composition, Reading, Writing*)

Borrowing (Money)

Before you borrow money from a friend, decide which you need more.
—Anonymous

Be not made a beggar by banqueting upon borrowing, when thou hast
nothing in thy purse.
—Apocrypha
Ecclesiasticus

Never ask of him who has, but of him who wishes you well.
—Spanish proverb

When a Friend Asks for Money, Try Saying "No": "Money has ruined
more friendships," says Lewis Altfest, a New York financial planner.
If friends are approached about a loan, he says, they should "try to
steer people into a normal loan situation whenever possible or co-sign
a loan rather than lend the money directly. . . ." Says Lawrence
Krause, a San Francisco financial planner, "you aren't doing the bor-
rower a favor by making it casual. As a lender you're playing banker
and you have the right to know where the money is going, and to
charge a fair interest rate."
—From a *Wall Street Journal* article

Advice to a creditor: Lose not thine own for want of asking for it; 'twill
get thee no thanks.
—Thomas Fuller

First commandment of a Swiss banker: Never lend money to someone
who must borrow money to pay interest.
—Quoted by Lester C. Thurow

(See *Economy, Money*)

Brotherhood

We must strengthen, defend, preserve and comfort each other. We must love one another. We must bear one another's burdens. We must not look only on our things, but also on the things of our brethren. We must rejoice together, mourn together, labor and suffer together.
> —John Winthrop
> Sermon to the Puritans, 1630, on
> approaching Massachusetts Bay aboard
> the ship
> *Arabella*

Be kindly affectioned to one another with brotherly love; in honor preferring one another.
> —New Testament
> Romans 12:10

However dark the prospects, however intractable the opposition, however devious and mendacious the diplomacy of our opponents, we ourselves have to carry so clear and intense a picture of our common humanity that we see the brother beneath the enemy and snatch at every opportunity to break through to his reason and his conscience, and, indeed, his enlightened self-interest.
> —Adlai E. Stevenson

Only connect.
> —E. M. Forster

We human beings ought to stand before one another as reverently, as reflectively, as lovingly, as we would before the entrance to hell.
> —Franz Kafka

If we are not our brother's keeper, let us at least not be his executioner.
> —Marlon Brando

(See *Communication—Personal, Love—Universal*)

C

Candor

The art of life is to show your hand. There is no diplomacy like candor. You may lose by it now and then, but it will be a loss well gained if you do. Nothing is so boring as having to keep up a deception.
—E. V. Lucas

Kiss the hand of him who can renounce what he has publicly taught, when convicted of his error; and who, with heartfelt joy, embraces the truth, though with the sacrifice of favorite opinions.
—Johann Kaspar Lavater

Take care never to seem dark and mysterious; which is not only a very unamiable character, but a very suspicious one too; if you seem mysterious with others, they will be really so with you, and you will know nothing. The height of abilities is to have . . . a frank, open and ingenuous exterior, with a prudent and reserved interior; to be upon your own guard, and yet, by a seeming, natural openness, to put people off of theirs. . . . Always look people in the face when you speak to them.
—Lord Chesterfield

Whenever one has anything unpleasant to say one should always be quite candid.
—Oscar Wilde

He who speaks the truth must have one foot in the stirrup.
—Armenian proverb

(See *Honesty, Truth*)

Career

No matter who you are or what you plan to do, learn to type!
—Liz Smith

Don't choose a profession just for money. Choose a profession as you would choose a wife—for love and for money.
—Advice quoted by John Huston

Integrate what you believe in every single area of your life. Take your heart to work and ask the most and best of everybody else, too. Don't let your special character and values, the secret that you know and no one else does, the truth—don't let that get swallowed up by the great chewing complacency.
—Meryl Streep

Find out what you like doing best and get someone to pay you for doing it.
—Katherine Whitehorn

Follow your bliss.
—Motto of James Campbell

First say to yourself what you would be; and then do what you have to do.
—Epictetus

Think . . .
Think about Appearance, Associations, Actions, Ambition, Accomplishment.
—Thomas J. Watson

Be absolutely determined to enjoy what you do.
                    —Gerry Sikorski

Starting as a secretary is a shrewd course for any ambitious young woman. It plugs you in at a higher level than most entry-level jobs. You can eavesdrop and learn a lot.
                    —Joan Manley

The best business you can go into you will find in your father's farm or in his workshop. If you have no family or friends to aid you, and no prospect open to you there, turn your face to the great West, and there build up a home and fortune.
                    —Horace Greeley

Start planning your second career while you're still on your first one.
                    —David Brown

(See *Job Hunting, Occupation*)

Caution

Never cut what you can untie.
                    —Joseph Joubert

Don't throw away the old bucket until you know whether the new one holds water.
                    —Swedish proverb

Be wary then; best safety lies in fear.
                    —Laertes in Shakespeare's *Hamlet*

Always count the cost.
                    —American proverb

Better to turn back than to lose your way.
                    —Russian proverb

Prefer a small certainty before a great uncertainty.
                    —English saying

Never play cards with a man named Doc. Never eat at a place called
Mom's. Never sleep with a woman whose troubles are worse than your
own.
                    —Nelson Algren

There is one exception to the rule "Never eat at a restaurant called
Mom's." If you're in a small town, and the only other place is called
Eats—then go to Mom's.
                    —Carl Waxman

(See *Discretion, Prudence, Restraint*)

Chance

You must take your chance.
                    —Portia in Shakespeare's
                    The Merchant of Venice

One should not underestimate ripeness as a factor facilitating discov-
eries which, as the saying goes, are "in the air"—meaning, that the
various components which will go into the new synthesis are all lying
around and only waiting for the trigger action of chance or the cata-
lyzing action of an exceptional brain, to be assembled and welded
together.
                    —Arthur Koestler

Keep an eye on the main chance.
                    —English proverb

Change

Observe always that everything is the result of change, and get used to thinking that there is nothing Nature loves so well as to change existing forms and make new ones like them.
—Marcus Aurelius

Childhood must pass away, and then youth, as surely as age approaches. The true wisdom is to be always seasonable, and to change with a good grace in changing circumstances. To love playthings well as a child, to lead an adventurous and honorable youth, and to settle when the time arrives, into a green and smiling age, is to be a good artist in life and deserve well of yourself and your neighbour.
—Robert Louis Stevenson

Do not feel certain of anything.
—Bertrand Russell

Let everyone try and find that as a result of daily prayer he adds something new to his life, something with which nothing can be compared.
—Mohandas K. Gandhi

Never change a winning game; always change a losing one.
—Bill Tilden

Let us resolve to be masters, not the victims, of our history, controlling our own destiny without giving way to blind suspicions and emotions.
—John F. Kennedy
Speech, University of Maine

Character

When the character of a man is not clear to you, look at his friends.
—Japanese proverb

When all those about you say of a man, "He is a man of talents and virtue," do not immediately believe them. When your great officers all say, "He is a man of talents and virtue," do not immediately believe them. When your people all say, "He is a man of talents and virtue," then examine into his character; and when you find that he is such indeed, then afterwards employ him.
—Mencius

Never underestimate a man who overestimates himself.
—Attributed to Franklin D. Roosevelt,
on General Douglas MacArthur

We should make a notch every day on our characters, as Robinson Crusoe on his stick. We must be at the helm at least once a day; we must feel the tiller-rope in our hands, and know that if we sail, we steer.
—Henry David Thoreau

Instill the love of you into all the world, for a good character is what is remembered.
—The Teaching for Merikare, 2135 B.C.

Judge not of a ship as she lies on the stocks: Wait till she has accomplished a voyage. Test everything by experience. Human beings cannot be added up like a column of figures: you can only know men by living with them. The Chinese say: "Every character must be chewed to get its juice."
—C. H. Spurgeon

Keep in mind that the true measure of an individual is how he treats a person who can do him absolutely no good.
—Ann Landers

Charity

Above all things have fervent charity among yourselves. For charity shall cover the multitude of sins.
—New Testament
I Peter 4:8

Let your hand feel for the afflictions and distresses of everyone, and let your hand give in proportion to your purse; remembering always the estimation of the widow's mite, that it is not everyone that asketh that deserveth charity; all, however, are worthy of the inquiry, or the deserving may suffer.
—George Washington
to his nephew

Despise not a small wound, a poor kinsman, or an humble enemy.
—English proverb

Scoff not at the natural defects of any which are not in their power to amend. Neither flout any for his profession, if honest, though poor and painful. Mock not a cobbler for his black thumbs.
—Thomas Fuller

Don't look at a torn dress.
—Malagasy proverb

If you see him riding on a bamboo-cane, say to him, Good health to your horse.
—Moroccan proverb

Don't use the impudence of a beggar as an excuse for not helping him.
—Rabbi Schmelke of Nicolsburg

Grasp the whole world of reason, life and sense,
In one close system of benevolence.
—Alexander Pope

(See *Compassion, Generosity, Kindness, Sympathy*)

Charm

Give me a few minutes to talk away my face and I can seduce the
Queen of France.
>   —Voltaire

Have something attractive about you, for it is the magic of civil in-
tercourse; use this smooth hook more to catch good will, than good
things; but always use it.
>   —Baltasar Gracián

We ought to defer our liking of those with whom we converse, till we
have taken some notice of the disposition of their minds; otherwise
the beauty of their person, or the charms of their wit, may make us
fond of those whom our reason or judgment will tell us we ought to
abhor.
>   —George Shelley

Cheerfulness

Be of good cheer.
>   —Proculeius in Shakespeare's
>   *Antony and Cleopatra*

Keep a green tree in your heart and perhaps the singing bird will
come.
>   —Chinese proverb

While there is a chance of the world getting through its troubles, I
hold that a reasonable man has to behave as though he were sure of
it. If at the end your cheerfulness is not justified, at any rate you will
have been cheerful.
>   —H. G. Wells

Fake feeling good. You may have the most legitimate reason in the world to be unhappy. You may have lost someone important to you, you may have lost your job, you may be a stranger in town, you may be recovering from a broken romance. But when you're with people, don't wear your depression like a badge. You're going to have to learn to fake cheerfulness. Believe it or not, eventually that effort will pay off: you'll actually start feeling happier.

—Jean Bach

Be of good cheer. And remember, my dear friends, what a wise man said—"A merry heart doeth good like a medicine, but a broken spirit dryeth the bones."

—Adlai E. Stevenson concession speech, 1956, in Chicago

If God gives you gaiety and cheer of spirits, lift up the careworn by it. Wherever you go, shine and sing. In every household there is drudgery. In every household there is sorrow. In every household there is a low-thoughted evil. If you come as a prince, with a cheerful, buoyant nature, in the name of God do not lay aside these royal robes of yours. Let humour bedew duty. Let gaiety take charge of dullness.

—Henry Ward Beecher

(See *Good Humor, Optimism/Pessimism*)

Children

Respect the child. Be not too much his parent. Trespass not on his solitude.

—Ralph Waldo Emerson

If you want a baby, have a new one. Don't baby the old one.

—Jessamyn West

I do not believe in a child world. . . . I believe the child should be taught from the very first that the whole world is his world, that adult and child share one world, that all generations are needed.
—Pearl S. Buck

Never help a child with a task at which he feels he can succeed.
—Maria Montessori

It's a great mistake, I think, to put children off with falsehoods and nonsense, when their growing powers of observation and discrimination excite in them a desire to know about things.
—Annie Sullivan

Parents think their children should keep their innocence as long as possible. The world doesn't work that way. If parents ever have a choice between mentioning something to children or not mentioning something to children, they should mention it. If there's a choice between talking and not talking, always choose talking, even if it's more difficult.
—Grace Hechinger

Let your children go if you want to keep them.
—Malcolm Forbes

Never say [to younger people] "that was before your time," because the last full *moon* was before their time.
—Bill Cosby

Never show a child what he cannot see. . . . While you are thinking about what will be useful to him when he is older, talk to him of what he knows he can use now.
—Jean-Jacques Rousseau

Accustom children to a true notion of things.
—George Shelley

Never threaten a child with a visit to the dentist.
—Jane E. Brody

You have to help the child understand the role of money. You want to establish that money doesn't grow on trees.
          —James Comer
            Professor of Child Psychology

If a child makes a mistake with an allowance, don't bemoan it. You have to trust them with the money.
          —Kathleen Rau

Remember, when they have a tantrum, don't have one of your own.
          —Dr. Judith Kuriansky

Re: *Child abuse:* Spare the rod and spare the child.
          —Susan Pouncey

Praise the child and you make love to the mother.
          —American proverb

Do but gain a boy's trust; convince him by your behaviour that you have his happiness at heart; let him discover that you are the wiser of the two; let him experience the benefits of following your advice and the evils that arise from disregarding it; and fear not you will readily enough guide him.
          —Herbert Spencer

(See *Family, Mother's Advice, Parenthood*)

Commitment

Always remember the distinction between contribution and commitment. Take the matter of bacon and eggs. The chicken makes a contribution. The pig makes a commitment.
          —John Mack Carter

Never reach out your hand unless you're willing to extend an arm.
          —Elizabeth Fuller

Do not turn back when you are just at the goal.
　　　　—Publilius Syrus

Two persons must believe in each other, and feel that it *can* be done and *must* be done; in that way they are enormously strong. They must keep up each other's courage.
　　　　—Vincent van Gogh

There are some people whom you have in life who have the capacity for real, passionate commitment to something, and sometimes you may be passionately committed to the same thing. You have to treasure these relationships, and if at times a relationship runs into rocky shoals, you have to treat yourselves as small Eastern European countries and exchange ambassadors. You have to keep that capacity for commitment alive.

　　　　—Warren Beatty

Commit yourself to a dream. . . . Nobody who tries to do something great but fails is a total failure. Why? Because he can always rest assured that he succeeded in life's most important battle—he defeated the fear of trying.
　　　　—Robert H. Schuller

(See *Involvement, Promises*)

Communication

Never awake me when you have good news to announce, because with good news nothing presses; but when you have bad news, arouse me immediately, for then there is not an instant to be lost.
　　　　—Napoleon I

If you have anything to tell me of importance, for God's sake begin at the end.
　　　　—Sara Jeanette Duncan

Rules for a White House spokesman: No. 1 is always tell the truth. I've got only one currency. That's the truth. There are 10,000 ways to say, "No comment," and I've used 9,999 of them. The second rule is don't be afraid to say, "I don't know." You may look dumb, but if you don't know you can't give them hot air because it always shows on your face.
    —Larry Speakes

Don't, Sir, accustom yourself to use big words for little matters.
    —Samuel Johnson

Is your child a computer thief? Ask what type of information he is obtaining via phone lines; request to see an electronic bulletin board screen. A very high phone bill indicates that your child is spending hours communicating with other computer users via modem—not necessarily an illegal activity. It's the very low phone bills that you should watch for. These may indicate calls are being illegally charged to someone else's number.
    —Hope Heymann

(See *Journalism, Media, Reporting, Television*)

Communication (Personal)

Say "I love you" to those you love. The eternal silence is long enough to be silent in, and that awaits us all.
    —George Eliot

If you want to "get in touch with your feelings," fine—talk to yourself, we all do. But if you want to communicate with another thinking human being, get in touch with your thoughts. Put them in order, give them a purpose, use them to persuade, to instruct, to discover, to seduce. The secret way to do this is to write it down, and then cut out the confusing parts.
    —William Safire

We all need somebody to talk to. It would be good if we talked to each other—not just pitter-patter, but real *talk*. We shouldn't be so afraid, because most people really like this contact; that you show you are vulnerable makes *them* free to be vulnerable too. It's so much easier to be together when we drop our masks.
                                                    —Liv Ullmann

Do not open your heart to the grim silent one; guard your tongue before the garrulous fool.
                                                    —Lin Yutang

(See *Brotherhood, Love—Universal*)

Companionship

Ever associate with the good.*
Associate not with the wicked man, even if thou canst learn from him.
                                                    —The Talmud

Keep gude company, and ye'll be counted one of them.
                                                    —Scottish proverb

Never have a companion who casts you in the shade.
                                                    —Baltasar Gracián

Value friendship for what there is in it, not for what can be gotten out of it.
                                                    —H. Clay Trumbull

Let your conversation therefore be with those by whom you may accomplish yourself best; for virtue never returns with so rich a cargo, as when it sets sail from such Continents: Company, like climates, alter complexions; And ill company by a kind of contagion, doth insensibly affect us. Soft and tender natures are apt to receive by

impression: Alexander learned his drunkenness of Leonidas, and Nero his cruelty from his barber.
—W. de Britaine

Avoid connecting yourself with characters whose good and bad sides are unmixed, and have not fomented together.
—Johann Kaspar Lavater

Do not choose for your friends and familiar acquaintances those that are of an estate or quality too much above yours. . . . You will hereby accustom yourselves to live after their rate in clothes, in habit, and in expenses, whereby you will learn a fashion and rank of life above your degree and estate, which will in the end be your undoing.
—Sir Matthew Hale

(See *Friendship*)

Compassion

Let no one underestimate the need of pity. We live in a stony universe whose hard, brilliant forces rage fiercely.
—Theodore Dreiser

Give him alms, woman. For there
is nothing in life, nothing,
So sad as to be blind in Granada.
—Francisco de Icaza
(Words cut into the Alhambra palace
watchtower, Granada, Spain)

Look for a long time at what pleases you, and for a longer time at what pains you.
—Colette

We ought not to treat living creatures like shoes or household belongings, which when worn with use we throw away.
—Plutarch

One cannot weep for the entire world. It is beyond human strength.
One must choose.
                    —Jean Anouilh

Never give up on anybody.
                    —Hubert H. Humphrey

(See *Charity, Generosity, Kindness, Sympathy*)

Complaint

The first lesson of life is to burn our own smoke; that is, not to inflict
on outsiders our personal sorrows and petty morbidness, not to keep
thinking of ourselves as exceptional cases.
                    —James Russell Lowell

Advice for consumers filing complaints:
Remember, the person reading your letters is not personally responsible
for your problem but may be responsible for solving it. Therefore,
avoid writing a sarcastic, threatening or angry letter. It may lessen your
chances of getting the complaint resolved. . . . Send copies of your
letter to a lawyer, the Better Business Bureau, Chamber of Commerce,
consumer advocates and so forth. This technique carries a lot of weight
and shows that you mean business.
                    —Michael Levine

Don't be the crazy or the zealot. Organizations have special people to
deal with those. And if you're angry, people will focus on your anger
instead of your problem.
                    —Stephen Pollan

Never begin at the top. Start by going through the normal customer-
complaint channels. . . . At every level your first choice should be a
personal visit, your second a phone-call, your third a letter; all discussions should be followed up with a letter of confirmation. Get the

first and last names of everyone you deal with. If someone says he'll get back to you, pleasantly nail down a date. . . .
—Katherine Davis Fishman

Conduct of Life

Let love be genuine; hate what is evil, hold fast to what is good; love one another with brotherly affection; outdo one another in showing honor. Never flag in zeal, be aglow with the Spirit, serve the Lord. Rejoice in your hope, be patient in tribulation, be constant in prayer.
—New Testament
Romans 12:9–12

People should think less about what they ought to do, and more about what they ought to be. If only their living were good, their work would shine forth brightly.
—Meister Eckhart

Let us endeavor to live that when we come to die even the undertaker will be sorry.
—Mark Twain

It may be that after this life we shall perish utterly, but if that is our fate, let us so live that annihilation will be unjust.
—Etienne de Sénancour

Twelve things to remember—1. The value of time. 2. The success of perseverance. 3. The pleasure of working. 4. The dignity of simplicity. 5. The worth of character. 6. The power of kindness. 7. The influence of example. 8. The obligation of duty. 9. The wisdom of economy. 10. The virtue of patience. 11. The improvement of talent. 12. The joy of origination.
—Marshall Field

In doing good, avoid fame. In doing bad, avoid disgrace. Pursue a middle course as your principle. Thus you will guard your body from

harm, preserve your life, fulfill your duties by your parents, and live your allotted span of life.
—Chuangtse, 275 B.C.

This is what you shall do: love the earth, and sun, and animals, despise riches, give alms to every one that asks, stand up for the stupid and crazy, devote your income and labour—to others, hate tyrants, argue not concerning God, have patience and indulgence towards the people, take off your hat to nothing known or unknown, or to any man or number of men; go freely with powerful uneducated persons, and with the young, and mothers of families; read these leaves [his own works] in the open air every season of every year of your life; re-examine all you have been told at school or church, or in any books, and dismiss whatever insults your own soul.
—Walt Whitman
Preface to *Leaves of Grass*

(See *Behavior*)

Confidence

Let not the cloud sit upon your brow; let not the canker sink into your heart. Look up, laugh loud, talk big, keep the colour in your cheek and the fire in your eye, adorn your person, maintain your health, your beauty, and your animal spirits. . . .
—William Hazlitt

Never let the fear of striking out get in your way.
—George Herman ("Babe") Ruth

You've got to take the initiative and play *your* game. In a decisive set, confidence is the difference.
—Chris Evert

Trust your hopes, not your fears.
—David Mahoney

Do not let people put you down. Believe in yourself and stand for yourself and trust yourself.
                        —Jacob Neusner

Don't accept that others know you better than yourself.
                        —Sonja Friedman

Of stealing bases: When you get on first, know you're going to second. Know you can beat the pitcher and the catcher and the two of them combined. You have to have an inner conceit to be a successful base stealer. You have to know you are better than either the pitcher or the catcher.
                        —Pete Reiser to Maury Wills

(See *Negativism, Positive Thinking, Self-Reliance, Self-Respect*)

(Over-Confidence)

Boast not thyself of tomorrow; for thou knowest not what a day may bring forth.
                        —Old Testament
                        Proverbs 27:1

Kings have long arms, but misfortune longer; let none think themselves out of reach.
                        —Benjamin Franklin

(See *Boasting*)

Conscience

Be fearful only of thyself; and stand in awe of none more than of thine own conscience. There is a Cato in every man; a severe censor of his

manners. And he that reverences this judge, will seldom do anything he need repent of.
　　　　　—Thomas Fuller

A man's first care should be to avoid the reproaches of his own heart, his next to escape the censures of the world.
　　　　　—English proverb

Never do anything against conscience even if the state demands it.
　　　　　—Albert Einstein

If you compromise with your own conscience, you will weaken your conscience. Soon your conscience will fail to guide you and you never will have real wealth based on peace of mind.
　　　　　—Napoleon Hill

　　　In your secret chamber ere you are judged;
　　　See you do nothing to blush for,
　　　Though but the ceiling looks down upon you.
　　　　　—Tse-sze
　　　　　(grandson of Confucius)

Never exchange a good conscience for the good-will of others, or to avoid their ill-will.
　　　　　—Charles Simmons

If your conscience won't stop you, pray for cold feet.
　　　　　—Elmer G. Leterman

(See *Goodness, Honor, Morality, Uprightness, Virtue*)

Consideration

Never give unnecessary pain. The cricket is not the nightingale; why tell him so? Throw yourself into the mind of the cricket . . . it is what charity commands.
　　　　　—Henry Amiel

Never despise a person's sensitivity. His sensitivity is his genius.
—Charles Baudelaire

Advice and reprehension require the utmost delicacy; and painful truths should be delivered in the softest terms. . . . A courteous man will mix what is conciliating with what is offensive; praise, with censure. . . . Advice, divested of the harshness and yet retaining the honest warmth of truth, "is like honey put around the brim of a vessel full of wormwood."
—William Cowper

Pay quickly what thou owest. The needy tradesman is made glad by such considerate haste.
—Walter Smith

You can't say yes to everything. When you do say yes, say it quickly. But always take a half hour to say no, so you can understand the other fellow's side too.
—Francis Cardinal Spellman's advice to his young associate, Terence (later Cardinal) Cooke

Never tell anyone they look tired; it only makes people feel worse.
—Susan Blond

Diminish your demands, especially on others.
—Leo C. Rosten

Every man should bear his own grievances and inconveniences, rather than detract from or abridge the comfort of others.
—Marcus Tullius Cicero

Constancy

Love him, and keep him for thy friend, who, when all go away, will not forsake thee, nor suffer thee to perish at the last.
—Thomas à Kempis

My Dear Sir:

Are you playing the same trick again, and trying who can keep silence longest? Remember that all tricks are either knavish or childish; and that it is as foolish to make experiments upon the constancy of a friend as upon the chastity of a wife.

—Samuel Johnson
(to James Boswell)

To have a true friendship, you have to do more than exchange Christmas cards or call each other once a year. There has to be some continued support and attention; otherwise the relationship is a sentimental attachment rather than a true friendship.

—Dr. Dolores Kreisman

Sigh no more, ladies, sigh no more,
　　Men were deceivers ever,
One foot in sea, and one on shore,
　　To one thing constant never.
　　　Then sigh not so, but let them go,
　　And be you blithe and bonny,
Converting all your sounds of woe
　　Into Hey nonny, nonny.

—Balthasar's Song in Shakespeare's
Much Ado About Nothing

(See *Fidelity/Infidelity*)

Contentment

Be content with such things as ye have.
　　—New Testament
　　Hebrews 13:5

Think contentment the greatest wealth.
　　—George Shelley

> Let us be content to work
> To do the things we can, and not presume
> To fret because it's little.
> —Elizabeth Barrett Browning

The secret of contentment is the realization that life is a gift, not a right.
> —Anonymous

I have not a word to say against contented people so long as they keep quiet. . . . If you are foolish enough to be contented, don't show it, but grumble with the rest.
> —Jerome K. Jerome

You can't have everything. Where would you put it?
> —Steven Wright

Control

Don't waste your time trying to control the uncontrollable, or trying to solve the unsolvable, or thinking about what could have been. Instead, think about what *can be* if you wisely control what you *can* control and solve the problems you *can* solve with the wisdom you have gained from both your victories and your defeats in the past.
> —David Mahoney

Conversation

Take rather than give the tone to the company you are in. If you have parts you will show them more or less upon every subject; and if you have not, you had better talk sillily upon a subject of other people's than of your own choosing.
> —Lord Chesterfield

It is a Secret known but to few, yet of no small use in the Conduct of Life, that when you fall into a man's Conversation, the first thing you should consider is, whether he has a greater inclination to hear you, or that you should hear him.

— Sir Richard Steele

It's all right to hold a conversation, but you should let go of it now and then.

— Richard Armour

Remember that talking is one of the fine arts,— the noblest, the most important, and the most difficult,— and that its fluent harmonies may be spoiled by the intrusion of a single harsh note. Therefore conversation which is suggestive rather than argumentative, which lets out the most of each talker's results of thought, is commonly the pleasantest and the most profitable.

— Oliver Wendell Holmes

Ask others about themselves, at the same time, be on guard not to talk too much about yourself.

— Mortimer Adler

How to begin and continue a conversation: Don't just say "Hello, my name is ——." A name is not a topic—you've got to be able to back it up with something immediately. . . . Don't lead with your name. . . . You have to *pierce* the beginning with a topic. . . . There are three topics to avoid—money, age and weight. Oh, and death and disease. [Do not just report facts.] Do not say, "I ate steak and mashed potatoes, and they had music." Say, "The steak was great, and they had sumptuous potatoes, and the music was so loud it went right through my body."

— Arthur Reel

> If someone asks you how you are,
> And 'though you don't feel up to par,
> Remember this: The only line
> He wants to hear is, "I'm just fine."
> — Marguerite Whitley May

How to break the ice: Move things off-center with a non-threatening question. . . . The best ice-breaker, in this age of everybody moving around is: "Where are you from?" Geography is the most neutral of subjects, but is pregnant with conversational possibilities. It opens up a whole range of secondary questions, allows you to compare impressions of places where you've both been, and prompts you to explain how you came to be where you are. More than that depends on chemistry.
—Glen Waggoner and Peggy Maloney

The art of conversation is to be prompt without being stubborn, to refute without argument, and to clothe grave matters in a motley garb.

The art of conversation consists of the exercise of two fine qualities; you must originate and you must sympathise; you must possess at the same time the habit of communicating and the habit of listening. The union is rather rare, but irresistible.
—Benjamin Disraeli
Beaconsfield's Maxims

(See *Talking*)

Counsel

What advice can one give to people who ask for it? If you see that they are determined to take a certain course, and ask for encouragement only, give it to them in abundance. If they still are undecided, try to help them find what they really want and what it would cost. Put the facts before them, as they themselves shy off from seeing them. Help them to see the situation as the consequences of taking one course of action rather than another. Then if they really want a decision, they can make it themselves.
—Bernard Berenson

Beware lest clamour be taken for counsel.
—Desiderius Erasmus

Though you are a prudent old man, do not despise counsel.
—Spanish proverb

Though thou hast never so many counsellors, yet do not forsake the counsel of your own soul.
—John Ray proverb

> Let no man value at a little price
> A virtuous woman's counsel; her wing'd spirit
> Is feather'd oftentimes with heavenly words.
> —George Chapman

He who calls in the aid of any equal understanding, doubles his own; and he who profits of a superior understanding, raises his powers to a level with the height of the superior understanding he unites with.

—Edmund Burke

What you always do before you make a decision is consult. The best public policy is made when you are listening to people who are going to be impacted. Then, once a policy is determined, you call on them to help you sell it.
—Elizabeth H. Dole

(See *Advice, Bad Advice, Facetious Advice, Questionable Advice*)

Couples

Before you run in double harness, look well to the other horse.
—Ovid

Don't compare your present lover with past ones. . . . Be realistic. Even with loving couples, sexual appetite waxes and wanes.
—Dr. Ruth Westheimer

You don't really know a person until you live with him, not just sleep with him. . . . I staunchly believe no two people should get married until they have lived together. The young people have it right.
—Doris Day

Better to be an old man's darling, than a young man's slave.
—English proverb

Straighten your problems out before you go to bed. That way you will wake up smiling.
—Louis Fromm
(married 55 years)

Pick a man for his human qualities, his values, his compatibility with you, rather than what he represents in status, power or good looks.
—Carol Botwin

Do not be in a hurry to tie what you cannot untie.
—English proverb

Do not think about trying to make it through a lifetime with a man. Just concentrate on making it through a year. . . . The reason a man will not try to split up with you after a year or so is his limitless fear of breaking in a new model.
—Stephanie Brush

(See *Dating, Husbands/Wives, Marriage, Relationships*)

Courage

We must face what we fear; that is the case of the core of the restoration of health.
—Max Lerner

Fear tastes like a rusty knife and do not let her into your house. Courage tastes of blood. Stand up straight. Admire the world. Relish the love of a gentle woman. Trust in the Lord.
—John Cheever

Never say you are walking on the last road.
—Song of the Jewish Resistance,
World War II

The world has no room for cowards. We must all be ready somehow to toil, to suffer, to die. And yours is not the less noble because no drum beats before you when you go out into your daily battlefields, and no crowds shout about your coming when you return from your daily victory or defeat.
—Robert Louis Stevenson

The bravest thing you can do when you are not brave is to profess courage and act accordingly.
—Corra Harris

Go on and increase in valor, O boy! this is the path to immortality.
—Virgil

I think I am pretty much of a fatalist. You have to accept whatever comes and the only important thing is that you meet it with courage and with the best that you have to give.
—Eleanor Roosevelt

(See *Adversity, Daring, Discouragement, Fortitude, Misfortune, Risk, Spirit*)

Courtesy

Never underestimate the power of simple courtesy. Your courtesy may not be returned or remembered, but discourtesy will.
—Princess Jackson Smith

Receive no satisfaction from premeditated impertinence; forget it, forgive it, but keep him inexorably at a distance who offered it.
> —Johann Kaspar Lavater

Treat your superior as a father, your equal as a brother, and your inferior as a son.
> —Persian proverb

Suit your manners to the man.
> —Latin proverb

(See *Etiquette, Manners*)

Courtship

Let every eye negotiate for itself
And trust no agent.
> —Claudio in Shakespeare's
> *Much Ado About Nothing*

Why don't you speak for yourself, John?
> —Priscilla Mullens to John Alden
> in Longfellow's "The Courtship of
> Miles Standish"

If you would have a good wife, marry one who has been a good daughter.
> —Thomas Fuller

Flatter and praise, commend, extol their graces;
Tho' ne'er so black, say they have angels' faces,
That man that hath a tongue, I say, is no man,
If with his tongue he cannot win a woman.
> —Valentine in Shakespeare's
> *Two Gentlemen of Verona*

Be warm but pure; be amorous but chaste.
—Lord Byron

Do not choose your wife at a dance, but in the field among the harvesters.
—Czech proverb

Please your eye and plague your heart.
—Adage quoted by William Cobbett

When a man goes a-courting, and hopes for success, he must begin with doing, and not saying.
—Royall Tyler

(See *Couples, Marriage—Contemplation of, Wooing*)

Creativity

You must create your own world. I am responsible for my world.
—Louise Nevelson

I think back when Alexander the Great visited Diogenes and asked whether he could do anything for the famous teacher. And Diogenes simply said, "Just stay out of my light." Sometimes the best way to heighten creativity is to stay out of the light.
—Alexander Kroll

'Tis well to borrow from the good and great;
'Tis wise to learn; 'tis god-like to create!
—J. G. Saxe

What to do when inspiration doesn't come: Be careful not to spook, get the wind up, force things into position. You must wait around until the idea comes.
—John Huston

Don't play the saxophone. Let it play you.
—Charlie Parker

Don't think! Thinking is the enemy of creativity. It's self-conscious, and anything self-conscious is lousy. You can't *try* to do things. You simply *must* do things.
—Ray Bradbury

(See *Originality*)

Creeds

Think in the morning. Act in the noon.
Eat in the evening. Sleep in the night.
—William Blake

Passion is a bad counsellor.
Quit vicious habits.
Encourage diligence.
Forget not past favours.
—Thomas Hardy

But what says the Greek? "In the morning of life, work; in the midday, give counsel; in the evening, pray."
—Hesiod

Be just: the unjust never prosper. Be valiant: die rather than yield. Be merciful: slay neither old men, children, nor women. Destroy neither fruit trees, grain, nor cattle. Keep your word, even to your enemies.
—Abu Bakr, Mohammed's father-in-law

To rise at six, to dine at ten,
To sup at six, to sleep at ten,
Makes a man live for ten times ten.
—Inscription over the door of
Victor Hugo's study

Support the strong, give courage to the timid, remind the indifferent, and warn the opposed.
—Whitney M. Young

Don't smoke too much, drink too much, eat too much or work too much. We're all on the road to the grave—but there's no reason to be in the passing lane.
—Robert Orben

As a grandfather I'm entitled to a few words of advice to the young, based upon my long and unvarying experience as a transgressor. I can sum them up with these answers to the oft-repeated questions, "What would you do or not do if you had it to do over again?"
I would spend more time with my children.
I would make my money before spending it.
I would learn the joys of wine instead of hard liquor.
I would not smoke cigarettes when I had pneumonia.
I would not marry a fifth time.
—John Huston

A *personal credo:*

Pay attention.
Respect others' rights and feelings.
Love all.
Avoid pleasure principle.
Refuse unnecessary gifts.
Don't be a rubber stamp.
—Chester F. Carlson
quoted by Sol Linowitz

Live your life, do your work, then take your hat.
—Henry David Thoreau

Don Quixote's creed:
Take a deep breath of life and consider how it should be lived.
Call nothing thine, except thy soul.
Love not what thou art, only what thou may become.
Do not pursue pleasure; for thou might have the misfortune of overtaking it.

Be just to all men, courteous to all women.
Live in the vision of the one for whom great deeds are done.
—quoted from *Man of La Mancha*,
screenplay by Dale Wasserman

(See *Mottoes*)

Crime

Keep thou from the opportunity and God will keep thee from the sin.
—Benjamin Franklin

If you choose to live outside the law, you must obey the law more
stringently than anyone. [You dare not be caught speeding—or even
jaywalking—because the smallest inquiry could open up your law-
lessness.]
—Bob Dylan

What ought not to be done do not even think of doing.
—Epictetus

Don't even think of parking here.
—New York Police Department sign at bus
stop on Fifth Avenue

There is a woman in every case; as soon as they bring me a report, I
say, "Look for the woman." [*Cherchez la femme.*]
—Alexandre Dumas

Do not buy stolen goods.
—The Talmud

Avoid carefully the first ill or mischief, for that will breed a hundred
more.
—Italian proverb

When thou art preparing to commit a sin, think not that thou wilt conceal it; there is a God that forbids crimes to be hidden.
—Tibullus

Never underestimate the effectiveness of a straight cash bribe.
—Claud Cockburn

Fathers, if you would see your children virtuous and happy, keep them far away from the tabernacles of bribery; teach them to loathe the wretch who has purchased the soul of another, or sold his own.
—William Cobbett

He who raises the black flag on any avenue of life is riding hard for a fall.
—Ralph Waldo Emerson

(See *Evil*, *Safety*, *Sin*)

Criticism

> We must not stint
> Our necessary actions, in the fear
> To cope malicious censurers; which ever,
> As rav'nous fishes, do a vessel follow
> That is new-trimm'd.
> —Wolsey in Shakespeare's
> *Henry VIII*

Before we blame, we should first see if we can't excuse.
—G. C. Lichtenberg

Never . . . attack whole bodies of any kind—individuals forgive sometimes; but bodies and societies never do.
—Lord Chesterfield

You must not pay a person a compliment, and then straightway follow
it with a criticism.
            —Mark Twain

Never criticize a man until you've walked a mile in his moccasins.
            —American Indian proverb

Never look a gift horse in the mouth. Never be too critical of anything
you have received as a gift. The condition of a horse's teeth is a good
guide to its age. If a man needs a horse and is offered one for nothing,
he should not examine its teeth too closely before accepting it.
            —Ronald Rideout and Clifford Whitting

Cast out the scorner and contention shall go out with him, and quarrels
and reproaches shall cease.
            —Old Testament
            Proverbs 22:10

Curiosity

One shouldn't be too inquisitive in life
Either about God's secrets or one's wife.
            —Chaucer

We must not always try to plumb the depths of the human heart; the
truths it contains are among those that are best seen in half-light or
in perspective.
            —François-Auguste-René de Chateaubriand

Be not curious in unnecessary matters.
            —Apocrypha

Be content with a little light, so it be your own. Explore, and explore.
Be neither chided nor flattered out of your position of perpetual inquiry. Neither dogmatize, nor accept another's dogmatism. Why
should you renounce your right to traverse the star-lit deserts of truth,

for the premature comforts of an acre, house and barn? Truth also has its roof, and bed, and board.
—Ralph Waldo Emerson
Oration, Dartmouth College

Go around asking a lot of damfool questions and taking chances. Only through curiosity can we discover opportunities, and only by gambling can we take advantage of them.
—Clarence Birdseye

(See *Inquiry, Questions*)

D

Dancing

Dancing is a sweat job. . . . When you're experimenting you have to try so many things before you choose what you want, and you may go days getting nothing but exhaustion. This search for what you want is like tracking something that doesn't want to be tracked. It takes time to get a dance right, to create something memorable. There must be a certain amount of polish to it. I don't want it to look anything but accomplished and if I can't make it look that way, then I'm not ready yet. I always try to get to know my routine so well that I don't have to think, "What comes next?" Everything should fall right into line and then I know I've got control of the bloody floor.
—Fred Astaire

. . . learn by practice. Whether it means to learn to dance by practicing dancing or to live by practicing living, the principles are the same. In each, it is the performance of the dedicated, precise set of acts, physical or intellectual, from which comes shape of achievement, a sense of one being, a satisfaction of spirit. One becomes, in some area, an athlete of God.
—Martha Graham

Danger

Attend my words, no place but harbors danger
In every region virtue finds a foe.
—John Milton

Do not stand in a place of danger trusting in miracles.
—Arab proverb

Better encounter a danger than live in continual fear.
—William H. Browne

The wise man in the storm prays God, not for safety from danger, but
for deliverance from fear.
—Ralph Waldo Emerson

When danger approaches, sing to it.
—Arab proverb

Think of thy deliverance, as well as of thy danger.
—Thomas Fuller

(See *Caution, Prudence, Risk, Safety*)

Daring

Let a man who has to make his fortune in life remember this maxim:
Attacking is the only secret. Dare and the world always yields; or if it
beats you sometimes, dare it again and it will succumb.
—William Makepeace Thackeray

I must tell you I take terrible risks. Because my playing is very clear,
when I make a mistake you hear it. If you want me to play only the
notes without any specific color dynamics, I will never make one

mistake. Never be afraid to dare. And never imitate. Play without asking advice.
—Vladimir Horowitz

Take a chance! All life is a chance. The man who goes farthest is generally the one who is willing to do and dare.
—*Dale Carnegie's Scrapbook*,
edited by Dorothy Carnegie

Something hidden. Go and find it.
Go, and look behind the Ranges—
Something lost behind the Ranges.
Lost and waiting for you . . . Go!
—Rudyard Kipling

(See *Courage, Fortitude, Risk, Spirit*)

Dating

Stop looking at the opposite sex as the enemy.

Don't tell your life story at a first meeting. Especially avoid talking about your personal problems. If the relationship has a future, there will be time for those discussions later.

Don't describe your long-term marital ambitions on the first date.
—Abby Hirsch

When a date takes you out for dinner, never order chicken or spaghetti because there's no way to eat either neatly.
—Mother's advice, quoted by Michele Slung

If a woman asks a man on a date, she should pay everything, including parking or taxi charges and coat check. After the first date if they want to see each other again, he should pay or they can agree to split everything. Of course, if he has money and wishes to keep paying all the time, that is fine. It's an equal world, but it's not.
—Letitia Baldrige

Never go out with anyone who says he loves you more than his wife or girlfriend.
—William Novak

Don't make love on your first date. Form a relationship first.
—Dr. Ruth Westheimer

Don't talk about ex-boyfriends or husbands, or how much you hate your job, or whatever other problems you have. Be positive and upbeat.

Try to get a man to reveal his fears, and offer advice. Give enough decent suggestions so that he starts to think, "This girl has ideas. She is interested in my life. I'll talk to her."
—Wendy Stehling

Six things not to talk about on your first date: former girl friends, sex, disease, pro wrestling, your work (at least not much) and money. Six things to talk about: Her, your hometown, food, travel, movies, politics (no longer a taboo, and if you're passionately opposed, better to find out sooner than later).
—Glen Waggoner and Kathleen Maloney

(See *Couples, Courtship, Relationships, Wooing*)

Death

Give up fearing death; it is at all times foolish to miss life's pleasures for fear of death.
—Disticha Moralia, A.D. 200

Fear not death, for it is your destiny.
—Ben Sira

We need to be reminded that there is nothing morbid about honestly confronting the fact of life's end, and preparing for it so that we may go gracefully and peacefully. . . . It was the Psalmist, one of the world's wisest men, who prayed, "So teach us to number our days, that we may apply our hearts unto wisdom." The fact is, we cannot truly face life until we have learned to face the fact that it will be taken away from us.

—Billy Graham

We must . . . consider our last hour, not as the punishment, but as the law of nature. . . . It is as great a folly to fear death as to fear old age. Nay, as to fear life itself; for he that would not die, ought not to live, since death is a condition of life: Besides that, it is a madness to fear a thing that is certain; for where there is no doubt, there is no place for fear.

—Seneca

We do not know whether it is good to live or to die. Therefore, we should not take delight in living nor should we tremble at the thought of death. We should be equiminded towards both. This is the ideal. It may be long before we reach it, and only a few of us can attain it. Even then, we must keep it constantly in view, and the more difficult it seems of attainment, the greater should be the effort we put forth.

—Mohandas K. Gandhi

Live riotously. It is foolish to sit around waiting for the collector when the collector may be late. Baseball coach Yogi Berra taught us that "It's not over till it's over." And if . . .the New Testament, Buddha, and the Koran are right, it may not be over even then. You'll either be with your pals in paradise or you won't feel a thing.

—David Brown

Perhaps the best cure for the fear of death is to reflect that life has a beginning as well as an end. There was a time when we were not: this gives us no concern—why then should it trouble us that a time will come when we shall cease to be? I have no wish to be alive a hundred years ago . . . why should I regret and lay it so much to heart that I shall not be alive a hundred years hence, in the reign of I cannot tell whom?

—William Hazlitt

(See *Immortality, Mortality*)

Defeat

How you handle defeat is not something to be taken lightly. You've got to think it through. Defeat is an art form. You've got to accept it, and you've got to go on. And once you do that, it's not bad.
　　　　　—Walter F. Mondale

If thou art a man, admire those who attempt great things, even though they fail.
　　　　　—Seneca

There is a time in life when you have to back off.
　　　　　—Attributed to Walter Annenberg

Oh, we all get run over—once in our lives. But one must pick oneself up again. And behave as if it were nothing.
　　　　　—Henrik Ibsen

The probability that we may fail in the struggle ought not to deter us from the support of a cause we believe to be just.
　　　　　—Abraham Lincoln
　　　　　Speech, 1839

One is defeated only when one accepts defeat, said Marshal Foch. . . . The essence of life: fight as if there were no death.
　　　　　—Guy de Rothschild

(See *Adversity, Disappointment, Discouragement, Failure, Positive Thinking*)

Deportment

If you don't already walk and sit as if you were brought up with the Bolshoi Ballet, work on your posture. The idea is to look as if you

own the world, not as if you're carrying it around on your shoulders.
—Elin Schoen

Another thing I would caution you against is not to pore over your books until you are bent almost double—a habit you will never be able to get the better of, and which you will find of serious ill consequence. *A stoop in the shoulders* sinks a man in public and in private estimation. You are at present straight enough, and you walk with boldness and spirit. Do nothing to take away the use of your limbs, or the spring and elasticity of your muscles. As to all worldly advantages, it is to the full of as much importance that all your deportment should be erect and manly as your actions.
—William Hazlitt

I know of no better way to acquire a beautiful walk than the time-tested one of walking with a book on one's head. Walk quickly, body held upright, without letting the book fall to the ground. Add a second book, then a third, and when you can carry up to four or five books on your head, you will begin to have a feeling about moving smoothly that will set you apart as a woman of elegance and magnificent carriage.
—Helena Rubinstein

On teaching executives to exude the right stuff: Walk slowly and purposefully. Plant some pauses along the way. . . . A modified West Point cadet look is critical for business.
—Benton Management Resources

If you carry yourself like a beauty, people will think of you as one.
—Mother's advice, quoted by Michele Slung

Depression

Be calm, my Dellius, and serene,
However fortunes change the scene;

In thy most dejected state
Sink not underneath the weight;
Nor yet, when happy days begin,
And the full tide comes rolling in,
Let a fierce, unruly joy
The settled quiet of thy mind destroy.
  —Anonymous verse quoted by
   Joseph Addison in *The Spectator*

We should feel sorrow, but not sink under its oppression; the heart of a wise man should resemble a mirror, which reflects every object without being sullied by any.
  —Confucius

Beware of allowing a tactless word, a rebuttal, a rejection to obliterate the whole sky.
  —Anaïs Nin

Change your thoughts and you'll change your moods. (1) *Get up and go.* When you most feel like moping, do something—anything. Try cleaning up a drawer. (2) *Make contact with people you care about.* You may not feel like socializing, but others can help to distract you from your depression, give you hugs, listen to you. (3) *Start smiling.* Studies show that your smile muscles send the same signals to your nervous system as when you are actually happy. (4) *Avoid drugs,* including alcohol, which may depress the nervous system and keep you feeling down.
  —Derived from Linda Tschirart and
   Mary Ellen Donovan

When I feel depressed I write my way out of it. If I told you anything more I'd go into business.
  —Bernard Malamud

(See *Anxiety, Melancholy/Blues, Stress, Worry*)

Desire

Rule your desires lest your desires rule you.
                    —Publilius Syrus

First deserve, and then desire.
                    —English proverb

Dwell not upon thy weariness, thy strength shall be according to the measure of thy desire.
                    —Arab proverb

Quench not your desires, when they tend to good.
                    —George Shelley

Learn to level down your desires rather than level up your means.
                    —Greek proverb

Tempt not a desperate man.
                    —Romeo, in Shakespeare's *Romeo and Juliet*

(See *Passions*)

Despair

Let us consult
What reinforcement we may gain from hope.
If not, what resolution from despair.
            —John Milton
            Lines favored by Sigmund Freud

You're gonna have your ups and downs and your moments when you call it quits. You gotta stick it out, because there's only one ball game

here, and it's your own life. You got no choice. You got to play to
win if you want to stay on this earth.
>   —Advice given to cancer patient James Brown
>   by another patient

We should never despair; our Situation before has been unpromising
and has changed for the better, so I trust, it will again.
>   —George Washington

Happy are they, my son, who shall learn . . . not to despair; but shall
remember, that though the day is past, and their strength is wasted,
there yet remains one effort to be made; that reformation is never
hopeless, nor sincere endeavors ever unassisted; that the wanderer may
at length return after all his errors; and that he who implores strength
and courage from above, shall find danger and difficulty give way
before him.
>   —Samuel Johnson

We all talk to ourselves, and many of our self-talks are needlessly
negative. Discipline yourself not to overreact emotionally. Why despair
when sadness is sufficient? Why be enraged when simple irritation will
get your message across?
>   —Robert S. Eliot and Dennis L. Breo

Keep making the movements of life.
>   —Thornton Wilder

(See *Courage, Depression, Fortitude*)

Destiny

Let us follow our destiny, ebb and flow. Whatever may happen, we
master fortune by accepting it.
>   —Virgil

One of the things your mother wrote you that hit me hard was her advice: "Let go your hold" as Wm. James says, "resign your destiny to higher powers."
> —Agnes Meyer to Adlai E. Stevenson

On the edge of destiny, you must test your strength.
> —Billy Bishop
> Canadian World War I Ace

People like us must have the religion of despair. One must be equal to one's destiny, that is to say impassible like it. By dint of saying: "That is so! That is so! That is so!" and of gazing down at the deep black hole at one's feet, one reaches calm.
> —Gustave Flaubert

(See *Fate, Luck*)

Determination

You can do what you have to do, and sometimes you can do it even better than you think you can.
> —Former president Jimmy Carter

They say you can't do it, but remember, that doesn't always work.
> —Casey Stengel
> quoted by Sol Linowitz

(See *Perseverance, Resolution*)

Dieting

Don't dig your grave with your knife and fork.
> —English proverb

The only way to change one's body weight is to begin a lifelong series of new habits. But the notion of going on some radical diet for a while and then stopping is a waste of time. [Ultimately] the thing that a person should do is to figure out what they can do forever. In terms of weight reduction it's simply taking in fewer calories and burning more. Whatever anyone can do to achieve that end is fine. But it has to be for keeps.

—Dr. Jules Hirsch

General Rules for Weight Control:
  Make up your mind you're going to lose weight.
  Don't talk about your diet. It bores others and soon will bore you.
  Eat bulky foods—spinach, cabbage, salad greens, and lean meat,
    so that you won't feel hungry.
  Never look at a menu. It's maddening.
  Don't think about rich foods. But if you crave a certain one, eat a
    tiny portion.
  Leave the table while you still feel you could eat a little more.

—Helena Rubinstein

Don't window shop at the bakery.

—Carol Weston

Know your calories. Hang a calorie chart on your kitchen wall or refrigerator door. . . . Reduce fat consumption. . . . Cut sugar consumption. . . . Eat smaller portions. . . . Watch what you drink. . . . Hold the sauces. . . . Watch your snacks.

—Dr. Jean Mayer and Jeanne Goldberg

Eat slowly. Put your fork down now and then—no one is going to take the food away. . . . *Don't be afraid to assert yourself.* I finally have the courage to go into a restaurant and wave away the rolls and tell them not to put butter on the fish. . . . *Restructure your kitchen.* Get rid of everything that isn't good for you. In other words, if it's not there, you're not going to eat it.

—James Coco

Cut out those intimate little dinners for two—unless there's someone with you.

—Joey Adams

Difficulties

Accustom yourself to master and overcome things of difficulty; for, if you observe, the left hand, for want of practice, is insignificant and not adapted to general business; yet it holds the bridle better than the right, from constant use.
　　　　—Pliny

When you can't solve the problem, manage it.
　　　　—Robert H. Schuller

Become a possibilitarian. No matter how dark things seem to be or actually are, raise your sights and see the possibilities—always see them, for they're always there.
　　　　—Norman Vincent Peale

Don't be crazy to do a lot of things you can't do.
　　　　—E. W. Howe

Be profound with clear terms, and not with obscure terms. What is difficult at last will become easy; but as one goes deep into things, one must still keep a charm, and one must carry into these dark depths of thought, into which speculation has only recently penetrated, the pure and antique clearness of centuries less learned than ours but with more light in them.
　　　　—Joseph Joubert

If you can't go over, you must go under.
　　　　—Jewish proverb

There are two ways of meeting difficulties: You alter the difficulties or you alter yourself to meet them.
　　　　—Phyllis Bottome

Diplomacy

Never answer a hypothetical question.
—Moshe Arens

I believe in the doctrine of constructive ambiguity. Don't tell people
what you're going to do—let them wonder about it.
—Vernon Walters

Grant graciously what you cannot refuse safely, and conciliate those
you cannot conquer.
—Charles Caleb Colton

Know the meaning of evasion. It is the prudent man's way of keeping
out of trouble; with the gallantry of a witty remark he is able to extricate
himself from the most intricate of labyrinths. He emerges gracefully
from the bitterest encounter and with a smile.
—Baltasar Gracián

You don't tell deliberate lies, but sometimes you have to be evasive.
—Margaret Thatcher

Women take naturally to it. [Diplomacy] The great trick in diplomacy
is to make some unwitting man think your idea is his idea, and women
have been doing that all their lives.
—Clare Boothe Luce

The best way to knock the chip off your neighbor's shoulder is to pat
him on the back.
—Anonymous

Wag your tongue as much as you please, but don't wave your gun.

Make yourself into a sheep, and you'll meet a wolf nearby.

Don't spit in the well: you'll be thirsty by and by.

We are related: the same sun dries our rags. . . . Don't hang all you
own on one nail.

Live and scratch—when you're dead the itching will stop.
        —Russian proverbs used by Soviet diplomats,
        quoted by James Reston

When you want to test the depth of a stream, don't use both feet.
        —Chinese proverb quoted by Leslie Stahl

Creep up carefully on the use of force. Violence is easy to escalate, hard to de-escalate. It should never be used just to provide a release for the user's frustration. (A veteran Japanese diplomat once gave me some good advice: "Never get angry except on purpose.")
        —Harlan Cleveland

If you are taken hostage: Keep faith and don't lose your will to survive. Don't lose faith in your inner strength to cope. Remember that law enforcement officers are working for your release. Statistics show that your chances for survival increase as time in captivity lengthens. Federal and local law-enforcement agencies have specially trained people and contingency plans to deal with hostage situations. . . . *Be realistic.* Any thoughts you have should first reflect: "Will my next step, word or action make the situation better or worse?" If you are unsure of yourself in attempting an escape, don't try it.
        —Al Santoli

(See *Government, Peace, Politics, Tact*)

Disappointment

I must say that the biggest lesson you can learn in life, or teach your children, is that life is not castles in the skies, happily ever after. The biggest lesson we have to give our children is truth. And that's what I'm saying: that we're all built with illusions. And they break.
        —Goldie Hawn

We had better prepare ourselves [and our children] for reality. . . . All of us must live with disappointment, accept limitations and imperfections. We live in a world of becoming and change. Inevitably you will sometimes be disappointed with friends. You will sometimes be disappointed in marriage, disappointed in institutions, and sometimes disappointed in yourselves. Thus, if you are to retain your joy in life you must find much of that joy in spite of disappointment, for the joy of life consists largely in the joy of savoring the struggle, whether it ends in success or in failure. Your ability to go through life successfully will depend largely upon your travelling with courage and a good sense of humor, for both are conditions of survival. It is for this reason that I stress the importance of living with reality and therefore with disappointment.

—John R. Silber
President, Boston University

Men will never disappoint us if we observe two rules: 1. To find out what they are; 2. To expect them to be just that.
—George Iles

(See *Discouragement, Negativism, Positive Thinking*)

Discernment

You have one failing you must overcome, one thing you must learn if you are to be a completely happy woman, maybe the most important lesson in living—you must learn to say no. You do not know how to say no, Sophia, and that is a serious deficiency.
—Charlie Chaplin to Sophia Loren

Judge not of actions by their mere effect;
Dive to the center and the cause detect;
Great deeds from meanest springs may take their course,
And smallest virtues from a mighty source.
—Alexander Pope

Do not value men according to their esteem of *thee,* but according to their worth and faithfulness.
—Charles Simmons

Never appeal to a man's "better nature." He might not have one.
—*Long's Notes*

When the fox preaches, look to your geese.
—German proverb

Weigh the meaning and look not at the words.
—Ben Jonson

(See *Appraisal*)

Discipline

You got to jump when I say jump, sleep when I say sleep. Otherwise you're wasting my time.
—Trainer Jack Blackburn to the
young Joe Louis

If you once turn on your side after the hour at which you ought to rise, it is all over. Bolt up at once.
—Sir Walter Scott

Would you live with ease, do what you ought, and not what you please.
—Benjamin Franklin

Know this for truth, and learn to conquer these:
Thy belly first; sloth, luxury, and rage.
Do nothing base with others or alone,
And, above all, thine own self respect.
—Pythagoras

Submit to the rule you laid down.
—English proverb

How parents should defend their disciplining decisions: One of the most reasonable of childish protests is "If you can do it, why can't I?" No sensible parent will admit that as a basis of argument. The best answer is: "Because."
　　　　　　　—Judith Martin
　　　　　　　"Miss Manners"

Don't blame the kids for everything. It's up to parents to control them. I say a smart mother should never give her boy all the allowance she can afford—keep some of it to bail him out.
　　　　　　　—Joey Adams

(See *Military*)

Discouragement

When one door shuts another opens. He that would struggle with the world, and bear up in adversity, ought still to resolve not to be discouraged, for resolution is the mother of fortitude, and not only necessary to our support, but very much conducive to our deliverance.
　　　　　　　—Samuel Palmer

Don't listen to those who say, "It's not done that way." Maybe it's not, but maybe you will. Don't listen to those who say, "You're taking too big a chance." Michelangelo would have painted the Sistine floor, and it would surely be rubbed out by today. Most importantly, don't listen when the little voice of fear inside of you rears its ugly head and says, "They're all smarter than you out there. They're more talented, they're taller, blonder, prettier, luckier and have connections. . . ." I firmly believe that if you follow a path that interests you, not to the exclusion of love, sensitivity, and cooperation with others, but with the strength of conviction that you can move others by your own efforts, and do not make success or failure the criteria by which you live, the chances are you'll be a person worthy of your own respect.
　　　　　　　—Neil Simon
　　　　　　　Commencement Address

Make a crutch of your cross.
—English proverb

As you attempt to make big differences, remember to appreciate the small differences. And remember that you don't always have to reach the goal you set in order to make a difference. T. H. White, in the last chapter of his story of King Arthur, tells of a discouraged king ready to enter his last battle. His dream of a just society, his roundtable, is destroyed. Then one of his loyal friends, a member of his council . . . tugs on his tunic and reminds him that his effort, his example, has made everything worthwhile.
—Win Borden

Don't be sad, don't be angry, if life deceives you! Submit to your grief—your time for joy will come, believe me.
—Aleksandr Sergeyevich Pushkin

(See *Disappointment, Negativism, Positive Thinking*)

Discretion

Remember, a closed mouth gathers no foot.
—Steve Post

Never make known one's wealth, one's remedies, one's lover, where one has hidden money, the good works one does, the insults one has received, or the debts one has contracted.
—Hindu proverb

Perish discretion when it interferes with duty.
—Hannah More

You cannot get anywhere with a fanatic; you must never point out to anyone the defects of his mistress, nor should you show the feebleness of a cause to those who are advocating it, nor offer reasons to one who is inspired.
—Voltaire

Never let people see the bottom of your purse or of your mind.
—Italian proverb

Do not give a present to one woman that another might recognize.
Change the time and place of your rendezvous, lest one of the others
should surprise you in a place whose mysteries she knows.
—Ovid

Never wrestle with a strong man nor bring a rich man to court.
—Latvian proverb

Never say "oops" in the operating room.
—Dr. Leo Troy

A man should live with his superiors as he does with his fire; not too
near, lest he burn; not too far off, lest he freeze.
—Diogenes

Be a father to virtue, but a father-in-law to vice. Be not always severe,
nor always merciful; choose a mean between these two extremes; for
that middle point is the center of discretion.
—Miguel de Cervantes

(See *Caution, Prudence, Restraint*)

Diversity

I take it to be a principal rule of life, not to be too much addicted to
any one thing.
—Terence

Keep out of ruts; a rut is something which
If traveled in too much, becomes a ditch.
—Arthur Guiterman

Shun no toil to make yourself remarkable by some talent or other. Yet
do not devote yourself to one branch exclusively. Strive to get clear

notions about all. Give up to no science entirely, for science is but one.
> —Seneca

I'm disturbed by the trend these days—all too prevalent in my view—of young people to narrow their sights too early, and to tailor their education or their career planning or their interests to one narrow specialty. Because it stifles that capacity to grow and change. Whether you go to college or not—stay as broad as you can, as long as you can!
> —James L. Ferguson

It is important not to draw lines around yourself. That is, if someone wants you to go to a boxing match, you should not say, "How vulgar. I don't go to boxing matches." Or, "I'm not interested in accountancy. I'm a musician." You should try to find out a bit about what is going on in other fields.
> —S. I. Hayakawa

Divorce

Better a tooth out than always aching.
> —Thomas Fuller

Never inform your spouse of your intention to divorce by having a lawyer send over papers. This is a red-hot poker, likely to incur bitter retaliation.
> —Mel Krantzler

Be wary how you marry one that hath cast her rider.
> —English proverb

How parents should explain their divorce to children: "I'm sorry, but this suits us, and you're going to have to live with it."
> —Judith Martin
> "Miss Manners"

Doing

Knowing is not enough; we must apply.
Willing is not enough; we must do.
—Johann Wolfgang von Goethe

The art of life, of a poet's life, is not having anything to do, to do something.
—Henry David Thoreau

The whole point about getting things done is knowing what to leave undone.
—Stella, Lady Reading

Think that day lost whose low descending sun
Views from thy hand no noble action done.
—Jacob Bobart

Never trouble another for what you can do for yourself.
—Thomas Jefferson

We must recoil a little, to the end we may leap the better.
—English proverb

Bury not your faculties in the sepulchre of idleness.
—George Shelley

(See *Beginnings, Enterprise, Initiative*)

Doubt

Tell that to the marines—the sailors won't believe it.
—Sir Walter Scott

Your doubt can become a good quality if you *train* it. It must become *knowing*, it must become criticism. Ask it, whenever it wants to spoil something for you, *why* something is ugly, demand proofs from it, test it, and you will find it perhaps bewildered and embarrassed, perhaps also protesting. But don't give in, insist on arguments, and act in this way, attentive and persistent, every single time, and the day will come when, instead of being a destroyer, it will become one of your best workers—perhaps the most intelligent of all the ones that are building your life.
—Rainer Maria Rilke

When in doubt, punt, anyway, anywhere.
—John William Heisman

NOTE: Heisman [after whom the Heisman trophy was named] thought it was a mistake to make first downs deep in your own territory because it wore out the team and gave away the plays. Instead, punt on first down if inside the 10-yard line, on second down if inside the 20 and on third down if inside the 30.
—Gene Griessman

Cleave ever to the sunnier side of doubt.
—Alfred, Lord Tennyson

In doubt if an action is just, abstain.
—Zoroaster

When in doubt who will win, be neutral.
—Swiss proverb

Teach yourself to work in uncertainty.
—Bernard Malamud

Dreams

If you don't daydream and kind of plan things out in your imagination, you never get there. So you have to start someplace.
—Robert Duvall

First, when everybody tells you that you are being idealistic or impractical, consider the possibility that everybody could be wrong about what is right for you. Look inside yourself the way nobody else can. Will the pursuit of your dream hurt anybody? Do you stand at least a fair chance of success? If you fail, will you be seriously damaged or merely embarrassed? If you succeed, will it change your life for the better? When you can persuade yourself that your dream is worthwhile and achievable—then say thank you to the doubters and take the plunge. . . . How much better to know that we have dared to live our dreams than to live our lives in a lethargy of regret.
—Gilbert E. Kaplan

If you want to enjoy success, fantasize about it. If you want a special love, fantasize about that, too. When it comes along you will be more comfortable. It won't be a new experience.
—Dr. Madeline Hirschfeld

Talk about a dream, try to make it real.
—Bruce Springsteen

Keep your sense of wonder. I suggest that you maintain that sense of wonder and that feeling of discovery because, speaking as a "hard-nosed businessman," it is also the road to success, because that is what fuels the fires of imagination. That is what powers your perseverance and inspires the creativity which the business world lacks in abundance.
—Paul Woolard

If you want your dreams to come true, don't sleep.
—Yiddish proverb

No one should negotiate their dreams. Dreams must be free to flee and fly high. No government, no legislature, has a right to limit your dreams. You should never agree to surrender your dreams.
—The Rev. Jesse Jackson
Commencement address

(See *Beliefs, Ideals, Principles, Vision*)

Dress (Men)

The way to go from rags to riches is to start by getting a decent set of rags.
—Leonard and Thelma Spinrad

Never underestimate the power of what you wear. . . . After all, there's a small bit of you yourself sticking out, at the cuff and at the neck. The rest of what the world sees is what you hang in the frame.
—Oscar E. Schoeffler

Learn that clothes are there to suit your life, not to run it.
—John Weitz

When in doubt, look at what the man who has the power to hire or fire you, or determine your raise or promotion, is wearing, and model yourself on that. And if he's a she, as may be the case, look at the nearest male authority figure you can find, if there still is one.
—Michael Korda

Remember, the shorter you are, the shorter the muffler.
Never buy shoes early in the day when your feet are their smallest.
—Francis Patiky Stein

Don't be too quick to mimic the expensive dress of a superior. The boss might resent an underling who tries to match a life style that's taken years of work to achieve.
—Consultant, Goodrich & Sherwood Co.

(See *Appearance, Fashion, Image*)

Dress (Women)

Your dresses should be tight enough to show you're a woman and loose enough to show you're a lady.
—Edith Head

Always buy one good dress instead of three cheap ones.
>   —Mother's advice quoted by Michele Slung

Hubert, I love your coat but you must give the women more room for comfort. A woman must move very easily in her clothes. It is not enough to have a coat or dress that is beautiful. . . . The dress must follow the body of a woman, not the body following the shape of the dress.
>   —Cristóbal Balenciaga's advice
>   to the young Hubert de Givenchy

[A woman] should never shop with another woman, who, sometimes consciously, and often unconsciously, is apt to be jealous.
>   —Elsa Schiaparelli

Be kind to the animal in you.
>   —Sign in women's store

Never buy a fur from a veterinarian.
>   —Joan Rivers

(See *Allure*, *Appearance*, *Beauty*, *Fashion*, *Grooming*, *Image*)

Drinking

Beware of drunkenness. It impairs the understanding, wastes the estate, banishes the reputation, consumes the body, and renders a man of the brightest parts, the common jest of an insignificant clown.
—George Shelley

Remember, it is your prerogative to drink or not. A firm "No, thank you" or "Plain soda, please" will not automatically label you a party pooper and may even win added respect. Remember this advice from Bernard Baruch: "Those who mind don't matter, and those who matter don't mind."
>   —Jane E. Brody

Remember that the purpose of a party is togetherness, not tipsiness. Good conversation is possible without a glass in hand. Alcohol should enhance conversation—not dominate it.
>   —From "Drinking Etiquette," a booklet from
>   the National Institute on Alcohol Abuse and
>   Alcoholism

Never be embarrassed to drink alone. But if you're smart, never take more than one drink at lunch.
>   —Letitia Baldrige

Drink water like an ox, wine like a king of Spain.
>   —Italian proverb

The first rule for dealing with a sommelier is not drastically different from that for dealing with a Marine sergeant or a brain surgeon: Don't panic. He is there to help you. Beyond that: (1) If you don't know anything about wine, don't fake it. . . . (2) If you are worried about the price, and you have seen the list, ask for something you can afford. (3) If you order wine, be sure to tip the wine steward. About $2 a bottle is the minimum.
>   —Frank J. Prial

When everybody says you are drunk, go to bed.
>   —Italian proverb

A man who has been drinking wine at all freely, should never go into a new company. With those who have partaken wine with him, he may be pretty well in unison; but he will, probably, be offensive, or appear ridiculous, to other people.
>   —Samuel Johnson

Drinking/Drugs/Addiction

Advice after returning from a treatment center: Stopping any addiction is basically an ongoing process. . . . You have to re-create what you

learned every day. Staying clean becomes a dedication. If you need to rekindle your promise, you have key people to call. Or you repeat the A.A. "Serenity Prayer"* whenever you need to.
—Elizabeth Taylor

The "Serenity Prayer":
> God grant me the serenity
> to accept the things I
> cannot change,
> Courage to change the
> things I can, and
> The wisdom to know the difference.
> —Reinhold Niebuhr
> *In the Way of Light,* 1933

In the house of a drunkard there is no happiness for anyone. All is uncertainty and anxiety. . . . Remember, therefore, that, while it is the duty of Kings and of Priests to abstain from wine and from strong drink, it is also a duty which belongs to ourselves. . . . Abstinence requires no aid to accomplish it. Our own will is all that is requisite, and, if we have not the will to avoid contempt, disgrace and misery, we deserve neither relief nor compassion.
—William Cobbett

Boys should abstain from all use of wine until their eighteenth year, for it is wrong to add fire to fire.
—Plato

If you drink, don't drive. Don't even putt.
—Dean Martin

Duty

Our duty is to be useful, not according to our desires, but according to our powers.
—Henry F. Amiel

Let a man begin with an earnest "I ought," and if he perseveres, by God's grace he will end in the free blessedness of "I will." Let him force himself to abound in small acts of duty, and he will, by and by, find them the joyous habit of his soul.
— F. W. Robertson

Love you lose. Honor has been gone for a long time. Duty you do.
— Ernest Hemingway

Our main business is not to see what lies dimly at a distance, but to do what lies clearly at hand.
— Thomas Carlyle

"Learn what is true in order to do what is right" is the summing up of the whole duty of mankind.
— Attributed to Thomas Henry Huxley

Do what you ought, and let what will come of it.
— Italian proverb

Never step over one duty to perform another.
— English proverb

E

Eating/Cooking

"Bless thy good creatures to our use, and us to thy table." This was the grace before meals at my school, and it seems to me to sum up admirably a truly balanced attitude to the pleasures of food and drink. We must keep these pleasures in proper perspective; we must indulge them reasonably, not grossly. . . . The savor of good food and good wine is one of the elements of true civilization, and no man who embarks upon a fine meal in that knowledge can rise from it without thinking something real has been added to his nature.
—Bernard Levin

You can't mix young food and old food. Don't order a poached egg with a strawberry margarita or boiled chicken garnished with a marijuana cookie.

Don't eat at any place called "The Di-Gel Diner."
—Phyllis Diller

Everything I've got I got from eating spaghetti. You try it. . . .

Spaghetti can be eaten most successfully if you inhale it like a vacuum cleaner.
—Sophia Loren

The secret of good cooking is first, having a love of it. . . . If you're convinced cooking is drudgery, you're never going to be any good at it, and you might as well warm up something frozen.
—James Beard

The Lonely Guy's Cooking Tips: Forget about measuring things. Just tear off hunks of things and toss them in. . . . Forget about shortening. Nobody really knows what it is. . . . In the middle of cooking, you may suddenly slump over, unable to continue. For this reason, it's good to have some late-night back up restaurants that serve bacon cheeseburgers and Chinese food.
—Bruce Jay Friedman

Never, never eat anything out of a carton, even if you are at home alone with the shades drawn. Doing so is wicked and constitutes Miss Manners' one exception to the generally genial rule about violations of etiquette not counting if you don't get caught.
—Judith Martin
"Miss Manners"

Economy

Work and save.
—Bernard M. Baruch
to a young Herbert Stein

If you want to know whether you are destined to be a success or failure in life, you can easily find out. One test is simple and infallible. Are you able to save money? If not, drop out. You will lose.
—James J. Hill

On money: Save it when you need it least. Spend it when you have it most.
—Franco Modigliani
Nobel Laureate

One of the Fidlers said, Gentlemen, I pray you to remember the Musicke, you have given us nothing yet. . . . Always those that dance must pay the Musicke.
—Jeremy Taylor

Get as much force of mind as you can. Live within your income. Always have something saved at the end of the year. Let your imports be more than your exports, and you'll never go far wrong.
                              —Samuel Johnson

Good people, hark ye: a few rules well observed, will contribute much to your happiness and independence. Never buy what you do not really want. Never purchase on credit what you can possibly do without. Take pride in being able to say, I owe no man.
                    —from *Poor Robert* essays by Helen Nearing

Spare no expense to make everything as economical as possible.
                    —Attributed to Samuel Goldwyn

(See *Borrowing—Money; Money*)

Education

I do beseech you to direct your efforts more to preparing youth for the path and less to preparing the path for youth.
                              —Judge Ben Lindsey

Prefer solid sense to wit; never study to be diverting, without being useful.
                              —George Shelley

When you feel discouraged or simply lazy, as is bound to happen sometimes, remember the millions of people in the world who have not had your privilege. Remember the poor and obscure lives of those countless millions who suffer from every sort of deprivation and frequently find themselves the unwilling victims of wars, and a variety of cruelties, perpetrated by man on man. Is it not significant that the first bid for self-realization, among the poor and downtrodden, is to assert their right to education?
                              —Jehan Sadat, widow of
                              President Anwar el-Sadat of Egypt

If you want one year's prosperity, grow grain. If you want ten years' prosperity, grow men and women.
        —Adage quoted by Harry J. Gray

Surely one of our highest charges in teaching is to teach what we ourselves have loved: *The Call of the Wild . . . Treasure Island . . . Huckleberry Finn . . .* We should want every student to know how mountains are made, and that for most actions there is an equal and opposite reaction. They should know who said "I am the state" and who said "I have a dream. . . ." They should know a little of how a poem works. . . . They should know the place of the Milky Way and DNA in the unfolding of the universe. They should know something about the Convention of 1787 and about the conventions of good behavior. . . . In certain places in America, there is a great zeal to remove certain things from study. Let us match that zeal for exclusion with a zeal for inclusion.
        —William J. Bennett
        Former Secretary of Education

The name of the game in the 1980s is quality. We must get back out of the wild growth of the curriculum and get back into some core of knowledge—history, philosophy, theology, language, literature, mathematics, science, art and music. Otherwise we are just graduating trained seals.
        —Theodore Hesburgh
        Former President, Notre Dame University

Let no youth have any anxiety about the upshot of his education. . . . If he keep faithfully busy each hour of the working-day, he may safely leave the final result to itself. He can with perfect certainty count on waking up some fine morning, to find himself one of the competent ones of his generation.
        —William James

Give a man a fish and you feed him for a day. Teach a man to fish and you feed him for a lifetime.
        —Chinese proverb

Don't ever dare to take your college as a matter of course—because, like Democracy and Freedom, many people you'll never know anything about have broken their hearts to get it for you.
                    —Alice Duer Miller

The best culture is not obtained from teachers when at school or college, so much as by our own diligent self-education when we have become men. Hence parents need not be in too great haste to see their children's talents forced into bloom. Let them watch and wait patiently, letting good example and quiet training do their work, and leave the rest to Providence. Let them see to it that the youth is provided, by free exercise of his bodily powers, with a full stock of physical health; set him fairly on the road of self-culture; carefully train his habits of application and perseverance; and as he grows older, if the right stuff be in him, he will be enabled vigorously and effectively to cultivate himself.
                    —Samuel Smiles

Educate the heart—educate the heart. Let us have *good* men.
                    —Hiram Powers

Be careful to leave your sons well instructed rather than rich, for the hopes of the instructed are better than the wealth of the ignorant.
                    —Epictetus

(See *Knowledge, Learning, Understanding, Wisdom*)

Education (Children)

Never educate a child to be a gentleman or lady only, but to be a man, a woman.
                    —Herbert Spencer

Education begins at home. You can't blame the school for not putting into your child what you don't put into him. You don't just take your child to ballet class. First, you dance with him when he is a baby.

Every family has its own rhythm, and if you dance with your children, that rhythm will become a part of them, and they will never forget it.
—Geoffrey Holder

The important thing is not so much that every child should be taught, as that every child should be given the wish to learn.
—John Lubbock

. . . children should be instructed in some useful things—for example, in reading and writing—not only for their usefulness, but also because many other sorts of knowledge are acquired through them. With a like view they may be taught drawing, not to prevent their making mistakes in their own purchases, or in order that they may not be imposed upon in the buying or selling of articles, but perhaps rather because it makes them judges of the beauty of the human form. To be always seeking after the useful does not become free and exalted souls.
—Aristotle

Begin to instruct as soon as a child has any notion of the difference between good and evil. And this is as soon as he knows your smile from your frown.
—Samuel Palmer

The Elderly (Advice to)

Old age must be resisted, and its deficiencies supplied by taking pains; we must fight it as we do disease. Care must be bestowed upon health; moderate exercise should be taken; food and drink should be sufficient to recruit, not overburden our strength. And not the body alone must be sustained, but the powers of the mind much more; unless you supply them, as oil to a lamp, they too grow dim with age. Whereas over-exertion weighs the body down with fatigue, exercise makes the mind buoyant.
—Marcus Tullius Cicero

If you're old, don't try to change yourself, change your environment.
—B. F. Skinner

Do not take the faults of youth into old age, for old age brings with it its own defects.
　　　　　—Johann Wolfgang von Goethe

Don't give them [young people] advice. Don't tell them about your ailments. And don't say, "When I was a young girl. . . ."
　　　　　—Sona Zeger Hodes

The secret of staying young is to live honestly, eat slowly, and lie about your age.
　　　　　—Lucille Ball

Don't stay in bed . . . unless you can make money in bed.
　　　　　—George Burns

Growing old gracefully: One must grow old. Do not weep, do not join supplicating hands, do not revolt; one must grow old. Repeat this word, not as a cry of despair, but as a signal for a necessary departure. Look at yourself, look at your eyelids, your lips, raise from your temples the curls of your hair: already you are beginning to drift away from your life, don't forget it, one must grow old! . . . Go away slowly, slowly, without tears; forget nothing! Take with you your health, your cheerfulness, your coquetry, the small amount of kindness that rendered life less bitter for you. . . . Go away adorned.
　　　　　—Colette

Regarding temptation: Don't worry about avoiding temptation. As you grow older—it will avoid you.
　　　　　—Joey Adams

(See *Longevity, Old Age, Retirement*)

Endurance

Endure, my heart: you once endured something even more dreadful.
　　　　　—Homer

Two frogs were playing on the rafters of a dairy barn one night. They fell into adjacent pails of cream. They jumped and hopped and scrambled for survival. One fought the good fight longer and harder than the other, and stayed the course. When the farmer came in the next morning, he found one frog floating on the top of a pail of cream, dead, and the other standing on a cake of butter, exhausted but happy to be alive.

When we let problems overwhelm us, when we stop jumping and hopping and scrambling for survival, we stop living. But when we hang in there and fight the good fight, we end up on a cake of butter.
—Father Giles Bello

Be still, be still my soul; it is but for a season:
Let us endure an hour and see injustice done.
—A. E. Housman
(Lines favored by William Faulkner)

You do what you can for as long as you can, and when you finally can't, you do the next best thing. You back up but you don't give up.
—Charles "Chuck" Yeager

(See *Patience*)

Energy/Stamina

The way to run faster is with a four-fifths effort. Just take it nice and easy. . . . Going all out is counterproductive. Our greatest athletes have been the sleepy-looking guys. Joe Louis. Joe DiMaggio. John Unitas. An athlete who wants to die for dear old Rutgers or San Jose State misses the point. He's no good dead.
—Bud Winters, track coach

The idea is to win, you win the way you have to. Sometimes it's a good idea to save all your energy for the really tough battles.
—Sugar Ray Robinson

I learned certain things about wasting energy. It hit me the hardest after the French [Open, which he lost]. The important thing is to learn a lesson every time you lose. Life is a learning process and you have to try to learn what's best for you. Let me tell you, life is not fun when you're banging your head against a brick wall all the time.
—John McEnroe

If you wish to begin life at forty, you must settle two large personal questions first of all. You must find work and play that call for no more energy than you can afford to spend on them. Then you must train your mind, eye and hand to the point of working and playing with ease, grace and precision.
—Walter B. Pitkin

All I'm thinking about is driving the ball through the strike zone. Drive the ball. Drive it. You're trying to get all your energies going towards home plate, physical and mental.
—Tom Seaver

Go to bed. Whatever you're staying up late for isn't worth it.
—Andrew A. Rooney

Enterprise

On starting your own business: Whatever you think it's gonna take, double it. That applies to money, time, stress. It's gonna be harder than you think and take longer than you think.
—Richard A. Cortese

Don't wait for your "ship to come in," and feel angry and cheated when it doesn't. Get going with something small.
—Dr. Irene C. Kassoria

Walk while ye have the light, lest darkness come upon you.
—New Testament
John 12:35

Try first thyself, and after call in God;
For to the worker God himself lends aid.
　　　—Euripides

In every enterprise consider where you would come out.
　　　—Publilius Syrus

Remember, if you are attempting the impossible, you will fail.
　　　—Anonymous

(See *Beginnings, Doing, Initiative*)

Entertaining

Invite the man that loves you to a feast, but let alone thine enemy.
　　　—Hesiod

Hostesses who entertain much must make up their parties as ministers make up their cabinets, on grounds other than personal liking.
　　　—George Eliot

Let the number of guests not exceed twelve . . . so chosen that their occupations are varied, their tastes similar . . . the dining room brilliantly lighted, the cloth pure white, the temperature between 60–68 degrees; the men witty and not pedantic, the women amiable and not too coquettish; the eating unhurried, dinner being the final business of the day.
　　　—Anthelme Brillat-Savarin

If you want a party where people are moving around, having fun, don't give them plates. Without plates they'll eat with their hands and talk to each other around the food. . . . When planning your party, imagine it. Walk it through.
　　　—Mary Risley
　　　Director, Tante Marie's Cooking School,
　　　San Francisco

On selecting restaurants: Stay away if there is a neon beer sign in the window. Never go to restaurants named after days of the week or months. . . . If I have to say to someone, "Should we meet Tuesday at Friday's? Or should it be Friday at Tuesday's?" I feel like I'm part of an Abbott and Costello routine.
—Alan King and Mimi Sheraton

Next time you're called on to give a toast, relax and speak from your heart. A fine toast improves the flavor of any drink, whether it's a Scotch on the rocks or a lemonade.
—Stanley Marcus

Never give a party if you will be the most interesting person there.
—Mickey Friedman

Support wildlife. Throw a party.
—Author unknown

Never be the first to arrive at a party or the last to go home and never, never be both.

Be careful not to impart your wisdom to a guest whose background you do not know. You may be instructing a Nobel laureate in his own field.
—David Brown

Be careful about giving any drink whatsoever to a bore. A lit-up bore is the worst in the world.
—David Cecil

(See *Hospitality, Visiting*)

Enthusiasm

Always give them the old fire, even when you feel like a squashed cake of ice.
—Ethel Merman

Be fanatics. When it comes to being and doing and dreaming of the best, *be maniacs*.
—A. M. Rosenthal

Think enthusiastically about everything; but especially about your job. If you do, you'll put a touch of glory in your life. If you love your job with enthusiasm, you'll shake it to pieces. You'll love it into greatness, you'll upgrade it, you'll fill it with prestige and power.
—Norman Vincent Peale

If you can give your son or daughter only one gift, let it be Enthusiasm.
—Bruce Barton

Don't ever let me catch you singing like that again, without enthusiasm. You're nothing if you aren't excited by what you're doing.
—Frank Sinatra to his son, Frank Jr.

Envy

Believe all the good you can of everyone. Do not measure others by yourself. If they have advantages which you have not, let your liberality keep pace with their good fortune. Envy no one, and you need envy no one.
—William Hazlitt

Never trust anyone who wants what you've got. Friend or no, envy is an overwhelming emotion.
—Blythe Holbrooke

Beware of envy: For to grudge any man an advantage in person and fortune, is to censure the liberality of providence, and be angry at the goodness of God.
—George Shelley

Do not measure another's coat on your own body.
—Malay proverb

The greatest of all secrets is knowing how to reduce the force of envy.
—Cardinal de Retz

Trust to me, ladies, and do not envy a splendor which does not constitute happiness.
—Josephine (first wife of Napoleon I)

Beware of covetousness; for a man's life consisteth not in the abundance of things which he possesseth.
—New Testament
Luke 12:15

Grudge not another what you cannot attain yourself.
—English proverb

Etiquette

Some table don'ts:

Don't lean back and announce, "I'm through"—just put your fork or spoon down.

Don't *ever* put liquid in your mouth if it is already filled with food.

Don't crook your finger when picking up your cup. It's an affected mannerism.
—Elizabeth Post

Whatever you do, girls, do not talk with the silverware in your hands. That is the complete pits. You never gesture with a knife and a fork.

Never be afraid to see what everybody else is doing. That happens in any social situation. Copy others! We all do that. I also believe you should not wait, when you're served, to begin eating. Just start. If someone says something to you about it, you say, "This is the way it's done in Europe."
—Charlotte Ford

Explain yourself without gestures. The moment you gesticulate you look common.

—Colette

Be aware that there is only one right way to shake hands—a firm clasp of the other person's *whole* hand (never just a few fingers) in a brief downward motion—no pumping, please. Use about as much pressure as you do when you grasp a doorknob to open a door. The gesture should take only two or three seconds. "People tend to think character matches a handshake," wrote Amy Vanderbilt. She also noted that it's not necessary to worry about who offers the hand first—these days, both men and women routinely do so.

—Julia Knowles

What should you do when you forget someone's name? . . . Honesty is always the best policy. Just admit the name has slipped your mind. Generally, you will be forgiven.

—Letitia Baldrige

Etiquette (Office)

It is definitely out of line to entertain friends in the office. It is rudeness in the extreme to drop in on someone unannounced at his office and have the receptionist call through.

—George Mazzei

On coping with unwelcome sexual advances: Try to reason with your colleague on the basis that it would be very bad for his career to have others talking in the office about his bad behavior when he's on the road. Explain that he is demonstrating a complete lack of professional respect for you. Tell him you know he didn't *really mean* to make that pass. Then leave because you're in a no-win situation. . . . When you see him the next day, act as though nothing happened.

—Letitia Baldrige

How to make them take your call: Tell them something they want to hear or something they will be afraid not to hear. I once received a

call from someone I didn't know, and the message was "I've got some great news." It turned out to be one of those telephone solicitations, but at least I did return the call.
—Mark McCormack

Former Postmaster General J. Edward Day revealed in his book an ingenious way to stop long-winded telephone callers. Day suggests you hang up while *you* are talking. The other party thinks you were accidentally cut off, because no one would hang up on his own voice.
—Judith Martin
"Miss Manners"

(See *Courtesy, Manners*)

Evil

Be sober, be vigilant; because your adversary, the Devil, as a roaring lion, walketh about seeking whom he may devour.
—New Testament
I Peter 5:8

When you choose the lesser of two evils, always remember that it is still an evil.
—Max Lerner

Resist the Devil, and he will flee from you.
—New Testament
James 4:7

If you have been tempted into evil, fly from it. It is not falling into the water, but lying in it, that drowns.
—Author unknown

He who sups with the Devil should have a long spoon.
—English proverb

Example 129

If you do evil, expect to suffer evil.
                    —Spanish proverb

(See *Crime, Sin*)

Example

Show yourself in all respects a model of good deeds.
                    —New Testament
                    Titus 2:7

Be careful how you live. You may be the only Bible some person ever reads.
                    —William J. Toms

If you would convince a man that he does wrong, do right. But do not care to convince him. Men will believe what they see. Let them see.
                    —Henry David Thoreau

My advice is, to consult the lives of other men, as he would a looking glass, and from thence fetch examples for his own imitation.
                    —Terence

Learn to admire rightly; the great pleasure of life is that. Note what the great men admired; they admired great things; narrow spirits admire basely, and worship meanly.
                    —William Makepeace Thackeray

Children learn as much from observing adults and then imitating and modeling our behavior, as they do from actual instruction. This means that parents must constantly demonstrate by their own actions and behavior what they are telling their children to do. The child gets two confusing messages when a parent tells him which is the right fork to use, and then proceeds to use the wrong one. So does the child who

listens to parents bicker and fuss, yet is told to be nice to his brothers and sisters.
—Dr. Michael Lewis

Watch me, learn from me and learn from my mistakes.
—Judy Garland's advice to her
daughter Liza Minnelli

Expectation

Don't pin much hope on the mail and when the phone rings don't expect anyone wonderful to be calling.
—Andrew A. Rooney

Never anticipate evils; or, because you cannot have things exactly as you wish, make them out worse than they are, through mere spite and wilfulness.
—William Hazlitt

One should not be in a hurry to be distressed; let us wait till what seems so bad comes to a head.
—Bernard le Bovier de Fontenelle

Make not the sauce till you have caught the fish.
—English proverb

People tend to have enormous expectations for what the holiday season will bring. Then in January, they realize it wasn't the answer. If you find yourself daydreaming that everything will be made right by the holiday season, be honest and admit that it really isn't going to have that much impact. We know that for some people this is easy and for others it's enormously difficult.
—Dr. Jerry M. Wiener

Look to be treated by others as you have treated others.
—Publilius Syrus

F

Facetious Advice

Lead us not into temptation. Just tell us where it is; we'll find it.
—Sam Levenson

Don't bother discussing sex with small children. They rarely have anything to add.
—Fran Lebowitz

RULES
1. The boss is always right.
2. When the boss is wrong, refer to Rule 1.
—Paul Dickson

BOREN'S WORK LAWS:
1. When in doubt, mumble.
2. When in trouble, delegate.
3. When in charge, ponder.

When all else fails, read the instructions.
—Arthur Bloch

Never accept an invitation from a stranger unless he offers you candy.
—Linda Festa

To teenagers: Straighten up your room first, *then* the world.
—Jeff Jordan

On crime detecting: Find the motive—and you've got the motive.
                                        —Groucho Marx

Personally, I find the best way to relieve anxieties is to shout an old-fashioned curse on your enemies. . . . Simply rear back and shout at them:
     May you get an obscene phone call from your psychiatrist!
     May you invest heavily in a solar heating system and may every day
       be cloudy.
     May your son work in Hawaii as a volcano sweep.
                                        —Phyllis Diller

How to open a childproof bottle: Leave the bottle in a room with a child.
                        —Michael Sorkin and Marguerite Howe

How to Get Out of Admitting You're Guilty Even Though You're Guilty: Deny it. Accuse him of doing it. Tell him he drove you to it. Tell him it doesn't count because you hated it.
                                        —Judith Viorst

Hartley's Second Law: Never sleep with anyone crazier than yourself.
                                        —Arthur Bloch

For job interviewers:
Never hire anybody whose résumé rhymes.

Never hire anybody whose résumé begins, *Call me Ishmael.*
                                        —Robert S. Wieder

It's so simple to be wise. Just think of something stupid to say, then say the opposite.
                                        —Sam Levenson

When all else fails, tell the truth.
                        —Line quoted by Donald T. Regan

Fill your mouth with marbles and make a speech. Every day reduce the number of marbles in your mouth and make a speech. You will

soon become an accredited public speaker—as soon as you have lost all your marbles.
—Brooks Hays

Never offend somebody with style when you can offend them with substance.
—Anonymous

Never run after your hat—others will be delighted to do it; why spoil their fun?
—Mark Twain

Never buy a car that's being sold at the bottom of a ravine.
—Joey Adams

Advice to a guest's child who is destroying your home: "Aaron, dear, why don't you go out and play in the traffic?"
—Judith Martin
"Miss Manners"

Never buy a portable TV set on the sidewalk from a man who's out of breath.
—Anonymous

How to drive a guy crazy: Send him a telegram and on top put "page 2."
—Henny Youngman

More than any other time in history, mankind faces a crossroads. One path leads to despair and utter hopelessness. The other, to total extinction. Let us pray we have the wisdom to choose correctly. . . . Summing up, it is clear the future holds great opportunities. It also holds pitfalls. The trick will be to avoid the pitfalls, seize the opportunities and get back home by six o'clock.
—Woody Allen
"My Speech to the Graduates"

Beware of the struggling young author, my friends. Whom God sees fit to starve, let not man presumptuously rescue from his own undoing.
—Mark Twain

Never steal a dure-mat. If ye do, ye'll be investigated, hanged and maybe reformed. Steal a bank, me boy, steal a bank.
                    —Finlay Peter Dunne

Marry a fat goil. They strong. Woik f'ya. Don't marry a face. Put ya under.
                    —Mel Brooks's Uncle Joe

Advice from an acupuncturist: Just take two thumbtacks and call me in the morning.
                    —Leo Steiner
                    quoted by Joey Adams

(See *Advice, Bad Advice, Counsel, Questionable Advice*)

Facts

Do not become archivists of facts. Try to penetrate to the secret of their occurrence, persistently search for the laws which govern them.
                    —Ivan Pavlov

The way to do research is to attack the facts at the point of greatest astonishment.
                    —Celia Green

Teach these boys and girls nothing but Facts. Facts alone are wanted in life. Plant nothing else, and root out everything else. You can only form the minds of reasoning animals upon Facts; nothing else will ever be of any service to them. This is the principle on which I bring up my own children, and this is the principle on which I bring up these children. Stick to Facts, sir!
                    —Thomas Gradgrind, in Charles Dickens'
                    Hard Times

Failure

Whenever you fall, pick something up.
—Oswald Avery

To bear failure with courage is the best proof of character that anyone can give. . . . You will find that people forget the failures of others very quickly. . . . My last piece of advice is not to let anyone see your mortification, but whatever you fancy people are saying about you to go on with your ordinary life as though nothing unpleasant had happened to you.
—W. Somerset Maugham

(See *Adversity, Defeat, Despair, Disappointment, Discouragement*)

Faith

Fight the good fight of faith.
—New Testament
I Timothy 6:12

Keep your faith in all beautiful things; in the sun when it is hidden, in the Spring when it is gone.
—Roy R. Gilson

If you believe, then you hang on. If you believe, it means you've got imagination, you don't need stuff thrown out for you in a blueprint, you don't face facts—what can stop you? If I don't make it today, I'll come in tomorrow.
—Ruth Gordon

. . . cling to Faith beyond the forms of Faith.
—Alfred, Lord Tennyson

I said to a man who stood at the gate of the year: "Give me a light that I may tread safely into the unknown." And he replied, "Go out into the darkness and put your hand into the hand of God. That shall be to you better than a light and safer than a known way."
—Minnie L. Haskins
(Quoted by King George VI of England, on Christmas Day 1939)

If you can't have faith in what is held up to you for faith, you must find things to believe in yourself, for a life without faith in something is too narrow a space to live.
—George E. Woodbury

We must have infinite faith in each other. If we have not, we must never let it leak out that we have not.
—Henry David Thoreau

I think that if I got a bicycle from my father, I should give a car to my son. In order to pass the exam of life, you have to give at least what you got from your parents, more or less in every sphere of life, or at least in the most basic ones: spiritual things and those for the body. I got faith from my parent, and I'm feeding faith, and I try to multiply in a maximum way what I have got. So instead of just making the sign of the cross, I say the Lord's Prayer.
—Lech Walesa

If I were dying, my last words would be, Have faith and pursue the unknown end.
—Oliver Wendell Holmes, Jr., at age 81

(See *God, Prayer, Skepticism, Trust*)

Fame

Let us satisfy our own consciences, and trouble not ourselves by looking for fame. If we deserve it, we shall attain it; if we deserve it not, we cannot force it.
—Seneca

Make your best bow to her and bid adieu,
Then, if she likes it, she will follow you.
—John Keats

Do not get excited over the noise you have made.
—Desiderius Erasmus

Kid, don't ever forget two things I'm going to tell you. One, don't believe everything that's written about you. Two, don't pick up too many checks.
—George Herman ("Babe") Ruth to
Harold ("Red") Grange, who had just
turned professional

The best way to handle celebrity status is for people to retain ties to where they came from—religion, family, hobbies—things that rooted them to life before they became celebrities.
—Dr. Howard A. Hoffman

Your first reaction when you become a public figure is, "Aren't I important! Who's going to call next?" But you can't let it turn your head, or you'll mess yourself up forever. You have to take your job seriously, but you can't take yourself seriously. This could pass so quickly.
—Brent Musburger

(See *Applause*, *Greatness*, *Praise*, *Reputation*)

Family

Stick with your family.
—Ida P. Safir
deathbed advice to her three sons

If you don't eat at least one meal with your children, you give up your best opportunity to teach concern for the needs of others. Let's face

it, chaotic meals contribute to self-oriented, pleasure-oriented values. The family meal is an excellent forum to learn about listening to others, taking turns and, in general, constraining instinctual needs in a social context.
—Dr. Lawrence J. Hatterer

Always tell your rich relatives how fast you are making money, and your poor ones how fast you are losing it.
—Author unknown

Do not be cool toward a close relative on account of some small quarrel; do not forget an old act of kindness because of a recent dispute.
—*Mr. Tut-Tut* (17th century)
Translated by Lin Yutang

A protective family can end up driving a child away. So you can forbid a youngster from going sky-diving, but you must realize that once you've forbidden it, that is all you can reasonably do. And you must be prepared for the fact that they may do it anyway. You must use all the moral suasion you can.
—Dr. Thomas Gamble

(See *Children, Mother's Advice, Parenthood*)

Fashion

Be not the first by whom the new are tried,
Nor yet the last to lay the old aside.
—Alexander Pope

Take great care always to be dressed like the reasonable people of your own age, in the place where you are; whose dress is never spoken of one way or another, as either too negligent or too much studied.
—Lord Chesterfield

As to your dress and manners, avoid as you would a pestilence those of a fop.
—Martha Wilson

Fashion is an industry rip-off. Forget it! Stay with the classics.
—Mortimer Levitt

Never try to wear a hat that has more character than you do.
—Lance Morrow

The trick of wearing mink is to look as though you were wearing a cloth coat. The trick of wearing a cloth coat is to look as though you were wearing mink.
—Pierre Balmain

Judge not a man by his clothes, but by his wife's clothes.
—Thomas R. Dewar

(See *Allure, Appearance, Beauty, Deportment, Dress, Grooming, Image*)

Fate

If Fate does not adjust itself to you, adjust yourself to Fate.
—Persian proverb

Seek not thou to find
The sacred counsels of almighty mind;
Involv'd in darkness lies the great decree,
Nor can the depths of fate be pierc'd by thee.
—Alexander Pope

Faith means that a man should regard any disaster simply as a fate-determined blow which must be endured.
—Anwar el-Sadat

One should treat one's fate as one does one's health; enjoy it when it is good, be patient with it when it is poorly, and never attempt any drastic cure save as an ultimate resort.
                    —François de La Rochefoucauld

(See *Destiny, Luck*)

Faults

It is better to be a crystal and be broken,
Than to remain perfect like a tile upon the housetop.
        —Kusakabe
        quoted by Robert Louis Stevenson

Never let the irregularities of your own life be the subject of your discourse, for men detest in others those vices which they cherish in themselves.
                    —Charles Palmer

Never exaggerate your faults. Your friends will attend to that.
                    —Robert C. Edwards

A man should be careful never to tell tales of himself to his own disadvantage. People may be amused and laugh at the time, but they will be remembered and brought out against him upon some subsequent occasion.
                    —Samuel Johnson

Face your deficiencies and acknowledge them; but do not let them master you. Let them teach you patience, sweetness, insight. . . . When we do the best we can, we never know what miracle is wrought in our life, or in the life of another.
                    —Helen Keller

Favor

Do not squander favor. Great friends are for great occasions; so do not waste a great generosity upon a matter trivial, for that is to squander good will.
> —Baltasar Gracián

If you want to make a dangerous man your friend, let him do you a favor.
> —Warden Lewis E. Lawes

Play no favorites: When Joseph got a many-colored coat, his brothers came to hate him.
> —Midrash, Genesis Rabbah

(See *Ability, Ancestry, Merit, Proficiency*)

Fear

Fear not, provided you fear; but if you fear not, then fear.
> —Blaise Pascal

It was a high counsel that I once heard given to a young person, "Always do what you are afraid to do."
> —Ralph Waldo Emerson

There is nothing wrong in admitting you are afraid. But whenever something threatens you, instead of running away, hold your ground and repeat the mantra Rama, Rama [God, God] over and over again in your mind. It can turn your fear into fearlessness.
> —Advice of an old family servant to
> Mohandas K. Gandhi, in his youth

When you're afraid, keep your mind on what you have to do. And if you have been thoroughly prepared, you will not be afraid.
      —Dale Carnegie

Be not afraid of sudden fear.
      —Old Testament
      Proverbs 3:25

Fear the goat from the front, the horse from the rear, and the man from all sides.
      —Russian proverb

The question is not whether you're frightened or not, but whether you or the fear is in control. If you say, "I won't be frightened," and then you experience fear, most likely you'll succumb to it, because you're paying attention to it. The correct thing to tell yourself is, "If I do get frightened, I will stay in command."
      —Dr. Herbert Fensterheim

We will not be driven by fear into an age of unreason if we . . . remember that we are not descended from fearful men, not from men who feared to write, to speak, to associate and to defend causes which were, for the moment, unpopular.
      —Edward R. Murrow
      "See It Now" Broadcast
      Report on Senator Joseph R. McCarthy

Fidelity/Infidelity

Hold faithfulness and sincerity as first principles.
      —Confucius

Don't trust a husband too far or a bachelor too near: Once, an officer of ancient Rome, called away to the wars, locked his beautiful wife in armor, gave the key to his best friend, a bachelor, with the admonition, "If I don't return in six months, use this key. To you, my

dear friend, I entrust it." He then galloped off to the wars. About ten miles from home, he turned to see a cloud of dust approaching. His trusted friend, on horseback, galloped up and said: "You gave me the wrong key."
—Maxwell Droke

Remember, if you can get along with one woman, you can get along with more.
—Arthur ("Bugs") Baer

In love affairs it is only the beginnings that are amusing. Therefore, you should start over again as soon as possible.
—Marquise de Sévigné

Never tell. Not if you love your wife. . . . In fact, if your old lady walks in on you, deny it. Yeah. Just flat out and she'll believe it. I'm tellin' ya. This chick came downstairs with a sign around her neck "Lay on Top of Me or I'll Die. . . ." I didn't know what I was gonna do. . . .
—Lenny Bruce

Thou shalt not commit adultery with the boss, because falling out of love will mean falling off the fast track.
—Marilee Hartley

(See *Constancy*)

Flattery

Flatter no man to gain his favor, for this will add falsehood and injury to hypocrisy, that will react with a sure and sore vengeance.
—Charles Simmons

I recommend to you . . . an innocent piece of art; that of flattering people behind their backs . . . This is, of all flattery, the most pleasing, and consequently, the most effectual.
—Lord Chesterfield

Be advised that all flatterers live at the expense of those who listen to them.

—Jean de La Fontaine

You must be very subtle. . . . You have to treat a highly intelligent man as a highly intelligent man. You must make him immediately aware that you are taking him very seriously. And you must enhance his confidence. Flattery is simply to make a man believe he can solve his problems.

—Henry A. Kissinger

Never accept flattery as though it were a compliment, and never treat a compliment as though it were mere flattery.

—Russell Lynes

Beware of softly whispered flatteries.

—Cato

Laugh when he laughs, so shalt thou be very agreeable to his heart and what thou doest will be very pleasant to his heart.

—Ptahhotep, 24th Century B.C.

Flirting

Wherever you plan to go, plan to flirt—with the wine merchant, your butcher, the man who handles your affairs at the bank. Flirting is an honorable pastime, good for everyone's ego, and without a doubt, it slims the waistline by sending hormones zipping around your body.

—Jeanine Larmoth

Flirtatious handshake: Finish with a tiny extra squeeze. This should not be tight, but merely a surge of energy. Then let go. Doing this signals that you are warm, confident, and something more than just pleased to meet someone—you are indicating there is a definite attraction.

There are times not to flirt. When you're sick. When you're with children. When you're on the witness stand.
—Joyce Jillson

Many a man has foolishly entered upon a flirtation—been drawn into an engagement, and compelled to marry against the strongest repulsion. . . . If you make a mistake, the moment you suspect it . . . stop . . . apologize . . . express your regrets, make any amends in your power . . . be sued, fight, do anything but marry.
—*The Illustrated Manners Book*, 1856

Key axioms for women who would be wives:
  Keep thinking of yourself as a soft, mysterious cat.
  Always sound delighted when a man calls.
  Do not make abrupt gestures of any kind.
  If he has a girlfriend, try to become a good friend of hers.
  Sarcasm is dangerous. Avoid it altogether.

This revisionist approach to romance may be difficult at first for women who thought that having your own American Express card meant never having to feign interest. But with enough practice, and enough leopard-skin scarfs, any woman should be able to act as feline as a cat. And avoid sarcasm—altogether.
—Maureen Dowd

Force

Let us first . . . entreat the man by gentle means, to let us in; . . . Then if all fayle, we will by force it win.
—Edmund Spenser

First, all means to conciliate; failing that, all means to crush.
—Cardinal Richelieu

There are two ways of contending, by law and by force; the first is proper to men; the second to beasts; but because many times the first is insufficient, recourse must be had to the second.
—Niccolò Machiavelli

(See *Freedom, Military, Oppression, Peace, Preparedness—Military, Warfare*)

Foresight

It's helpful to look at your life and ask: "If I had one more year to live, what would I do?" We all have things we want to achieve. Don't just put them off—do them now!
—John Goddard

We should go warily into the future, looking for ways to be more useful, listening more carefully for signals, watching our step and having an eye out for partners.
—Dr. Lewis Thomas

It will not always be summer: build barns.
—Hesiod

The surest way to get a thing in this life is to be prepared for doing without it, to the exclusion even of hope.
—Jane Welsh Carlyle

Always look ahead. Look far ahead as a racing motorist looks, through his telescopic sight, at the horizon which he will have reached before he knows it.
—Arnold J. Toynbee

Forgiveness

If your brother sins, call him to task, and if he repents, forgive him.
　　　　—New Testament
　　　　Luke 17:3

Do as the heavens have done, forget your evil;
With them forgive yourself.
　　　　—Cleomenes in Shakespeare's
　　　　The Winter's Tale

Forgive, son; men are men, they needs must err.
　　　　—Euripides

Let us no more contend, nor blame
Each other, blam'd enough elsewhere, but strive
In offices of love, how we may lighten
Each other's burden, in our share of woe.
　　　　—John Milton

We must develop and maintain the capacity to forgive. He who is devoid of the power to forgive is devoid of the power to love. There is some good in the worst of us and some evil in the best of us. When we discover this, we are less prone to hate our enemies.
　　　　—Dr. Martin Luther King, Jr.

Forgive your enemies, but never forget their names.
　　　　—Edward I. Koch

Once, but in our time, there was a war transcending greed and miscalculation. Once, in our time, there existed a satanic force that aspired not only to conquer and plunder but to establish a bestial order in half the globe. And in our time, a kindred people fell enthusiastically under the spell of this fascist demon. . . .

On days of remembrance, the proper prayer is . . . carved into stone at the Bergen-Belsen concentration camp: EARTH CONCEAL NOT THE BLOOD SHED ON THEE!
—Editorial, *New York Times*

(See *Mercy, Remembrance*)

Fortitude

Bear, do not blame, what cannot be changed.
—Publilius Syrus

Bear the ills you have, lest worse befall you.
—Phaedrus

You gotta play the hand that's dealt you. There may be pain in that hand, but you play it. And I've played it.
—James Brady
Presidential Press Secretary (shot during assassination attempt on President Reagan)

Never give up!—if adversity presses,
Providence wisely has mingled the cup.
And the best counsel, in all your distresses,
Is the stout watchword, "Never give up!"
—Martin Farquhar Tupper

Whatever you do . . . don't whimper, but take the consequences.
—T. S. Eliot
Address to students

Bite on the bullet, old man, and don't let them think you're afraid.
—Rudyard Kipling

You have to learn to live with your chances. It's not easy, but if you are honest, it becomes easy. Then you can laugh at it, and you can hope, too, because that gives you a hold on life.
—Cancer patient Christa Freund

(See *Courage, Daring, Despair, Risk, Spirit*)

Freedom

Hereditary bondsmen! know ye not,
Who would be free, themselves must strike the blow?
—Lord Byron

It is better to die on your feet than to live on your knees.
—Dolores Ibarruri (known as La Pasionaria)
Speech in Paris, 1936

It is far better to fight on your feet than on your knees, but you can still fight on your knees.
—Alexander Solzhenitsyn

If A Plant's Roots Are Too Tight, Repot.
—Headline, *New York Times,*
on gardening

America is a passionate belief in freedom and in the worth and dignity of the human personality. We must not let the song die on our lips.
—Harry Emerson Fosdick

An artist should never be: prisoner of himself, prisoner of a style, prisoner of success, etc. Did not the Goncourts write that the artists of the great age of Japanese art changed names many times during their careers? I like that: they wanted to safeguard their freedom.
—Henri Matisse

(See *Diplomacy, Force, Oppression, Peace, Preparedness—Military, Warfare*)

Freedom of the Press

Be not intimidated, therefore, by any terrors, from publishing with the utmost freedom whatever can be warranted by the laws of your country, nor suffer yourselves to be wheedled out of your liberty by any pretenses of politeness, delicacy, or decency. These, as they are often used, are but three different names for hypocrisy, chicanery and cowardice.

—John Adams, 1765

Friendship

Develop the art of friendliness. One can experience a variety of emotions staying home and reading or watching television; one will be alive but hardly living. Most of the meaningful aspects of life are closely associated with people. Even the dictionary definition of life involves people.

—William L. Abbott

Treat your friends as you do your pictures, and place them in their best light.

—Jennie Jerome Churchill

Hold a true friend with both hands.

—Nigerian proverb

Don't put your friend in your pocket.

—Irish proverb

Above all things, be not made an ass to carry the burdens of other men: if any friend desire thee to be his surety, give him a part of what

thou hast to spare; if he presses thee further, he is not thy friend at all, for friendship rather chooseth harm to itself than offereth it.
> —Sir Walter Raleigh
> Advice to his son

Some of the most rewarding and beautiful moments of a friendship happen in the unforeseen open spaces between planned activities. It is important that you allow these spaces to exist.
> —Christine Leefeldt and Ernest Callenbach

In choosing a friend, go up a step.
> —Jewish proverb

The art of life is to keep down acquaintances. One's friends one can manage, but one's acquaintances can be the devil.
> —Edward Verall Lucas

Treat your friends like family and your family like friends.
> —Mother's advice quoted by Michele Slung

Put not so much into a friend's power that, if hostilely disposed, he can do you an injury.
> —Saadi

On loss of friends
> Let no man grumble when his friends fall off,
> As they will do like leaves at the first breeze:
> When your affairs come round, one way or t'other,
> Go to the coffee house, and take another.
> —Lord Byron

Do not make a surfeit of friendship through over-sanguine enthusiasm, nor expect it to last forever. . . . Do not keep on with a mockery of friendship after the substance is gone—but part, while you can part friends.
> —William Hazlitt

> Where you are liberal of your loves and counsels,
> Be sure you be not loose; for those you make friends
> And give your hearts to, when they once perceive

The least rub in your fortunes, fall away
Like water from ye, never found again
But where they mean to sink ye.
> —Duke of Buckingham in
> Shakespeare's *King Henry VIII*

(See *Companionship*)

Fulfillment

If I could get the ear of every young man but for one word, it would be this; make the most and best of yourself. There is no tragedy like a wasted life—a life failing of its true end, and turned to a false end.
> —T. T. Munger

Strange that any human being should be content with less than the fullness of life! I take that back. We are not content to be less than we might be, but at times we do fail in courage, or we become tired and need a hand on our shoulder to hearten us. I need it often. When my spirits are a bit low, I give myself Goethe's advice:
"Remember to live."
> —John Erskine

Think it more satisfaction to live richly than die rich.
> —Sir Thomas Browne

Don't evaluate your life in terms of achievements, trivial *or* monumental, along the way. If you do, you will be destined to the frustration of always seeking out other destinations, and never allowing yourself actually to be fulfilled. . . . Instead, wake up and appreciate everything you encounter along your path. Enjoy the flowers that are there for your pleasure. Tune in to the sunrise, the little children, the laughter, the rain and the birds. Drink it all in . . . *there is no way to happiness; happiness IS the way.*
> —Dr. Wayne W. Dyer

Be All That You Can Be.
   —U.S. Army Slogan

(See *Happiness, Purpose*)

The Future

Build on resolve and not upon regret
The structure of the future.
Waste no tears upon the blotted record of lost years,
But turn the leaf and smile.
   —Adlai E. Stevenson

Just remember—when you think all is lost, the future remains.
   —Quoted by Bob Goddard

Never look at the future with eyes of fear.
   —Anonymous

Don't add to the difficulties and problems of today by worrying about what is going to happen tomorrow. "Take therefore no thought for the morrow; for the morrow shall take thought for the things of itself. Sufficient unto the day is the evil thereof."—New Testament, Matthew 6:33–34
   —Ronald Rideout and Clifford Whitting

We must respect the past, and mistrust the present, if we wish to provide for the safety of the future.
   —Joseph Joubert

If you try to measure the future you will never risk the present. Playing it safe. A ghastly game.
   —Catherine Deneuve

G

Gambling

The best throw of the dice is to throw them away.
—English proverb

Keep flax from fire, youth from gaming.
—Benjamin Franklin

If you must play, decide upon three things at the start: the rules of the game, the stakes, and the quitting time.
—Chinese proverb

"Son," the old man said, "as you go around and about in this world, some day you will come upon a man who will lay down in front of you a new deck of cards with the seal unbroken and offer to bet he can make the jack of spades jump out of the deck and squirt cider in your ear. Son," the old man continued, "do not bet him because as sure as you do, you are going to get an earful of cider."
—Damon Runyon

Generosity

Give soon and you give twice.
—Publilius Syrus

Put justice before generosity.
>—Irish proverb

Give a grateful man more than he asks.
>—Portuguese proverb

We should give as we would receive, cheerfully, quickly, and without hesitation; for there is no grace in a benefit that sticks to the fingers.
>—Seneca

If you have much give of your wealth, if you have little give of your heart.
>—Arab proverb

As long as you give yourself and your time to a man, you can be as ambitious as you want. *Giving* is the key. The more independent you want to be, the more generous you must be with yourself as a woman.
>—Diane von Furstenberg

(See *Charity, Compassion, Kindness, Sympathy*)

Gifts

Never look a gift horse in the mouth. A gift ought to rise in our esteem in proportion to the friendship and respect of the donor; not to the intrinsic excellency or worth. . . . To make a judgment of the donor's affection by the value of the present is often a false estimate; for if it be but a small matter, 'tis more than you could insist upon, and may be the effect of the giver's sincerest affection, as well as equal to his fortunes.
>—Samuel Palmer

Women are never what they seem to be. There is the woman you see and there is the woman who is hidden. Buy the gift for the woman who is hidden.
>—Erma Bombeck

Let him that desires to see others happy, make haste to give while his gift can be enjoyed, and remember that every moment of delay takes away something from the value of his benediction.
—Samuel Johnson

International gift-giving etiquette:
Flowers are appreciated when visiting a home in Japan, but never give chrysanthemums: they are part of the Imperial Family's personal crest.

Never inquire about an Arab's wife; worse, never bring a gift for her— you may be suspected of ulterior motives.

Never bring red roses to your host's home in Germany; red roses are reserved for lovers.

Don't give perfume to a French business woman; this is considered far too personal a gesture.
—Dr. Kathleen Reardon

Never give an Argentinian a set of knives. It signals a desire to cut off the business relationship.
—Letitia Baldrige

Office gifts: An employee should never give a present to a superior— under any circumstances. It takes it out of the realm of a business relationship. A boss, on the other hand, should gift only his immediate secretary, not all of the people who work under him.
—George Mazzei

God

Be strong and of good courage; be not afraid, neither be thou dismayed: for the Lord thy God *is* with thee whithersoever thou goest.
—Old Testament
Joshua 1:9

Render unto Caesar the things which are Caesar's; and unto God the things that are God's.
>—New Testament
>Matthew 22:21

Be not deceived; God is not mocked; for whatsoever a man soweth, that shall he also reap.
>—New Testament
>Galatians 6:7

Let us weigh the gain and the loss in wagering that God *is*, but let us consider the two possibilities. If you gain, you gain all; if you lose you lose nothing. Hesitate not, then, to wager that He is.
>—Blaise Pascal

And I say to mankind, be not curious about God. For I, who am curious about each, am not curious about God—I hear and behold God in every object, yet understand God not in the least.
>—Walt Whitman

Don't bargain with God.
>—Yiddish proverb

Let us fear God and we shall cease to fear man.
>—Mohandas K. Gandhi

(See *Faith, Skepticism, Trust*)

Good Humor

To be wildly enthusiastic, or deadly serious—both are wrong. Both pass. One must keep ever present a sense of humour. It depends entirely on yourself how much you see or understand. But the sense of humour I have found of use in every single occasion of my life.
>—Katherine Mansfield

Do not take life too seriously. You will never get out of it alive.
>—Elbert Hubbard

Look for the ridiculous in everything and you will find it.
—Jules Renard

Once you can laugh at your own weaknesses, you can move forward.
Comedy breaks down walls. It opens up people. If you're good, you
can fill up those openings with something positive. Maybe you can
combat some of the ugliness in the world.
—Goldie Hawn

Do not think that your Learning and Genius, your Wit or Sprightliness,
are welcome everywhere. I was once told that my Company was disagreeable because I appeared so uncommonly happy.
—Johann Georg von Zimmerman

(See *Cheerfulness, Optimism*)

Goodness

In the time of your life, live—so that in that good time there shall be
no ugliness or death for yourself or for any life your life touches. Seek
goodness everywhere, and where it is found, bring it out of its hiding-
place and let it be free and unashamed.
—William Saroyan

No man should be praised for his goodness if he lacks the strength to
be bad; in such cases goodness is usually only the effect of indolence
or impotence of will.
—François de La Rochefoucauld

Don't be too worthwhile. Always keep a few character defects handy.
People love to talk about your frailties. If you must be noble, keep it
to yourself.
—Edward D. Stone

If you would succeed, you must not be too good.
—Italian proverb

(See *Conscience, Honor, Morality, Uprightness, Virtue*)

Gossip/Rumor

Be not a witness against thy neighbour without cause; and deceive *not* with thy lips.
—Old Testament
Proverbs 24:28

Let us suspect all rumours whether about events or persons. When Napoleon's marshals told him they had won a victory, he said, "Show me your prisoners." When you are told a rumour do not swallow it like a hungry pike. Say "Show me your facts." And before you accept them be sure they are the whole facts and not half facts.
—Author unknown

Refrain your tongue from backbiting.
—Apocrypha

What you don't see with your eyes, don't witness with your mouth.
—Jewish proverb

Wives of corporate directors who babble indiscreetly at lunch are a rich source of financial information. Listen carefully and buy them another drink.
—David Brown

Bored with your present enemies? Make new ones! Tell two of your women friends that they look alike.
—Mignon McLaughlin

(See *Slander/Scandal*)

Government

Do not expect Plato's ideal republic; be satisfied with even the smallest step forward, and consider this no small achievement.
—Marcus Aurelius

If, to please the people, we offer what we ourselves disapprove, how can we afterward defend our work? Let us raise a standard to which the wise and honest can repair. . . .
—George Washington

Unite for the public safety, if you would remain an independent nation.
—Napoleon I

Cherish, therefore, the spirit of our people, and keep alive their attention. Do not be too severe upon their errors, but reclaim them by enlightening them. If once they become inattentive to public affairs, you and I, and Congress and Assemblies, Judges and Governors, shall all become wolves.
—Thomas Jefferson

Of government interference: *Laissez faire, laissez passer.* Leave it alone, and let it happen.
—François Quesnay

Rudyard Kipling recommended that the leaders of nations study the art of "judicious leaving alone." Chief Justice Burger has a little warning sign on his desk: "L.I.S.—let it simmer."
—James Reston

If you are to stand up *for* your Government, you must be able to stand up *to* your Government.
—Sir Harold Caccia

Never for a day let them forget that you can pick up your marbles and go home.
—Douglas Dillon to Sol Linowitz
on appointment to government post

Pray for the welfare of the government, since if it were not for the awe which it inspires, men would swallow each other alive.
— The Talmud

In governing others you must do what you can do, not all you would do.
— Italian proverb

Free the state from the past. Weed it out. Fumigate it. Put it back on the job of serving the present.
— Raymond Moley

Let the people think they govern and they will be governed.
— William Penn

To gain the hearts of the people, among other things, I have two chiefly to recommend: One is, to be affable, courteous, and fair to all the world; I have already told thee of that: And for the other, to take care that plenty of provisions be never wanting, for nothing afflicts or urges more the spirits of the poor, than scarcity or hunger.

Do not put out many new orders, and if thou dost put out many, see that they be wholesome and good, and especially that they be strictly observ'd; for laws not well obey'd, are not better than if they were not made, and only shew that the Prince who had the wisdom and authority to make them, had not resolution to see 'em executed; and laws that only threaten, and are not kept, become like the log that was given to the frogs to be their king, which they fear'd at first, but soon scorn'd and trampled on. . . .

Visit the prisons, the shambles, and the publick markets, for the Governor's presence is highly necessary in such places.

Comfort the prisoners that hope to be quickly dispatched.
— Miguel de Cervantes
Don Quixote

(See *Diplomacy, Politics*)

Gratitude

Let not thine hand be stretched out to receive and shut when thou shouldst repay.
> —Apocrypha
> Ecclesiasticus

When eating bamboo sprouts, remember the man who planted them.
> —Chinese proverb

Don't drown the man who taught you to swim.
> —English proverb

To a grateful man, give money when he asks.
> —English proverb

Do not neglect gratitude. Say thank you. Better still, say it in writing. A simple note of thanks is money in the bank and you will be remembered.
> —Princess Jackson Smith

Do not refuse a wing to the person who gave you the whole chicken.
> —R. G. H. Siu

When befriended, remember it; when you befriend, forget it.
> —Benjamin Franklin

Greatness

To achieve great things we must live as though we were never going to die.
> —Marquis de Vauvenargues

Be substantially great in thyself, and more than thou appearest unto others.
> —Sir Thomas Browne

Study to be eminent: Mediocrity is below a brave soul: Eminence in a high employment will distinguish you from the vulgar, and advance you into the Catalogue of Famous Men: to be eminent in a low profession, is to be great in little, and something in nothing.
　　　　—W. de Britaine

Be great in act, as you have been in thought.
Let not the world see fear and sad distrust
Govern the motion of a kingly eye.
　　　　—Philip the Bastard in
　　　　Shakespeare's *King John*

The longer you live and the more you learn, the more clearly you will feel the difference between the few men who are truly great and the mere *virtuosi*. . . . I must deny myself the applause of the crowd. . . . The point is not to take the world's opinion as a guiding star but to go one's way in life and work unerringly, neither depressed by failure nor seduced by applause. A true "personality" . . . is like a robust organism that, with unconscious sureness, seeks out and digests the nourishment appropriate to it and vigorously rejects that which is unsuitable. You must renounce all superficiality, all convention, all vanity and delusion. . . .
　　　　—Gustav Mahler, advice to his wife Alma

Envie not greatness; for thou mak'st thereby
Thyself the worse, and so the distance greater.
　　　　—George Herbert

Don't bunt. Aim out of the ball park. Aim for the company of the immortals.
　　　　—David Ogilvy

(See *Applause, Fame, Reputation*)

Grief

I think many people need to learn that it is OK to cry and that they do not have to be strong all the time . . . We all have the right to be

human, to feel, to cry. There is no need to deprive ourselves of the natural healthy release of emotional tears. The next time you feel tears coming and struggle to hold them back, think of Mr. Bumbles' lines from Charles Dickens' *Oliver Twist*: "It opens the lungs, washes the countenance, exercises the eyes, and softens down the temper. So cry away!"
                            —Dr. William H. Frey II

Weeping is perhaps the most human and universal of all relief measures.
                            —Dr. Karl Menninger

Believe in dreams. Never believe in hurts. . . . You can't let the grief and the hurts and the breaking experiences of life control your future decisions.
                            —Robert H. Schuller

There can be no resolution of mourning and loss until you put the question of "Why?" behind. . . . [Better questions might be] "How do I survive and find courage? How can I take this life-shattering trauma and make it a basis for growing?"
                            —Mrs. A. J. Levinson and Harold S. Kushner

Let mourning stop when one's grief is fully expressed.
                            —Confucius

Face grief without any expectation of miraculous healing, but with the knowledge that if we are courageous and resolute we can live as our loved ones would wish us to live, not empty, morose, self-centered, and self-pitying, but as brave and undismayed servants of the greater life. . . . If a dear one has passed away, an invalid to whose welfare we have been devoted for years, then we must find some other person or persons in need of our loving care, and that very devotion which we lavish on life will be the substitute therapy, the miraculous healing that will come to our torn spirits. . . .
                            —Joshua Loth Liebman

Grooming (Women)

For years, in every one of my advertisements, I insisted on a line of copy which is still very dear to my heart. "There are no ugly women, only lazy ones." Remember this.

Always make up in a good light, and study the final effect in a magnifying mirror near an uncurtained window.

Whether you are sixteen or over sixty, remember, understatement is the rule of a fine makeup artist. Adjust your makeup to the light in which you wear it. Daylight reveals color; artificial light drains it.
—Helena Rubinstein

There are no old women in America—you only choose to make yourself old by dating yourself. The best advice is to do everything you can to be good-looking forever. If you're always changing, it keeps you young. As you grow older, your makeup should be softer. And, above a certain age, you don't want to have long hair—you want to have shorter hair, or pull it back away from the face.
—Halston

No one should hide behind a mask of make-up; the older we are, the less we need. A more natural, translucent look makes everyone appear fresher.
—Sylvie Chantecaille

Wear makeup. It's so conceited not to!
—Gabrielle ("Coco") Chanel
quoted by Estée Lauder

If you look at a picture of yourself taken 20 years ago and realize that you're still doing your makeup the same way, then it's time to rethink it. In most cases, it won't look good—not just because of what's happened to fashion, but because of how your face has changed in the interim. . . . I'm a firm believer that nature is doing the right thing at the right time. If you absolutely have to do something with gray

hair, then put in brown and honey streaks and warm it up. But to make silver hair black again is absurd.
　　　—Rick Gillette

The most basic facial at home: steam face over a sink filled with hot water.
　　　—Lia Schorr

(See *Allure, Appearance, Beauty, Deportment, Dress, Fashion, Image*)

H

Habit/Custom

Every habit and faculty is preserved and increased by correspondent actions; as the habit of walking, by walking; of running, by running. If you would be a reader, read; if a writer, write. After sitting still for ten days, get up and attempt to take a long walk; and you will find how your legs have weakened. Whatever you would make habitual, practise it; and if you would not make a thing habitual, do not practise it, but habituate yourself to something else.
> —Epictetus

Set out wisely at first; custom will make every virtue more easy and pleasant to you than any vice can be.
> —English proverb

Break the legs of an evil custom.
> —Italian proverb

How to develop good moral habits:
We must take care to launch ourselves with as strong and decided an initiative as possible. . . . Never suffer an exception to occur till the new habit is securely rooted in your life. . . . Seize the very first opportunity to act on every resolution you make, and on every emotional prompting you may experience in the direction of the habits you aspire to gain.
> —William James

Make sobriety a habit, and intemperance will be hateful; make prudence a habit and reckless profligacy will become revolting . . . Even happiness itself can become habitual. There is a habit of looking at the bright side of things, also of looking at the dark side. Dr. Johnson has said that the habit of looking at the best side of a thing is worth more to a man than a thousand pounds a year. . . . And to bring up men and women with a genial nature of this sort, a good temper, and a happy frame of mind, is perhaps of even more importance, in many cases, than to perfect them in much knowledge and many accomplishments.

—Samuel Smiles

Handicaps

Here is how to live without resentment or embarrassment in a world in which you are different from everyone else; be indifferent to that difference.

—Al Capp
From *My Well-Balanced Life on a
Wooden Leg*

Do not feel shame at being helped. It is your purpose to perform the task before you, as a soldier does in a siege. What if you, being lame, cannot reach the battlements alone but can do so with another's assistance?

—Marcus Aurelius

(See *Illness, Health*)

Happiness

There is only one way to happiness and that is to cease worrying about things which are beyond the power of our will.

—Epictetus

Happiness is equilibrium. Shift your weight. Equilibrium is pragmatic. You have to get everything into proportion. You compensate, rebalance yourself so that you maintain your angle to your world. When the world shifts, you shift.
—Tom Stoppard

A man should always consider how much he has more than he wants, and how much more unhappy he might be than he really is.
—Joseph Addison

If you cannot be happy in one way, be in another, and this felicity of disposition wants but little aid from philosophy, for health and good humor are almost the whole affair. Many run about after felicity, like an absent man hunting for his hat, while it is in his hand or on his head.
—James Sharp

Compare what you want with what you have, and you'll be unhappy; compare what you deserve with what you have, and you'll be happy.
—Evan Esar

Talk happiness. The world is sad enough
Without your woe. No path is wholly rough.
—Ella Wheeler Wilcox

Never believe that anyone who depends on happiness is happy.

He who would be truly happy must think his own lot best, and so live with men, as considering that God sees him, and so speak to God, as if men heard him.
—Seneca

Always leave something to wish for; otherwise you will be miserable from your very happiness.
—Baltasar Gracián

If you would be happy for a week, take a wife; if you would be happy for a month, kill a pig; but if you would be happy all your life, plant a garden.
—Ancient Chinese proverb

Your best shot at happiness, self-worth and personal satisfaction—the things that constitute real success—is not in earning as much as you can but in performing as well as you can something that you consider worthwhile. Whether that is healing the sick, giving hope to the hopeless, adding to the beauty of the world, or saving the world from nuclear holocaust, I cannot tell you.
                              —William Raspberry

The secret of happiness is to find a congenial monotony.
                              —V. S. Pritchett

Never fear spoiling children by making them too happy. Happiness is the atmosphere in which all good affections grow.
                              —Ann Eliza Bray

Just try to be happy. Unhappiness starts with wanting to be happier.
                              —Sam Levenson

Happiness is like a cat. If you try to coax it or call it, it will avoid you. It will never come. But if you pay no attention to it and go about your business, you'll find it rubbing against your legs and jumping into your lap. So forget pursuing happiness. Pin your hopes on work, on family, on learning, on knowing, on loving. Forget pursuing happiness, pursue these other things, and with luck happiness will come.
                              —William Bennett

To be happy in this world, especially when youth is past, it is necessary to feel oneself not merely an isolated individual whose day will soon be over, but part of the stream of life flowing on from the first germ to the remote and unknown future.
                              —Bertrand Russell

If you want to know the single most important insight I've learned in living my own life, it is the right understanding of happiness. The modern understanding of happiness is confused with pleasure or satisfaction, having a good time. Aristotle used the Greek word *eudaimonia*, and that translates into "good life." He meant the good life as a whole. But how can you experience the good life? What you can have is the moral aim of leading a whole good life—by building it the way one builds part of a play.

—Mortimer Adler

(See *Fulfillment, Purpose*)

Hatred

If you must hate, if hatred is the leaven of your life, which alone can give flavor, then hate what should be hated: falsehood, violence, self-ishness.

—Ludwig Boerne

When evil men plot, good men must plan. When evil men burn and bomb, good men must build and bind. When evil men shout ugly words of hatred, good men must commit themselves to the glories of love.

—Dr. Martin Luther King, Jr.

Take care that no one hate you justly.

—Publilius Syrus

Hate. Just scratch that word from your vocabulary. If you're going to talk about a man you don't like, just say you don't like him. Don't say you hate him. "Hate" is the dirtiest, ugliest word in the language—any language.

—Barry Goldwater

Love as if you would one day hate, and hate as if you would one day love.

—Bias, 570 B.C.

Don't hold grudges; it's pointless. Jealousy too is a non-cathartic negative emotion.

—Liz Smith

Health

Above all, do not lose your desire to walk.
>—Søren Kierkegaard

If you be not ill, be not ill-like.
>—Scottish proverb

You must not pledge your own health.
>—John Ray proverbs

Don't worry about your children, walk at least a mile a day, eat as little meat as possible and as little processed food as possible.
>—David Davies, gerontologist
>(Advice based on a study of people of Vilcambabba, Ecuador, among the longest-lived in the world)

Quit worrying about your health. It'll go away.
>—Robert Orben

Eat what you like and let the food fight it out inside.
>—Mark Twain

Let the covering of your neck be light and loose; the covering of your feet tight and close, and avoid streams of wind, streams of alcohol, and torrents of passion, if you would escape colds, storms, and tempests within.
>—Charles Simmons

Now that I'm gone, I tell you: don't smoke, whatever you do, don't smoke.
>—Yul Brynner, cancer victim, in a posthumous anti-smoking commercial

Heart

Some guys play with their heads, and sure, you need to be smart to be number one in anything you try. But most important, you've got to play with your heart. If you're lucky enough to find a guy with a lot of head and a lot of heart, he'll never come off the field second.
—Vince Lombardi

Find the seed at the bottom of your heart and bring forth a flower.
—Shigenori Kameoka

Your mind must control, but you must have heart. . . . Give your feeling free.
—Vladimir Horowitz

Remember that the real duties of religion are independent of human institutions; that righteous heart is the true temple of the Godhead; that in every land, in every sect, to love God above all things and to love our neighbor as ourself is the whole law; remember there is no religion which absolves us from our moral duties; that these alone are really essential, that the service of the heart is the first of these duties and that without faith there is no such thing as true virtue.
—The Savoyard priest in
Jean-Jacques Rousseau's *Emile*

Hedonism

Fly the pleasure that will bite tomorrow.
—English proverb

It's all right letting yourself go, as long as you can get yourself back.
—Mick Jagger

Try everything once except incest and folk-dancing.
                              —Sir Thomas Beecham

Don't lose the peace of years by seeking the rapture of moments.
                              —English proverb

Let the good times roll.
                              —Cajun motto

Choke not thy soul with immoderate pouring-in the cordial of pleasures.
                              —Thomas Fuller

(See *Leisure, Pleasure*)

Help

Never look down on anybody unless you're helping him up.
                              —The Rev. Jesse Jackson

High-Mindedness

Seek the lofty by reading, hearing and seeing great work at some moment every day.
                              —Thornton Wilder

Give not thyself up, then, to fire, lest it invert thee, deaden thee; as for a time it did me. There is a wisdom that is woe; but there is a woe that is madness. And there is a Catskill eagle in some souls that can alike dive down into the blackest gorges, and soar out of them again and become invisible in the sunny spaces. And even if he forever flies within the gorge, that gorge is in the mountains; so that even in his lowest swoop the mountain eagle is still higher than other birds upon the plain, even though they soar.
                              —Herman Melville

Enlarge your consciousness. If your consciousness is small, you will experience smallness in every department of your life.*
—Robert Pante

**Ed. Note:* Or, as the anonymous saying goes: "All the thoughts of a turtle are turtle."

Live like a bourgeois, and think like a demigod.
—Gustave Flaubert

Honesty

But play no tricks upon thy soul, O man;
Let fact be fact, and life the thing it can.
—Arthur Hugh Clough

Whatever games are played with us, we must play no games with ourselves, but deal in our privacy with the last honesty and truth.
—Ralph Waldo Emerson

I desire you would use all your skill to paint my picture truly like me; but remark all these roughnesses, pimples, warts, and everything as you see me, otherwise I will not pay a farthing for it.
—Oliver Cromwell, to Peter Lely, who was
about to paint his portrait

(See *Affectation, Candor, Hypocrisy, Sincerity, Truth*)

Honor

Be noble-minded! Our own heart, and not other men's opinions of us, form our true honor.
—Friedrich Schiller

Be honorable yourself if you wish to associate with honorable people.
—Welsh proverb

Avoid "affairs of honor." . . . These duels are the tempters of good sense, and it is safer to flee from them, than to win through them.
—Baltasar Gracián

. . . see that you come
Not to woo honor, but to wed it.
—King in Shakespeare's
All's Well That Ends Well

Be not ashamed of thy virtues; honor's a good brooch to wear in a man's hat at all times.
—Ben Jonson

Run away from dishonor, but don't run after honors.
—Jewish proverb

On the achievement of fame in government service: Of this be wary. Honor and fame are often regarded as interchangeable. Both involve an appraisal of the individual . . . but I suggest this difference. Fame is morally neutral.
—Edward R. Murrow

(See *Reputation, Virtue*)

Hope

Hope humbly then; with trembling pinions soar,
Wait the great teacher, Death, and God adore:
What future bliss, He gives not thee to know,
But gives that Hope to be thy blessing now.
Hope springs eternal in the human breast:

Man never Is, but always To be blest:
The soul, uneasy, and confin'd from Home,
Rests and expatiates in a life to come.
—Alexander Pope

Lay hold upon the hope set before us: which hope we have as an anchor of the soul, both sure and stedfast.
—New Testament
Hebrews 6:18–19

Know then, whatever cheerful and serene
Supports the mind, supports the body too;
Hence, the most vital movement mortals feel
Is hope, the balm and lifeblood of the soul.
—John Armstrong

Beware how you take away hope from any human being.
—Dr. Oliver Wendell Holmes

If you do not hope, you will not find what is beyond your hopes.
—St. Clement of Alexandria

In Israel, in order to be a realist, you must believe in miracles.
—David Ben-Gurion

Hope to the end.
—New Testament
I Peter 1:13

Never cease loving a person, and never give up hope for him, for even the prodigal son who had fallen most low, could still be saved; the bitterest enemy and also he who was your friend could again be your friend; love that has grown cold can kindle again.
—Søren Kierkegaard

Hold your head high, stick your chest out. You can make it. It gets dark sometimes but morning comes. . . . Keep hope alive.
—The Rev. Jesse Jackson

Hospitality

Sign in the entranceway of an English castle open to the public:
  It is the duty of the host to make his guests feel at home.
  It is the duty of the guests to remember that they are not.
                    —J. S. Groenfeldt

To revolutionize a whole house on the coming of a few visitors betrays
not only poor taste, but an absolute lack of character. Let your friends
come into your life; let them see you as you are, and not find you
trying to be somebody else.
                    —Emma Whitcomb Babcook
                    Household Hints, 1881

Two safe rules for entertaining are: Seldom apologize; never pretend.
                    —Mrs. S. D. Power, 1884

Measure not thy entertainment of a guest by his estate, but thine
own.—Because he is a lord, forget not that thou art but a gentleman;
otherwise, if with feasting him thou breakest thyself, he will not cure
thy rupture, and (perchance) rather deride than pity thee.
                    —Thomas Fuller

(See *Entertaining, Visiting*)

House/Home

Never build after you are five and forty; have five years' income in
hand before you lay a brick; and always calculate the expense at double
the estimate.
                    —Henry Katt

Have nothing in your houses that you do not know to be useful, or
believe to be beautiful.
                    —William Morris

Please—place the curtain on the *inside* of the tub.
>—Conrad Hilton

No matter how carefully you plan, and no matter how rationally you justify your behavior, trying to run two homes at the same time is a crazy, difficult task that produces more frustrations than rewards. . . . Don't try it if you scare easily.
>—James A. Michener

Touch the lightbulbs in your house with scent and watch your rooms turn into a garden.
>—Estée Lauder

Always leave home with a tender good-bye and loving words. They may be the last.
>—*Hill's Manual of Social and Business Forms,*
>1887

On moving: Once the decision has been made to relocate, concentrate on the positive aspects of the move. Children are especially prone to picking up a parent's negative reaction to the transfer. . . . Children need to be reassured that they will not lose their old friends. . . . Once the relocation has been made, moving veterans and psychologists agree, getting involved in the new community is important. "Establish very quickly someone you can call on for babysitting or for help in the middle of the night."
>—Richard Raymond

On interior decorating: When you are decorating, you must learn to break some rules, but not all of them. Take the case of pattern on pattern. Some decorators today think you can willy-nilly mix prints. Not so. That just results in confusion. . . . It is very important when mixing furnishings of different provenance that there be some kind of connection, so that they can be good neighbors, such as placing a superb modern table next to an antique chair. It would look all wrong. There wouldn't be any connection of quality.
>—Billy Baldwin

Find a designer who has the ability to reflect you; don't reflect the designer.

If you are unable to express verbally your visual intentions to a designer, I suggest collecting photographs from magazines of furnishings that you like. Sooner or later a pattern will emerge and will give the designer a sense of your style and personality.
—Carol Siegmeister

Don't expect perfect products unless you are willing to pay for perfection.
—Robert Siegmeister

The desire to build a house is the tired wish of a man content thenceforward with a single anchorage. The desire to build a boat is the desire of youth, unwilling yet to accept the idea of a final resting place. . . . You must build to regain your freedom.
—Arthur Ransome

(See *Servants*)

Humility

Always remember there are two types of people in this world. Those who come into a room and say, "Well, here I am!" and those who come in and say, "Ah, there you are!"
—Frederick L. Collins

Be aware that a halo has to fall only a few inches to be a noose.
—Dan McKinnon

Whatever you may be sure of, be sure of this: that you are dreadfully like other people.
—James Russell Lowell

Make way for your betters.
—Latin proverb

Let us be a little humble; let us think that the truth may not perhaps be entirely with us.
                    —Jawaharlal Nehru

Acquire the art of detachment, the virtue of method, and the quality of thoroughness, but above all the grace of humility.
                    —Sir William Osler

Place yourself in the background. Write in a way that draws the reader's attention to the sense and substance of the writing, rather than to the mood and temper of the author.
                    —E. B. White

Never send to know for whom the bell tolls. It tolls for thee.
                    —John Donne

Stay humble. Always answer your phone—no matter who else is in the car.
                    —Jack Lemmon

Husbands/Wives

A husband should tell his wife everything that he is sure she will find out, and before anyone else does.
                    —Thomas Robert Dewar

Never strike your wife, even with a flower.
                    —Hindu proverb

Have the courage to listen to your wife when you should and not to listen when you should not.
                    —Stanislaw Leszczyński, King of Poland

The good Husband keeps his Wife in the wholesome ignorance of unnecessary Secrets. . . . He knows little who will tell his Wife all he knows.
                    —Sir Richard Steele

Never feel remorse for what you have thought about your wife, she has thought much worse things about you.
                    —Jean Rostand

Depart not from a wise and good wife, whom
thou hast gotten in the fear of the Lord, for
the grace of her modesty is above gold.
                    —Apocrypha

He that will thrive must ask leave of his wife.
                    —John Heywood proverbs, 1546

Never refer to your wedding night as the "original amateur hour."
                    —Phyllis Diller

So live that when a man says he's married to you, he'll be boasting.
                    —Anonymous

What advice would you give to a young woman about to marry an executive who is likely to be successful?—Wall Street Journal

Grow with your husband. Remember that he lives in an enlarging world. Make yours the same.
                    —A wife in her sixties

Make the home a refuge from the pressures of the business world, a place he is anxious to go and does so every chance he gets, a place where he will not be hassled or nagged at or where expectations are heaped on him. Find time to sit with him and talk every time he gets home. Don't try to solve all his problems for him.
                    —A wife in her thirties

Don't settle for living through his successes. Create your own successes. Don't expect him to be everything for you. There will be times when he is drained and has nothing to give.
                    —A wife in her thirties

Put off your shame with your clothes when you go in to your husband, and put it on again when you come out.
                    —Theano, 420 B.C.

Trust your husband, adore your husband, and get as much as you can in your own name.
>—Joan Rivers

(See *Couples, Marriage, Relationships*)

Hypocrisy

Woe unto them that call evil good, and good evil; that put darkness for light, and light for darkness; that put bitter for sweet, and sweet for bitter!
>—Old Testament
>Isaiah 5:20

Thou hypocrite, first cast out the beam out of thine own eye; and then shalt thou see clearly to cast out the mote out of thy brother's eye.
>—New Testament
>Luke 6:42

>Better to live as a rogue and a bum,
>   a lover all treat as a joke
>to hang out with a crowd of comfortable drunks,
>   than crouch in a hypocrite's cloak.
>>—Mahsati
>>(12th century)

You should not live one way in private, another in public.
>—Publilius Syrus

It is of great consequence to disguise your inclination, and to play the hypocrite well.
>—Niccolò Machiavelli

(See *Affectation, Candor, Sincerity, Truth*)

I

Ideals

In framing an ideal we may assume what we wish, but should avoid impossibilities.
> —A dictum of Aristotle
> quoted by Aldous Huxley

You always need to make ideals clear to yourself. You always have to be aware of them, even if there is no direct path to their realization. Were there no ideals, there would be no hope whatsoever. Then everything would be hopelessness, darkness—a blind alley.
> —Dr. Andrei Sakharov

If there is anything in the world a person should fight for, it is freedom to pursue his ideal, because in that is his great opportunity for self-expression, for the unfoldment of the greatest thing possible to him.
> —Orison S. Marden

So we are all idealists. We are all visionaries. Let it not be said of this Atlantic generation that we left ideas and visions to the past, nor purpose and determination to our adversaries. We have come too far, we have sacrificed too much, to disdain the future now. And we shall ever remember what Goethe told us—that the "highest wisdom, the best that mankind ever knew" was the realization that "he only earns his freedom and existence who daily conquers them anew."
> —John F. Kennedy
> Speech in Germany, 1963

My child,

In the life ahead of you, keep your capacity for faith and belief, but let your judgment watch what you believe. Keep your love of life, but throw away your fear of death. Life must be loved or it is lost, but it should never be loved too well. Keep your wonder at great and noble things, like sunlight and thunder, the rain and the stars, and the greatness of heroes. Keep your heart hungry for new knowledge. Keep your hatred of a lie, and keep your power of indignation. . . . I am ashamed to leave you an uncomfortable world, but someday it will be better. And when that day comes, you will thank God for the greatest blessing man can receive, living in peace.

> —Letter from an executed Yugoslav partisan to
> his unborn child in World War II

(See *Beliefs, Dreams, Principles, Vision*)

Identity

For God's sake, choose a self and stand by it!
> —William James

Somewhere along the line of development we discover what we really are, and then we make our real decision for which we are responsible. Make that decision primarily for yourself because you can never really live anyone else's life, not even your own child's. The influence you exert is through your own life and what you become yourself.
> —Eleanor Roosevelt

Let the world know you as you are, not as you think you should be, because sooner or later, if you are posing, you will forget the pose, and then where are you?
> —Fanny Brice

Be on the alert to recognize your prime at whatever time of your life it may occur.
> —Muriel Spark

(See *Introspection, Meditation, Self-Improvement*)

Idleness

If you are idle, be not solitary; if you are solitary, be not idle.
    —Samuel Johnson

Never be entirely idle; but either be reading, or writing, or praying, or meditating, or endeavouring something for the public good.
    —Thomas à Kempis

This habit of uselessly wasting time is the whole difficulty; it is vastly important to you, and still more so to your children, that you should break the habit. It is more important to them, because they have longer to live, and can keep out of an idle habit before they are in it, easier than they can get out after they are in.
    —Abraham Lincoln

Be sure to keep busy, so the devil may always find you occupied.
    —Flavius Vegetius Renatus

Do anything innocent rather than give yourself up to reverie. I can speak on this point from experience; for at one period in my life, I was a dreamer and a castle-builder. Visions of the distant and future took the place of present duty and activity. I spent hours in reverie. The body suffered as much as the mind. The imagination threatened to inflame the passions, and I found, if I meant to be virtuous, I must dismiss my musings. The conflict was a hard one; but I resolved, prayed, resisted, sought refuge in occupation, and at length triumphed.
    —William Ellery Channing

Do not allow idleness to deceive you; for while you give him to-day, he steals tomorrow from you.
    —H. Crowquill

Shun idleness. It is the rust that attaches itself to the most brilliant metals.
    —Voltaire

(See *Labor*)

Illness (Serious)

Let great physicians cure the dangerous ills.
　　　　　—Juvenal

It is better to live and be done with it than to die daily in the sick-room. By all means begin your folio; even if the doctor does not give you a year, even if he hesitates about a month, make one brave push and see what can be accomplished in a week . . . does not life go down with a better grace, foaming in full body over a precipice, than miserably straggling to an end in sandy delta? . . . For surely, at what-ever age it overtake the man, this is to die young.
　　　　　—Robert Louis Stevenson

If you believe that God gave this affliction to you, believe He can take it away.
　　　　　—Rabbinical saying

Never deny the diagnosis, but do deny the negative verdict that may go with it.
　　　　　—Norman Cousins

—In spite of illness, in spite even of the archenemy sorrow, one *can* remain alive long past the usual date of disintegration if one is unafraid of change, insatiable in intellectual curiosity, interested in big things, and happy in small ways.
　　　　　—Edith Wharton

Before undergoing a surgical operation, arrange your temporal affairs. You may live.
　　　　　—Ambrose Bierce

Illness/Infirmity

Don't feel guilty if you decide to take the rosy view. Accentuating the positive turns out to be medically sound.
                    —Daniel Goleman

In afflictions without remedy, advice can be given only as palliatives. I ask you to remember that to pity a sick person is not to blame him . . . Let us leave the right to judge to Him who alone can read our hearts.
                    —Choderlos de Laclos

(*Illness—less serious*)
Feed a cold and starve a fever.
                    —American proverb

> The best of remedies is a beefsteak
> Against sea-sickness; try it before
> You sneer, and I assure you this is true,
> For I have found it answer—so may you.
>   —Lord Byron

Make not thy stomach an apothecary's shop.
                    —English proverb

(See *Handicaps, Health, Physicians/Medicine*)

Illusion

Don't mock the faith . . . to hell with the truth! As the history of the world proves, the truth has no bearing upon anything. It's irrelevant

and immaterial. . . . The lie of a pipedream is what gives life to the whole misbegotten mad lot of us, drunk or sober.
—Larry Slade in Eugene O'Neill's
The Iceman Cometh

Never give up; and never, under any circumstances, no matter what—*never* face the facts.
—Ruth Gordon

Don't part with your illusions. When they are gone you may still exist but you have ceased to live.
—Mark Twain

Illusions commend themselves to us because they save us pain and allow us to enjoy pleasure instead. We must therefore accept it without complaint when they sometimes collide with a bit of reality against which they are dashed to pieces.
—Sigmund Freud

(See *Practicality, Reality, Reason, Truth*)

Image

We should gain more by letting ourselves be seen such as we are, than by attempting to appear what we are not.
—François de La Rochefoucauld

Looking good is not an end in itself. It's a metaphor for our inner being. Ponder this. Society doesn't applaud people's looking bad. Looking bad means we feel bad about ourselves. It also suggests that things aren't right with our character.
—Charles Hix

If you're going into politics, never let anyone take a picture of you with a drink in your hand—whether it's a Coke or anything else—because it projects the wrong image.
—Walter F. Mondale

Act apologetic and you will lose. Act certain and you will win.
                                    —Robert Pante

I used to be very self-conscious. I used to wish I was pretty. My cousin
Georgia always taught me that if you *smile*, people will like you.
Sometimes people will say something you don't like, and you get angry
a bit, but you just smile. You let it go by, even if you really would
like to choke 'em. By smiling, I think I've made more friends than if
I was the other way.
                                    —Ella Fitzgerald

On looking good: Fashion designers can't make anybody look good. If
you look good, my clothes support that in you. But looking good is
feeling good and feeling good is being at peace with yourself. If you're
not sexy before you buy a dress, forget the dress.
                                    —Perry Ellis

Never "just run out for a few minutes" without looking your best. This
is not vanity—it's self-liking. Your face is always on display.
                                    —Estée Lauder

Each of us has a mental picture of himself, a self-image which governs
much of his conduct and outlook. To find life reasonably satisfying
you must have a self-image that you can live with.
                                    —Dr. Maxwell Maltz

On first impression, many people judge the financial worth of a woman
by her handbag and briefcase. You can't fake leather.
                                    —Nancy Thompson

Never offend the eyes of other people. If you don't make yourself as
attractive as possible, you are very egoistic.
                                    —Erte (Romain de Tirtoff)

(See *Allure, Appearance, Beauty, Deportment, Dress, Fashion,*
                    Grooming)

Immortality

Hath man no second life?—Pitch this one high!
  —Matthew Arnold

> O my soul, do not aspire to immortal
> life, but exhaust the limits of the possible.
>   —Pindar

We must remember that the word "decease" literally means an "exodus" or "going out." And that's what death is—a departure, not to oblivion but to a new horizon. The Psalmist wrote not of disappearing into "the valley of the shadow of death," but going *through* it.
  —Billy Graham

> Listen to the rumblings of the clouds, a heart of man.
> Be brave, right through and leave for the unknown.
>   —Rabindranath Tagore

> He is forever free who has broken
> Out of the ego-cage of *I* and *mine*
> To be united with the Lord of Love.
> This is the supreme state. Attain thou this
> And pass from death to immortality.
>   —Sri Krishna in the Bhagavad Gita
>   (A meditation of Gandhi's)

I have no wish to be deprived of the happiness of believing in a future life. . . . But these incomprehensible matters are too remote to be an object of daily meditation; such speculations ruin the brain. . . . An honest man who hopes to achieve something while he is still here on earth and is working and striving and struggling every day to that end, will let the other world take care of itself and bestir himself usefully in this one.

  —Johann Wolfgang von Goethe

(See *Death, Mortality*)

Independence

Try to arrange your life in such a way that you can afford to be disinterested. It is the most expensive of all luxuries, and the one best worth having.
—W. R. Inge

Favour is to be esteemed, but not depended on. He that stands on another man's legs, knows not how soon they may fail him. Be sure therefore never to lean too hard upon any man, that if he sinks he may give thee a fall.
—George Shelley

You should aim to be independent of any one vote, of any one fashion, of any one century.
—Baltasar Gracián

The only way to attain superiority in dealing with men, is to let it be seen that you are independent of them. And in this view it is advisable to let everyone of your acquaintance—whether man or woman—feel now and then that you could very well dispense with their company. This will consolidate friendship.
—Arthur Schopenhauer

Read, every day, something no one else is reading. Think, every day, something no one else is thinking. Do, every day, something no one else would be silly enough to do. It is bad for the mind to be always part of a unanimity.
—Christopher Morley

When it comes time to do your own life, you either perpetuate your childhood or you stand on it and finally kick it out from under.
—Rosellen Brown

(See *Individuality, Self-Reliance*)

Individuality

Whatever you think, be sure it is what you think; whatever you want, be sure that it is what you want; whatever you feel, be sure that it is what you feel. It is bad enough to think and want the things that your elders want you to think and want, but it is still worse to think and want just like all your contemporaries.
—T. S. Eliot
Advice to students

Adhere to your own act, and congratulate yourself if you have done something strange and extravagant, and broken the monotony of a decorous age.
—Ralph Waldo Emerson

I beg you to keep alive the integrity of the individual, and his ability to judge and compare and create. May your writers write secretly and hold their writing for the time when this gray anaesthetic has passed as pass it must. The free world outside your prison still lives. You will join it again and it will welcome you. Everything around you is cynically designed to destroy you as individuals. You must remember and teach your children that they are precious, not as dull cogs in the wheel of party existence, but as units, complete and shining in themselves.
—John Steinbeck
Broadcast to Eastern Europe

Do not quench your inspiration and your imagination; do not become the slave of your model.
—Vincent van Gogh

Cultivate your garden. . . . Do not depend upon teachers to educate you . . . follow your own bent, pursue your curiosity bravely, express yourself, make your own harmony. . . . In the end, education, like happiness, is individual, and must come to us from life and from ourselves. There is no way; each pilgrim must make his own path.

"Happiness," said Chamfort, "is not easily won; it is hard to find it in ourselves, and impossible to find it elsewhere."
—Will Durant

Men like Socrates and Einstein are what William James called "quarto and folio editions of mankind." You and I are paperbacks. Still, paperbacks vary in quality. Each of us is unique, and life is one long experiment in self-discovery. Be your unique self.
—Brand Blanchard

Know how to draw away. . . . Do not belong so wholly to others that you do not belong to yourself.

Neither be all, nor give all to anyone; neither blood, nor friendship, nor the most pressing obligation, justifies it, for there is a big difference between the bestowal of your affection and the bestowal of yourself.
—Baltasar Gracián

Perhaps one day we will indeed learn to guide the state—that would be true civilization—but to do so we must learn to understand ourselves. Carl Jung wrote to Laurens van der Post: "I cannot prove to you that God exists, but my work has proved empirically that the pattern of God exists in every man and that this pattern in the individual has at its disposal the greatest transforming energies of which life is capable. Find this pattern in your own individual self and life is transformed."
—Prince Charles
Lecture, Cambridge University

Live your own life, for you will die your own death.
—Latin proverb

(See *Independence, Self-Reliance*)

Influence

We must not, in trying to think about how we can make a big difference, ignore the small daily differences we can make which, over time,
add up to big differences that we often cannot foresee.
—Marion Wright Edelman

Initiative

Awake and sing.
—Old Testament
Isaiah 26:19

Awake, arise, or be forever fall'n!
—John Milton

Sitting still and wishing
Makes no person great.
The good Lord sends the fishing
But you have to dig the bait.
—Anonymous

Go to the ant, thou sluggard; consider her ways and be wise:
Which having no guide, overseer, or ruler,
Provideth her meat in the summer, and gathereth her food in the
harvest.
—Old Testament
Proverbs 6:6–8

You cannot plough a field by turning it over in your mind.
—Anonymous

You don't just stumble into the future. You create your own future.
—Roger Smith

(See *Beginnings, Doing, Enterprise*)

Inquiry

If you wish to strive for peace of soul and pleasure, then believe; if you wish to be a devotee of truth, then enquire.
—Heinrich Heine

Never answer a question until it is asked.
—American legal maxim

Don't ask questions you don't want answers to.
—Captain Schroeder, USCG
Quoted by Paul Dickson

Do not betray even to your friend too much of your real purposes and thoughts; in conversation ask questions oftener than you express opinions; and when you speak offer data and information rather than beliefs and judgments.
—Will Durant

(See *Curiosity, Questions*)

Interests

I have lived to know that the great secret of human happiness is this: Never suffer your energies to stagnate. The old adage of "too many irons in the fire," conveys an untruth—you cannot have too many— poker, tongs—and all, keep them going.
—Adam Clark

. . . the man who pursues happiness wisely will aim at the possession of a number of subsidiary interests in addition to those central ones upon which his life is built.
—Bertrand Russell

The whole secret of life is to be interested in one thing profoundly and in a thousand other things well.
—Hugh Walpole

One must learn to be bored.
—French proverb

Never interest yourself in anything you don't care about. This is not the rule for conduct, but it's the rule for art, and for artists in their work.
—J. B. Yeats to his son
William Butler Yeats

When one's ill or unhappy, one needs something outside oneself to hold one up. It is a good thing, I think, when one has been knocked out of one's balance . . . to have some external job or duty to hang on to.
—Aldous Huxley

(See *Pursuits*)

Introspection

Get to know yourself: Know your own failings, passions, and prejudices so you can separate them from what you see. Know also when you actually have thought through to the nature of the thing with which you are dealing and when you are not thinking at all. . . . Knowing yourself and knowing the facts, you can judge whether you can change the situation so it is more to your liking. If you cannot—or if you do not know how to improve on things—then discipline yourself to the adjustments that will be necessary.
—Bernard M. Baruch

Know thyself, presume not God to scan;
The proper study of mankind is man.
                              —Alexander Pope

Know thyself! A maxim as pernicious as it is ugly. Whoever observes himself arrests his own development. A caterpillar that wanted to know itself well would never become a butterfly.
                              —André Gide

Keep no secrets of thyself from thyself.
                              —Greek proverb

Do not divert your attention to the directing minds of others; look straight ahead to where Nature is leading you, to the nature of the Whole through what befalls you, and your own nature through what you must do, for every man must do what is compatible with his own make-up.
                              —Marcus Aurelius

You must try to observe yourself more and more objectively, to look at everything in yourself as though in another person.
                              —Sigmund Freud

Let mystery have its place in you; do not be always turning up your whole soil with the ploughshare of self-examination, but leave a little fallow corner in your heart ready for any seed the winds may bring, and reserve a nook of shadow for the passing bird; keep a place in your heart for the unexpected guest, an altar for an unknown God.
                              —Henri-Frédéric Amiel

(See *Identity, Meditation, Self-Improvement*)

Intuition

To believe your own thought, to believe that what is true for you in your heart is true for all men,—that is genius. . . . A man should

learn to detect and watch that gleam of light which flashes across his mind from within, more than the lustre of the firmament of bards and sages.
                    —Ralph Waldo Emerson

. . . there is no prescribed route to follow to arrive at a new idea. You have to make the intuitive leap. But the difference is that once you've made the intuitive leap you have to justify it by filling in the intermediate steps. In my case, it often happens that I have an idea, but then I try to fill in the intermediate steps and find that they don't work, so I have to give it up.
                    —Stephen W. Hawking
                    Cambridge cosmologist

You must train your intuition—you must trust that small voice inside you which tells you exactly what to say, what to decide. Your intuition is your instrument. If you can imagine, I throw a spear into the dark. That is my intuition, and then I have to send an expedition into the jungle to find the spear and to find a way to the spear. And that is absolutely another process. That is my intellect.
                    —Ingmar Bergman

Begin to observe your life more and try to awaken the observer in you, the high self. Thinkers from Plato to Freud have talked about the three selves we have within us. I call them the high self, the conscious self, and the basic self. The conscious self is the personality; the basic self is the child. When the conscious self decides to go on a diet, the basic self eats chocolate cake. The high self is the God within us, the part that is eternal and divine. It is always there but we need to activate it. . . . Listen to the slow, still voice we call intuition.
                    —Arianna Stassinopoulos Huffington

Trust your hunches. . . . Hunches are usually based on facts filed away just below the conscious level. Warning! Do not confuse your hunches with wishful thinking. This is the road to disaster.
                    —Dr. Joyce Brothers

Involvement

What I want to tell you today is not to move into that world where you're alone with your self and your mantra and your fitness program or whatever it is that you might use to try to control the world by closing it out. I want to tell you to just live in the mess. Throw yourself out into the convulsions of the world. I'm not telling you to make the world better, because I don't believe progress is necessarily part of the package. I'm just telling you to live in it, to look at it, to witness it. Try and get it. Take chances, make your own work, take pride in it. Seize the moment.
> —Joan Didion
> Commencement Address

Plunge boldly into the thick of life!
> —Johann Wolfgang von Goethe

Do not bind yourself to what you cannot do.
> —George Shelley

What you can't get out of, get into wholeheartedly.
> —Mignon McLaughlin

Remember, people support that which they help create. . . . Always get the commitment of others in any undertaking. Have them take a piece of the action so it's their action as well as yours. Involvement begets commitment. Commitment begets power.
> —Herb Cohen

Pick battles big enough to matter, small enough to win.
> —Jonathan Kozol

Life is a great big canvas; throw all the paint on it you can.
> —Danny Kaye

(See *Commitment, Promises*)

J

Job Hunting

If you have a job now, keep it until you find a better one—even if it's driving you crazy. Potential employers are much more likely to hire someone who's already working.
—Ron Berman

When you want something, go back and go back and go back, and don't take no for an answer. And when rejection comes, don't take it personally. It goes with the territory. Expose yourself to as much humiliation as you can bear, then go home and go do it all again tomorrow.
—Betty Furness

You will find it a very good practice always to verify your references.
—M. J. Routh
President of Magdalen College
Oxford, 1847

There are moments in life when it is imperative to behave like Mr. Micawber and wait for Something to Turn Up, not try too hard to turn it up oneself, as though one were looking for a centipede under a stone.

—Aldous Huxley

Don't just grab at the first thing that comes along. . . . Know when to refuse something that won't get you anywhere.
—Will Rogers

1. Never show up for an interview in bare feet.
2. Do not read your prospective employer's mail while he is questioning you as to qualifications.
—W. C. Fields

(See *Career, Occupation*)

Joking

You must bring to an art some measure of respect and affection, or it will not be wooed and won. *Funny stories should be told only by those persons who enjoy telling them.* If you look upon the telling of tales as an ordeal . . . if you feel foolish and uncomfortable in relating humorous incidents, then the funny story is not your meat or métier. Leave funny stories alone.
—Maxwell Droke

Better lose a jest than a friend.
—Thomas Fuller

Be careful in selecting jokes that will be appropriate for the time, place and audience. . . . If a joke fails to get a laugh, either continue with your talk or turn the joke on yourself by using a gag about why you failed.
—Dr. Laurence J. Peter

How to Tell a Joke: (1) *Know the joke cold.* Rehearse first if you have to. There's nothing worse than stopping in the middle and trying to re-track who's who or who did what. (2) *Don't start out apologizing.* Too many women begin badly by putting themselves (or the joke) down, saying: "I'm lousy at telling jokes but here goes"; "I hope I can remember the punchline"; "This isn't very funny, but . . ." Or the

coy come-on, "I heard a good joke, but, no, I can't tell you." After a few "Please, tell it's" and "No, I can'ts," who cares?
—Lys Marigold

As you launch into your joke, show that you enjoy it: smile, chuckle, spread cheer. Don't look dour and self-conscious, even when you deliver a one-liner. . . . Above all else: prepare the exact wording and rhythm of your climax. Deliver the final line crisply, cheerfully, confidently.
—Leo C. Rosten

(See *Good Humor, Laughter*)

Journalism

. . . always fight for progress and reform, never tolerate injustice and corruption, always fight demagogues of all parties, never belong to any party, always oppose privileged classes and public plunderers, never lack sympathy with the poor, always remain devoted to the public welfare, never be satisfied with merely printing news; always be drastically independent; never be afraid to attack wrong, whether by predatory plutocracy or predatory poverty.
—Joseph Pulitzer
Statement of policy for the *New York World* and *St. Louis Post-Dispatch*, on retirement, 1907

Print all the news, but see more in the news than other editors do. . . . Get young people around you. . . . Let them get excited. . . . Let them do things. Let them make a few mistakes. Maybe the public will like the mistakes. . . . I am getting old, running down, going to sleep like a top before it keels over. Don't let the papers run down. They must not go to sleep. Get in a lot of youngsters who don't know it can't be done.
—William Randolph Hearst, to his editors on his seventieth birthday

Arthur Brisbane gave me this advice: "Learn to write for people who follow a line with their finger and move their lips when they read, and when you have learned that, you will be understood by presidents of corporations, colleges, and the United States. . . ."
—John Reagan ("Tex") McCrary

Go after big game. Select a federal judge, a governor or, best of all, the president. The second rule, as military men recognize, is not to fire all your ammunition at one time.

If these two rules . . . are followed, then the editor has a bully chance of bringing down big game, to his credit and to the credit of the public weal.
—Vermont Royster

Afflict the comfortable.
Comfort the afflicted.
—Journalistic credo

All you need to run a news division is common sense and a good deal of concern for humanity.
—Edward R. Murrow's advice to
CBS's Richard Salant

Never argue with people who buy ink by the barrel.
—Anonymous

Keep in mind always . . . that you are likely to write best what you understand best. One successful journalist, Ernest Hemingway, tested himself with this question: "What did I know about truly and care for the most?"
—Leonard Ray Teel and Rod Taylor

Write, write, write anything. The world's a fine believing world, write news!
—John Fletcher

Advice for would-be sportswriters: Well, loving sports would be the very least recommendation for someone who wants to be a sportswriter. First, he should really feel he wants to be a newspaperman. Then I

would suggest he get as much formal education as possible, not necessarily in a school of journalism, but reading languages, philosophy,
history, economics, sociology. Then go out and hound a city editor
for a job and work on the local side of the paper under the discipline
of a city desk. Learn what the newspaper business is all about. After
that, it's easy to get a transfer into sports.
                                    —Red Smith

Get it first, but first get it right.
                                    —Seymour Berkson
                                     International News Service

Guidelines for journalists working in Latin America:
    If authorities can't guarantee your safety, get out of the country.
    Never carry a gun or other weapon. . . .
    Resist abuse by authorities and always protest such abuse of yourself
        and other professionals. But don't become abusive yourself. . . .
    Avoid reporting from both sides of a conflict. Crossing from one to
        the other is often dangerous.
    Always carry a white flag.
    Never point your finger; it may be mistaken for a gun.
    Never wash your car. Tampering can be detected more easily on a
        dirty car.
    If guerrillas at roadblocks ask you for a "war tax," give something.
                                    —Inter American Press Association

Biting journalists should allow no hand to feed them.
                                    —Sinclair Lewis
                                     declining an invitation by the U.S. State
                                     Department to visit and report on a foreign
                                     country

You can write a column about one thing, or you can write a column
about three things and tie them up with an overarching theme. But
a two-thing column will never hang together.
                                    —Suzanne Garment, quoting advice from a
                                     fellow columnist

(See *Communication, Media, Reporting, Television*)

Joy

Find joy in simplicity, self-respect, and indifference to what lies between virtue and vice. Love the human race. Follow the divine.
—Marcus Aurelius

"On with the dance, let joy be unconfined" is my motto, whether there's any dance to dance or any joy to unconfine.
—Mark Twain

You have your brush, you have your colors, *you paint paradise*, then *in* you go.
—Nikos Kazantzakis

The trick is not how much pain you feel—but how much joy you feel. Any idiot can feel pain. Life is full of excuses to feel pain, excuses not to live, excuses, excuses, excuses.
—Erica Jong

Find expression for a sorrow, and it will become dear to you. Find expression for a joy, and you will intensify its ecstasy.
—Oscar Wilde

Judging

No one should be a judge in his own case.
—Legal maxim

A man should not act as a judge either for someone he loves or for someone he hates. For no man can see the guilt of someone he loves or the good qualities in someone he hates.
—Babylonian Talmud
Tractate Ketubbot

Judge nothing before the time. Let us not with rash judging thrust all into the pit of hell whom we see walking near the brink thereof.
—Thomas Fuller

If you judge, investigate.
—Seneca

Do not judge your fellow man until you have stood in his place.
—Hillel

Do not be too hasty in accusing, or approving, anyone.
—Publilius Syrus

Judge everyone with the scale weighted in his favor.
—Joshua ben Perahyah

Do not judge of the ship from the land.
—English proverb

As in all human situations, there is a paradox here. "Judge not" . . . and yet, at the same time, choose what seems to be right, reasonable, decent. In other words, judge but don't judge—judge in the sense of discriminating, but don't judge in the sense of condemning. Even when there seems to be a moral evil, don't judge in a condemnatory way.
—Aldous Huxley

Justice

Let justice be done, even though the heavens fall.
—Roman jurist's saying

When it is our duty to do an act of justice it should be done promptly. To delay is injustice.
—Jean de La Bruyère

Never expect justice in the world. That is not part of God's plan. Everybody thinks that if they don't get it, they're some kind of odd man out. And it's not true. Nobody gets justice—people get good luck or bad luck.

—Orson Welles

Be just, and fear not.
                    —Wolsey in Shakespeare's
                    King Henry VIII

K

Kindness

The true and noble way to kill a foe,
Is not to kill him,—you, with kindness, may
So change him, that he shall cease to be so,
And then he's slain.
—Alain

Never lose a chance of saying a kind word.
—William Makepeace Thackeray

Happiness, grief, gaiety, sadness, are by nature contagious. Bring your health and your strength to the weak and sickly, and so you will be of use to them. Give them, not your weakness, but your energy, so you will revive and lift them up. Life alone can rekindle life.
—Henri-Frédéric Amiel

The way to make yourself pleasing to others is to show that you care for them. . . . The seeds of love can never grow but under the warm and genial influence of kind feelings and affectionate manners.
—William Wirt to his daughter

It's a bit embarrassing to have been concerned with the human problem all one's life and find at the end that one has no more to offer by way of advice than "Try to be a little kinder."
—Aldous Huxley

Be not too critical of others, and love much.
                    —Julia Huxley
                    (Aldous Huxley's mother), to her son

(See *Charity, Compassion, Generosity, Sympathy*)

Knowledge

Receive my instruction, and not silver; and knowledge rather than choice gold.
For wisdom *is* better than rubies; and all the things that may be desired are not to be compared to it.
                    —Old Testament
                    Proverbs 8:10–11

While young, hoard up a great stock of knowledge; though in that season of dissipation, you may not have occasion to spend much of it, yet, a time will come, when you will need it to maintain you.
                    —Lord Chesterfield

If we would have new knowledge, we must get a world of new questions.
                    —Susanne K. Langer

        In this world and the next
        There is impurity and impurity:
        When a woman lacks dignity,
        When a man lacks generosity.

        But the greatest impurity is ignorance.
        Free yourself from it.
        Be pure.
                    —The Dhammapada
                    Sayings of the Buddha

Never carry your shotgun or your knowledge at half-cock.
                    —Austin O'Malley

It is never enough for us simply to *know*. We must also *weigh*.
—John MacCunn

If you seek the kernel, then you must break the shell. And likewise, if you would know the reality of Nature, you must destroy the appearance, and the farther you go beyond the appearance, the nearer you will be to the essence.
—Meister Eckhart

(See *Education, Learning, Understanding, Wisdom*)

L

Labor

Let every man be occupied, and occupied in the highest employment of which his nature is capable, and die with the consciousness that he has done his best.
—Sydney Smith

It's necessary to be slightly underemployed if you are to do something significant.
—James Watson
Nobel Laureate, co-discoverer of the DNA double helix

Love labour: for if thou dost not want it for food, thou mayst for physic. It is wholesome for thy body, and good for thy mind. It prevents the fruits of idleness which many times comes of nothing to do, and leads too many to do what is worse than nothing.
—William Penn

Toil and be strong. By toil the flaccid nerves grow firm, and gain a more compacted tone.
—John Armstrong

Derive happiness in oneself from a good day's work, from illuminating the fog that surrounds us.
—Henri Matisse

Einstein's three rules of work:
(1) Out of clutter find simplicity.
(2) From discord make harmony.
(3) In the middle of difficulty lies opportunity.
                    —Albert Einstein

(See *Work Psychology*)

Language/Writing

All we can do is hang on to our colons: punctuation is bound to change, like the rest of language; punctuation is made for man, not man for punctuation; a good sentence should be intelligible without the help of punctuation in most cases; and if you get in a muddle with your dots and dashes, you may need to simplify your thoughts, and shorten your sentence.
                    —Philip Howard

Fumblerules of grammar:
   Don't use no double negatives.
   Proofread carefully to see if you any words out.
   Take the bull by the hand and avoid mixed metaphors.
   If I've told you once, I've told you a thousand times, resist hyperbole.
   "Avoid overuse of 'quotation "marks." ' "
   Avoid commas, that are not necessary.
   If you reread your work, you will find on rereading that a great deal
      of repetition can be avoided by rereading and editing.
   Avoid clichés like the plague.
   Never use a long word when a diminutive one will do.
   Avoid colloquial stuff.
                    —William Safire
                    based on suggestions from readers

Place yourself in the background; write in a way that comes naturally; work from a suitable design; write with nouns and verbs; do not overwrite; do not overstate; avoid the use of qualifiers; do not affect a breezy style; use orthodox spelling; do not explain too much; avoid fancy

words; do not take shortcuts at the cost of clarity; prefer the standard to the offbeat; make sure the reader knows who is speaking; do not use dialect; revise and rewrite.
—E. B. White

Hanging is too good for a man who makes puns; he should be drawn and quoted.
—Fred Allen

Beware the elongated yellow fruit: Have no unreasonable fear of repetition. . . . The story is told of a feature writer who was doing a piece on the United Fruit Company. He spoke of bananas once; he spoke of bananas twice; he spoke of bananas yet a third time, and now he was desperate. "The world's leading shippers of the elongated yellow fruit," he wrote. A fourth bananas would have been better.
—James J. Kilpatrick

Bad spellers of the world, untie!
—Graffito

(See *Authorship, Books, Literary Composition, Reading, Words, Writing*)

Laughter

Frame your mind to mirth and merriment,
Which bars a thousand harms and lengthens life.
—Servant, in Shakespeare's
The Taming of the Shrew

Life can be wildly tragic at times, and I've had my share. But whatever happens to you, you have to keep a slightly comic attitude. In the final analysis, you have got not to forget to laugh.
—Katharine Hepburn

Once you get people laughing, they're listening and you can tell them almost anything.
—Herbert Gardner

Beware of too much laughter, for it deadens the mind and produces oblivion.
—The Talmud

Never make people laugh. If you would succeed in life, you must be solemn, solemn as an ass. All the great monuments are built over solemn asses.
—Thomas Corwin

Laugh at yourself first, before anyone else can.
—Elsa Maxwell

All you earnest young men out to save the world . . . please, have a laugh.
—Reinhold Niebuhr

(See *Good Humor, Joking*)

Law

Let reverence for the laws be breathed by every American mother to the lisping babe that prattles on her lap; let it be taught in schools, seminaries, and in colleges; let it be written in primers, spelling books, and in almanacs; let it be preached from the pulpit, proclaimed in legislative halls, and enforced in courts of justice. And, in short, let it become the political religion of the nation.
—Abraham Lincoln

Do not first suffer the punishment of the law, and then learn of its nature; but, before thou suffer, anticipate it by thy respect for it.
—Menander

Never create by law what can be accomplished by morality.
—Charles-Louis de Secondat
Baron de Montesquieu

Let all the laws be clear, uniform and precise; to interpret laws is always almost to corrupt them.
—Voltaire

Agree, for the law is costly.
—English proverb

Learning

Take fast hold of instruction; let her not go; keep her; for she is thy life.
—Old Testament
Proverbs 4:13

The chief art of learning, as Locke has observed, is to attempt but little at a time. The widest excursions of the mind are made by short flights frequently repeated; the most lofty fabrics of science are formed by the continued accumulation of single propositions.
—Samuel Johnson

Learn of the skilful; he that teaches himself, hath a fool for his master.
—Benjamin Franklin

It is not always possible to know what one has learned, or when the dawning will arrive. You will continue to shift, sift, to shake out and to double back. The synthesis that finally occurs can be in the most unexpected place and the most unexpected time. My charge . . . is to be alert to the dawnings.
—Virginia B. Smith
President, Vassar College

Swallow all your learning in the morning, but digest it in company in the evenings.
—Lord Chesterfield

The more you study, the more you find out you don't know, but the more you study, the closer you come.
—Cozy Cole

As long as you live, keep learning how to live.
—Seneca

(See *Education, Knowledge, Understanding, Wisdom*)

Leisure

If you are losing your leisure, look out! You are losing your soul.
—Logan Pearsall Smith

Leisure should be relaxing. Possibly you like complicated puzzles or chess, or other demanding intellectual games. Give them up. If you want to continue to be intellectually productive, you must risk the contempt of your younger acquaintances and freely admit that you read detective stories or watch Archie Bunker on television.
—B. F. Skinner

The art of leisure lies, to me, in the power of absorbing without effort the spirit of one's surroundings; to look, without speculation, at the sky and sea; to become part of a green plain; to rejoice, with a tranquil mind, in the feast of colour in a bed of flowers.
—Dion Calthrop

(See *Hedonism, Pleasure, Travel*)

Letters

"Gentlemen" is no longer acceptable as a salutation when writing to a corporation or partnership. "Ladies/Gentlemen" sounds like a unisex bathroom. The best of the lot is "Dear Sir or Madam". . . .
—Ann Landers

A *formula for answering controversial letters (without even reading the letters)*:
Dear Sir (or Madame):
  You may be right.
                          —H. L. Mencken
                          (quoted by Alexander Woollcott in a letter
                          to Felix Frankfurter)

The best time to frame an answer to the letters of a friend, is the moment you receive them. Then the warmth of friendship, and the intelligence received, most forcibly co-operate.
                          —William Shenstone

I consider it a good rule for letter writing to leave unmentioned what the recipient already knows, and instead tell him something new.
                          —Sigmund Freud

Years ago a famous lawyer gave me a very good piece of advice: "Never write a letter," he said, "and never destroy one." That does not always hold true, but it certainly does when you're angry. Don't write the angry letter. If you must, say it in person. And don't tell secrets in a letter. Once that letter is in the mail, it is out of your control.
                          —Barbara Walters

Life

  Reflect that life, like every other blessing
  Derives its value from its use alone.
  —Samuel Johnson

Life is an unanswered question, but let's still believe in the dignity and importance of the question.
                          —Tennessee Williams

Teach him [your child] to live rather than to avoid death; life is not breath, but action, the use of our senses, our mind, our faculties,

every part of ourselves which makes us conscious of our living. Life consists less in length of days than in the keen sense of living.
— Jean-Jacques Rousseau

The great art of life is how to turn the surplus life of the soul into life for the body.
— Henry David Thoreau

Look, I really don't want to wax philosophic, but I will say that if you're alive, you got to flap your arms and legs, you got to jump around a lot, you got to make a lot of noise, because life is the very opposite of death. And therefore, as I see it, if you're quiet, you're not living . . . you've got to be noisy, or at least your *thoughts* should be noisy and colorful and lively.
— Mel Brooks

The art of life is to know how to enjoy a little and to endure much.
— William Hazlitt

Life can only be understood backwards, but it must be lived forwards.
— Søren Kierkegaard

You don't get to choose how you're going to die. Or when. You can only decide how you're going to live. Now.
— Joan Baez

I dreamed I had a child, and even in the dream I saw that it was my life, and it was an idiot, and I ran away. But it always crept into my lap again, clutched at my clothes. Until I thought, if I could kiss it, whatever in it was my own, perhaps I could sleep. And I bent over the broken face, and it was horrible . . . but I kissed it. I think that one must finally take one's life into one's arms.
— Arthur Miller
After the Fall

It's a very short trip. While alive, live.
— Malcolm Forbes

We must leave our mark on life while we have it in our power, lest it should close up, when we leave it, without a trace.
— Isak Dinesen
(nom de plume of Karen Blixen)

Epictetus would also say that there were two faults far graver and fouler than any others—inability to bear, and inability to forbear, when we neither patiently bear the blows that must be borne, nor abstain from the things and the pleasures we ought to abstain from. "So," he went on, "if a man will have only these two words at heart, and heed them carefully by ruling and watching over himself, he will for the most part fall into no sin, and his life will be tranquil and serene." He meant the words "BEAR AND FORBEAR."

—*The Golden Sayings of Epictetus,*
The Harvard Classics

(See *Living, Quality of Life*)

Limitations

Seek not out the things that are too hard for thee, neither search the things that are beyond thy strength.

—Apocrypha

Be careful. A man who is used to serving his sentence at Brest cannot get accustomed to Toulon. Stick to the jail you know.

—Heine's advice to Balzac,
recommending him to confine himself to
the writing of novels

If thy heart fails thee, climb not at all.

—Thomas Fuller

(See *Resignation/Acceptance, Restraint*)

Listening

Keep some opinions to yourself. Say what you please of others, but never repeat what you hear said of them to themselves. If you have

nothing to offer yourself, laugh with the witty, assent to the wise; they will not think the worse of you for it. Listen to information on subjects you are unacquainted with, instead of always striving to lead the conversation to some favourite one of your own. By the last method you will shine, but will not improve. I am ashamed myself ever to open my lips on any question I have ever written upon.
—William Hazlitt

When a woman is speaking to you, listen to what she says with her eyes.
—Victor Hugo

Listening, not imitation, may be the sincerest form of flattery. . . . If you want to influence someone, listen to what he says. . . . When he finishes talking, ask him about any points that you do not understand. Then tell him what it is you want and point out the areas where you are in agreement and those where you do not agree. He will be flattered that you have listened intently, that you take him seriously, and that you truly want to understand his position.
—Dr. Joyce Brothers

Be a good listener. Your ears will never get you in trouble.
—Frank Tyger

The only way to entertain some folks is to listen to them.
—Kin Hubbard

Bend from the lofty perch of your own disciplines and listen with regard to disciplines not your own. If you are an engineer, listen to the artist; if you are a physicist, listen to the philosopher; if you are a logician, listen to the religionist; and especially if you are in a position of power, listen, listen. We need to listen to one another if we are to make it through this age of permanent apocalypse and avoid the chaos of the crowd.
—Chaim Potok

Avoid interruptive thinking. Everyone—and I mean everyone—has something good to offer you if you are astute enough to find it. Sometimes it means picking a small kernel out of a lot of chaff, but the kernel is always there. One way to get the best from people is to learn to avoid what I call interruptive thinking. This is where someone is saying something to you and you interrupt—and probably change the subject in doing so.

—David Mahoney

Literary Composition

When writing a novel a writer should create living people; people not characters. A *character* is a caricature.

Never write about a place until you're away from it, because that gives you perspective. Immediately after you've seen something you can give a photographic description of it and make it accurate. That's good practice, but it isn't creative writing.

Don't get discouraged because there's a lot of mechanical work to writing. . . . I rewrote the first part of A *Farewell to Arms* at least fifty times. . . . The first draft of anything is shit. When you first start to write you get all the kick and the reader gets none, but after you learn to work it's your object to convey everything to the reader so that he remembers it not as a story he has read but something that has happened to himself. That's the true test of writing.

—Ernest Hemingway

Keep your hands from literary picking and stealing. But if you cannot refrain from this kind of stealth, abstain from murdering what you steal.

—Augustus Montague Toplady

Read over your compositions and whenever you meet with a passage that you think is particularly fine, strike it out.

—Samuel Johnson, quoting a college tutor

Life goes on, and for the sake of verisimilitude and realism, you cannot positively give the impression of an ending: you must let something hang. A cheap interpretation of that would be to say that you must always leave a chance for a sequel. People die, love dies, but life does

not die, and so long as people live, stories must have life at the end.
                           —John O'Hara

Don't *explain* your characters—make 'em live!
                           —Sinclair Lewis
                           Advice to a woman author on excess of
                           earnestness

Find a subject you care about and which you in your heart feel others
should care about. It is this genuine caring, and not your games with
language, which will be the most compelling and seductive element
in your style.
                           —Kurt Vonnegut

The way to become boring is to say *everything*.
                           —Voltaire

Never dare to tell me again anything about "green grass." Tell me
how the lawn was flecked with shadows. I know perfectly well that
grass is green. So does everybody else in England. . . . Make me see
what it was that made your garden distinct from a thousand others.
                           —Robert Louis Stevenson
                           to young Adelaide Boodle

Whatever you write should, on the surface, out of respect for the
sources from which you borrow, and for the sake of language, offer a
sense of direction however indifferent.
                           —Stéphane Mallarmé

Throw yourself away when you write.
                           —Maxwell Perkins

Generalizations are no use—give one specific thing and let the action
say it. . . . When you have people talking, you have a scene. You
must interrupt with explanatory paragraphs but shorten them as much
as you can. Dialogue is *action*. . . . You tend to explain too much.
You must explain, but your tendency is to distrust your own narrative
and dialogue. . . . You need only to intensify throughout what actually is there—and I think you would naturally do this in revision,
anyhow. It is largely a matter of compression, and not so much of

that really. . . . You can't know a book until you come to the end of it, and then all the rest must be modified to fit that.
                    —Maxwell Perkins to Marcia Davenport

Beware of creating tedium! I know no guard against this so likely to be effective as the feeling of the writer himself. When once the sense that the thing is becoming long has grown upon him, he may be sure that it will grow upon his readers.
                    —Anthony Trollope

Resolve not to use the passive voice. Simply fly in the face of convention and begin your sentences with "I" or "we" or "the writer."
                    —Sheridan Baker

When you say something, make sure you have said it. The chances of your having said it are only fair.
                    —E. B. White

Let the writer not scorn the word "technique." . . . The tyro says we can do without tricks. . . . Art, he says, is "above" craftsmanship. "If you have a hundred thousand francs' worth of craftsmanship," Degas told a pupil, "spend five sous to buy more."
                    —Catherine Drinker Bowen

To write well, combine strong metaphor with subdued metaphor, strongly marked forms with indefinite forms.

A writer should never give forth the whole of his thought, unless it be of a kind that it is well to be rid of. Breathe out all your anger, but not all your kindness; all your abuse, but not all your praise. Do not quench the mind's fire; still more do not empty it. Keep back always a little of its produce and leave something of its honey to the bee itself for nourishment.
                    —Joseph Joubert

Sit down to write what you have thought, and not to think about what you shall write.
                    —William Cobbett

(See *Authorship, Books, Language/Writing, Reading, Words, Writing*)

Living

Pray, let us live without being drawn by dogs, Esquimaux-fashion, tearing over hill and dale, and biting each other's ears.
—Henry David Thoreau

Let us not go hurrying about and collecting honey, bee-like buzzing here and there for a knowledge of what is not to be arrived at, but let us open our leaves like a flower, and be passive and receptive, budding patiently under the eye of Apollo, and taking truths from every noble insect that favours us with a visit.
—John Keats

Don't forget until too late that the business of life is not business, but living.
—B. C. Forbes

If you feel that you are lacking in ambition, be assured that meditation and contemplation . . . is a more certain joy in life. Anyone can indulge ambition; only those who have the spirit can revel in passive enjoyment.
—Advice from Samuel White
to his son, E. B. White

We live in the midst of details that keep us running round in circles and never getting anywhere but tired, or that bring on nervous breakdowns and coronary thrombosis. The answer is not to take to the woods, but to find out what we really want to do and then cut out the details that fritter away what is most valuable in life. *Live deep instead of fast*. I think this is what Thoreau meant.
—Henry Seidel Canby

(See *Life*, *Quality of Life*)

Loneliness

How to fight loneliness:

Plan ahead nightly for the next day's work. Don't get up at 7 o'clock and think the day will take care of itself. The day is not going to take care of itself.

Get out of the house every day. Rain, shine or snow, be sure to stay out at least two or three hours and meet people of all ages.
—Dr. Michael Vaught

Always have some project under way . . . an ongoing project that goes over from day to day and thus makes each day a smaller unit of time.
—Dr. Lillian Troll

Plan well ahead to be with family and close friends during holidays and weekends. These are the cruelest periods for those living alone. If you can't be with family or friends, draft a list of time-consuming chores that will occupy you and avert self-pity.
—Henry Lee

Go not to hell for company.
—English proverb

(See *Solitude*)

Longevity

Prefer a noble life before a long.
—Coriolanus in Shakespeare's *Coriolanus*

If you wouldst live long, live well; for folly and wickedness shorten life.
—Benjamin Franklin

Do you desire to master the art of prolonging life? Rather apply yourself to the art of enduring it.
                    —Ernst von Feuchtersleben

The secret of a long life is double careers. One to about age 60, then another for the next 30 years.
                    —David Ogilvy

Go to bed the same day you get up.
                    —Miles B. Carpenter, age 93

Pick the right grandparents, don't eat or drink too much, be circumspect in all things, and take a two-mile walk every morning before breakfast.
                    —Harry S. Truman on his 80th birthday

Let thy vices die before thee.
                    —English proverb

(See *The Elderly, Old Age, Retirement*)

Love

If you'd be loved, be worthy to be loved.
                    —Ovid

          Prepare,
          You lovers, to know Love a thing of moods
          Not like hard life, of laws.
                    —George Meredith

Never confuse "I love you" with "I want to marry you."
                    —Le Roy King

Let us love temperately, things violent last not.
                    —Philip Massinger

Beware of all the paradoxical in love. It is simplicity which saves, it is simplicity which brings happiness. . . . Love should be love.
—Charles Baudelaire

Be secret to thyself and trust none in matters of love as thou lovest life.
—John Lyly

> And let us mind, faint heart ne'er won
> A lady fair.
> Wha does the utmost, that he can
> Will shyles do mair.
> —Robert Burns

Love doesn't drop on you unexpectedly; you have to give off signals, sort of like an amateur radio operator.
—Helen Gurley Brown

Love not at the first look.
—John Clarke

> Before you love,
>   Learn to run through snow,
>   Leaving no footprints.
> —Turkish proverb

Love for the joy of loving, and not for the offerings of someone else's heart.
—Marlene Dietrich

You need someone to love you while you're looking for someone to love.
—Shelagh Delaney

> Never love with all your heart,
> It only ends in aching.
> —Countee Cullen

Treasure each other in the recognition that we do not know how long we shall have each other.
—Joshua Loth Liebman

Gather the rose of love whilst yet is time.
—Edmund Spenser

I don't think you can look for love. All you can do is get yourself in a situation where you don't discourage something that may be rather nice.
—Linda Ronstadt

If you want something very, very badly, let it go free. If it comes back to you, it's yours forever. If it doesn't, it was never yours to begin with.
—Anonymous

Hold fast to whatever fragments of love are left, for sometimes a mosaic is more beautiful than an unbroken pattern.
—Dawn Powell

Love is as strict as acting. If you want to love somebody, stand there and do it. If you don't, don't. There are no other choices.
—Tyne Daly

When one feels oneself smitten by love for a woman, one should say to oneself, "Who are the people around her? What kind of life has she led?" All one's future lies in the answer.
—Alfred de Vigny

True love comes quietly, without banners or flashing lights. If you hear bells, get your ears checked.
—Erich Segal

Love (Universal)

This is my commandment, that ye love one another, even as I have loved you. Greater love hath no man than this, that a man lay down his life for his friends.
>   —New Testament
>   John 15:12–13

Scorn no man's love though of a mean degree:
Love is a present for a mighty king;
Much less make any one thine enemy.
>   —George Herbert

Keep love in your heart. A life without it is like a sunless garden when the flowers are dead. The consciousness of loving and being loved brings a warmth and richness to life that nothing else can bring.
>   —Oscar Wilde

Do not love your neighbor as yourself. If you are on good terms with yourself it is an impertinence; if on bad, an injury.
>   —George Bernard Shaw

Make love now, by night and by day, in winter and in summer. . . . You are in the world for that and the rest of life is nothing but vanity, illusion, waste. There is only one science, love, only one riches, love, only one policy, love. To make love is all the law, and the prophets.
>   —Anatole France

Love many things, for therein lies the true strength, and whosoever loves much performs much, and can accomplish much, and what is done in love is well done.
>   —Vincent van Gogh

You must love all that God has created, both his entire world and each single tiny sand grain of it. Love each tiny leaf, each beam of sunshine. You must love the animals, love every plant. If you love

all things, you will also attain the divine mystery that is in all things. For then your ability to perceive the truth will grow every day, and your mind will open itself to an all-embracing love.
—Fyodor Dostoyevsky

(See *Brotherhood, Communication—Personal*)

Love (Unrequited)

Take not the first refusal ill:
Tho' now she won't, anon she will.
—Thomas D'Urfey

If you cannot inspire a woman with love of you, fill her above the brim with love of herself; all that runs over will be yours.
—Charles Caleb Colton

You who seek an end of love, love yields to business; be busy, and you will be safe.
—Ovid

Quit, quit for shame; this will not move;
If of herself she will not love,
Nothing will make her, the devil take her!
—Sir John Suckling

(See *Affection*)

Luck

Be grateful for luck. Pay the thunder no mind—listen to the birds. And don't hate nobody.
—Eubie Blake

Do not reveal your thoughts to everyone, lest you drive away your good luck.
　　　　　—Apocrypha

　　　Don't envy men
　　　Because they seem to have a run of luck,
　　　Since luck's a nine day's wonder,
　　　Wait their end.
　　　　　—Euripides

Las Vegas Law: Never bet on a loser because you think his luck is bound to change.
　　　　　—Arthur Bloch

Once, a *petit fonctionnaire* came blubbering in to thank foreign minister Talleyrand for an assignment, tears of gratitude in his eyes as he explained, "This is the first break I've ever gotten." "What? Unlucky?" said Talleyrand, immediately withdrawing the appointment. Moral? Only report those stories that enhance your aura—not of ability (which others might resent) but of beautifully dumb, irresistible luck. Whom the fates adore, their fellows admire.
　　　　　—Blythe Holbrooke

(See *Destiny, Fate*)

M

Magnanimity

Give losers leave to talk.
    —English proverb

You, I am sure, will forgive me for sincerely remarking that you might curb your magnanimity, and be more of an artist, and load every rift of your subject with ore.
    —John Keats, in a letter to
    Percy Bysshe Shelley

Leave the field, thou art victorious; it is noble to spare the vanquished.
    —Statius

When you have gained a victory, do not push it too far; 'tis sufficient to let the company and your adversary see 'tis in your power but that you are too generous to make use of it.
    —Eustace Budgell

In War: Resolution. In Defeat: Defiance.
In Victory: Magnanimity. In Peace: Good Will.
    —Sir Winston Churchill
    Preface to *The Second World War*

Manners

Frame your manners to the time.
> —Lucentio in Shakespeare's
> *The Taming of the Shrew*

Speak not of doleful things in a time of mirth or at the table.

Sleep not when others speak, sit not when others stand, speak not when you should hold your peace, walk not when others stop.

In the presence of others sing not to yourself with a humming noise, nor drum with your fingers or feet.
> —George Washington, age 15, in his "Rules
> of Civility and Decent Behavior"

Eat as it becometh a man, those things which are set before thee; and devour not, lest thou be hated. . . . When thou sittest among many, reach not thy hand out first of all. . . . Be not insatiable in any dainty thing, nor too greedy upon meats.
> —Ben Sira
> Apocrypha

How to survive common sticky social situations like being seated at dinner between two people whom you have never met . . . and have absolutely nothing in common with: Be ready to draw from a large group of topics, one of which *must* strike a responsive chord. Be sure these are topics on which you can lead a discussion during an entire meal course. Following are examples:
  Landscape gardening
  Professional wrestling
  The use of hypnotism to stop smoking
  Robots doing housework
  What you'd put in a time capsule
  The contents of the Smithsonian Institution
> —Letitia Baldrige

When confronted with rudeness: What you don't do is respond with equally rude behavior . . . When someone says, "God, you look awful"—a typical remark these days—and you respond, "Well, you don't look so hot yourself," you are going down to their level. But if you look them in the eye and reply, "How kind of you to say so," it might give them pause.
> —Judith Martin
> "Miss Manners"

Don't look at the ground when you say, "I'm sorry." Hold your head up and look the person in the eye, so he'll know you mean it.
> —Susan Jacoby

Never answer a telephone that rings before breakfast. It is sure to be one of three types of persons: a strange man in Minneapolis who has been up all night and is phoning collect; a salesman who wants to come over and demonstrate a combination Dictaphone and music box that also cleans rugs; or a woman out of one's past.
> —James Thurber

(See *Courtesy, Etiquette*)

Marriage

The goal of our life should not be to find joy in marriage, but to bring more love and truth into the world. We marry to assist each other in this task. The most selfish and hateful life of all is that of two beings who unite in order to enjoy life. The highest calling is that of the man who has dedicated his life to serving God and doing good, and who unites with a woman in order to further that purpose.
> —Leo Tolstoy
> Letter to his son

If you have respect and consideration for one another, you'll make it.
> —Mary Durso (married 58 years)

Think not because you now are wed
That all your courtship's at an end.
—Antonio Hurtado de Mendoza

If the husband and wife can possibly afford it, they should definitely have separate bathrooms for the sake of their marriage.
—Doris Day

Guidelines for dual-career couples wanting to avoid trouble: Make an appointment to, at least once a week, be with each other outside the house. . . . Every six weeks, go away for 36 hours. . . . To avoid bickering over housework, sit down and list all household tasks. Divide them equitably. . . . Don't set too-high standards for housework. . . . Never accept an invitation to a party or after-hours business meeting without discussing it with your spouse. . . . Set up a household communication system. Get a household calendar. Get together once a week and keep each other informed of social commitments and work schedules.
—Marjorie Shaevitz

To keep the fire burning brightly there's one easy rule: Keep the two logs together, near enough to keep each other warm and far enough apart—about a finger's breadth—for breathing room. Good fire, good marriage, same rule.
—Marnie Reed Crowel

Whatever you may look like, marry a man your own age—as your beauty fades, so will his eyesight.
—Phyllis Diller

(See *Couples, Husbands/Wives, Relationships*)

Marriage (Advice to Women)

Better have an old man to humour, than a young rake to break your heart.
—Thomas Fuller

Marriage (Contemplation of)

First thrive, then wive.
—English proverb

In marriage do thou be wise; prefer the person before money; virtue before beauty; the mind before the body.
—William Penn

When marrying, ask yourself this question: Do you believe that you will be able to converse well with this person into your old age? Everything else in marriage is transitory.
—Friedrich Nietzsche

When you marry . . . make sure your lives are different enough so that you have something to tell each other in the evening.
—Brett Daniels

If I lay it down as a general rule, Harriet, that if a woman *doubts* as to whether she should accept a man or not, she certainly ought to refuse him. If she can hesitate as to "Yes," she ought to say "No," directly.
—Jane Austen

Never marry a man who can't please you. If you'd rather be with someone else, then don't make the commitment.
—Dr. Joyce Brothers

Choose a wife rather by your ear than by your eye.
—English proverb

My mother said: "Marry a man with good teeth and high arches." She thought I should get that into the genetic structure of the family.
—Jill Clayburgh

Let still the woman take
An elder than herself; so wears she to him,
So sways she level in her husband's heart.
For, boy, however we do praise ourselves,
Our fancies are more giddy and unfirm,
More longing, wavering, sooner lost and worn,
Than women's are.
 —The Duke, in Shakespeare's
 Twelfth Night

Let there be no great disproportion in age. They that marry ancient people in expectation to bury them, hang themselves in hope that one will come and cut the halter.
 —Thomas Fuller

Men who love to command must be especially careful not to marry imperious, women's-rights women; while those who willingly "obey orders" need just such. A timid woman should never marry a hesitating man, lest, like frightened children, each keep perpetually re-alarming the other by imaginary fears.
 —Victorian etiquette advice quoted
 by Russel Crouse

When you meet someone who can cook and do housework—don't hesitate a minute—marry him.
 —Graffito on back of a bus reported
 by Joey Adams

A person of genius should marry a person of character. Genius does not herd with genius.
 —Oliver Wendell Holmes

The things which you ought to desire in a wife are, 1. Chastity; 2. sobriety; 3. industry; 4. frugality; 5. cleanliness; 6. knowledge of domestic affairs; 7. good temper; 8. beauty. . . .
 —William Cobbett

In choosing a wife, and buying a sword, we ought not to trust another.
 —English proverb

If you ever marry, I would wish you to marry the woman you like. Do not be guided by the recommendation of friends. Nothing will atone for or overcome an original distaste.
—William Hazlitt

It is very important to make sure the person you're marrying is like-minded. It's crucial for a couple to have shared goals and values. The more you have in common the less you have to argue about.
—Barbara Friedman
Director of Divorce and Remarriage Counseling Center

Don't get married to an actress, because they're also actresses in bed.
—Roberto Rossellini

(See *Couples, Courtship, Relationships, Wooing*)

Maturity

Make up your mind . . . before it is too late, that the fitting thing for you to do is to live as a mature man who is making progress, and let everything which seems to be best for you be a law that must not be transgressed.
—Epictetus

Each age, like every individual, has its own characteristic intoxication; we must seek in each decade the joys natural to our years. If play is the effervescence of childhood, and love is the wine of youth, the solace of age is understanding. If you would be content in age, be wise with Solon and learn something every day. Education is not a task, it is a lifelong happiness, an ennobling intimacy with great men, an unhurried excursion into all realms of loveliness and wisdom. If in youth we fell in love with beauty, in maturity we can make friends with genius.
—Will Durant

I've never been impressed by mellowing. Usually the people who have mellowed always have just a touch of sadness, because maybe they shouldn't have survived. You just can't sit there and say, "I'm in the prime of life, isn't it wonderful. Lose 10 lbs. I'll be better than ever." You always have to doubt yourself. The only security I ever feel is that I won't turn pious. But that's a dangerous remark to make, because the devil's always listening.
—Norman Mailer

Love of life, passion for life. Perhaps one feels it also in one's youth, but differently and with different words. One must liberate oneself, at least to some extent, from complexities, from taking one's fate too much to heart, before being able to rejoice simply because one is alive and among the living.
—Czeslaw Milosz

(See *Aging*, *Mid-life*)

Meddling

Enquire not what boils in another's Pot.
—Thomas Fuller

Media

News should be covered, but not exploited. A hostage incident should be reported but not turned into a "round the clock circus." I believe that we must learn again that people are persons, not generic footage. We must not trample on privacy, even if we risk losing a dramatic bit of tape.
—Daniel Schorr

In dealing with the press, do yourself a favor, stick with one of three responses: (a) I know and I can tell you; (b) I know and I can't tell you; (c) I don't know.
—Dan Rather

Advice to bureaucrats on dealing with the news media: When in doubt, put it out.
—Joseph Laitin

If you've got some news that you don't want to get noticed, put it out Friday afternoon at 4 P.M.
—David Gergen

When you're talking to the media, be a well, not a fountain.
—Michael Deaver

Never trust a reporter who has a nice smile.
—William Rauch

(See *Communication, Journalism, Reporting, Television*)

Meditation

If thou may not continually gather thyself together, do it some time at least once a day, morning or evening.
—Thomas à Kempis

> Nor let soft slumber close your eyes
> Before you've recollected thrice
> The train of actions through the day:
> Where have my feet chose out the way?
> What have I learnt where'er I've been
> From all I've heard, from all I've seen?
> What know I more that's worth the knowing?
> What have I done that's worth the doing?

What have I sought that I should shun?
What duty have I left undone;
Or into what new follies run?
These self inquiries are the road
That leads us to virtue and to God.
        —Isaac Watts

Do not dissect things too much. . . . There is a place for analysis, but it is apt to be quite fatal in prayer and meditation. . . . Pray more with your heart and less with your brain. . . . Do you remember the old verse which says:

A centipede was happy quite,
Until a frog in fun
Said, "Pray, which leg comes after which?"
This raised her mind to such a pitch,
She lay distracted in the ditch,
Considering how to run.

Don't be a theoretical centipede.
        —Emmett Fox

(See *Identity, Introspection, Self-Improvement*)

Melancholy/Blues

Never give way to melancholy; resist it steadily, for the habit will encroach.
        —Sydney Smith

Be your own palace or the world's your jail.
        —Anonymous

If it makes you happy to be unhappy, then be unhappy.
        —Anonymous

"Keep aloof from sadness," says an Icelandic writer of the 12th century, "for sadness is a sickness of the soul." Life has, indeed, many ills, but the mind that views every object in its most cheering aspect, and every doubtful dispensation as replete with latent good, bears within itself a powerful and perpetual antidote. The gloomy soul aggravates misfortune, while a cheerful smile often dispels those mists that portend a storm.
—Lydia H. Sigourney

How to shake those holiday blues: Do your Christmas shopping early, go easy on the eggnog [alcohol], watch out for family confrontations—and keep expectations in check.
—*Business Week*

Love him (or her)—and let her (or him) alone. Let him enjoy his troubled moments. He may need occasional withdrawal or self inquiry. Don't intrude upon the private mood; it does not necessarily mean he hates you or resents his mother or should be carried off to a couch.
—Leo C. Rosten

(See Anxiety, Depression, Despair, Peace of Mind, Stress, Worry)

Men (Advice to Women About Men)

The best way to get most husbands to do something is to suggest that perhaps they're too old to do it.
—Shirley MacLaine

The best way to find out if a man has done something is to advise him to do it. He will not be able to resist boasting that he has done it without being advised.
—Comtesse Diane

You have to understand that men can be awfully sluggish about making decisions of the heart. Remember, please, that evolution is a slow process. Amphibians didn't exactly *decide* to become reptiles. One day, one brave, scaly green guy took a long walk on land and cautiously said, "Okay, okay, I can handle this." That's how life science is.
—Stephanie Brush

Remember, a woman wins an aged husband by listening to him, and a young man by talking to him.
—William H. Browne

Mercy

Let not mercy and truth forsake thee: bind them about thy neck; write them upon the table of thine heart:

So shalt thou find favour and good understanding in the sight of God and man.
—Old Testament
Proverbs 3:3–4

Though justice be thy plea, consider this,
That in the course of justice, none of us
Should see salvation. We do pray for mercy,
And that same prayer doth teach us all to render
The deeds of mercy.
—Portia in Shakespeare's
The Merchant of Venice

Dost thou wish to receive mercy? Show mercy to thy neighbor.
—St. John Chrysostom

In case of doubt it is best to lean to the side of mercy.
—Legal maxim

(See *Forgiveness, Remembrance*)

Merit

We should try to succeed by merit, not by favor. He who does well will always have patrons enough.
   —Plautus

If you have but the magnanimity to allow merit wherever you see it—understanding in a lord or wit in a cobbler—this temper of mind will stand you instead of many accomplishments.
   —William Hazlitt

Don't overestimate your own merits.
   —Bertrand Russell

(See *Ability, Ancestry, Favor, Proficiency*)

Mid-Life

The most important words in midlife are—Let Go. Let it happen to you. Let it happen to your partner. Let the feelings. Let the changes. . . . You are moving out of roles and into the self. . . . It would be surprising if we didn't experience some pain as we leave the familiarity of one adult stage for the uncertainty of the next. But the willingness to move through each passage is equivalent to the willingness to live abundantly. If we don't change, we don't grow. If we don't grow, we are not really living.
   —Gail Sheehy

Keep in mind that your level of best performance after forty will probably be at least one step below that on which you succeeded before forty. Normally your energies would not slump much at that age. They may not slump appreciably until close to fifty. But slump they will,

and it seems the better part of valor to anticipate the change and train yourself for a new and somewhat gentler mode of living.
                    —Walter B. Pitkin

Just remember, once you're over the hill you begin to pick up speed.
                    —Charles Schulz

(See *Aging, Maturity*)

Military

Yield, ye arms, to the toga.
                    —Cicero

Advice to officers: . . . be strict in your discipline; that is, to require nothing unreasonable of your officers and men, but see that whatever is required be punctually complied with. Reward and punish every man according to his merit, without partiality or prejudice; hear his complaints; if well founded, redress them; if otherwise, discourage them, in order to prevent frivolous ones. Discourage vice in every shape, and impress upon the mind of every man, from the first to the lowest, the importance of the cause, and what it is they are contending for.

                    —George Washington to William Woodford

One should never risk one's whole fortune unless supported by one's entire forces.
                    —Niccolò Machiavelli

If it moves, salute it.
If it doesn't move, pick it up.
If you can't pick it up, paint it.

Keep your mouth shut, your bowels open and never volunteer.

Shape up or ship out.
                    —World War II U.S. Army maxims

In the councils of government, we must guard against the acquisition of unwarranted influence, whether sought or unsought, by the military-industrial complex. The potential for the disastrous rise of misplaced power exists and will persist.
—Dwight D. Eisenhower

(See *Discipline, Force, Peace, Preparedness—Military, Warfare*)

Misfortune

Yield not thy neck
To fortune's yoke, but let thy dauntless mind
Still ride in triumph over all mischance.
—King Lewis in Shakespeare's
King Henry VI

Do not wake misfortune while she sleeps.
—Baltasar Gracián

It is our duty to make the best of our misfortunes, and not to suffer passion to interfere with our interest and the public good.
—George Washington

When it has happened to thee to be unfortunate, master, remember the saying of Euripides and then wilt thou be more easy—"There is no man who is happy in every way." Then imagine thyself to be one of the great crowd of mankind.
—Philippides

Meditate upon exile, torture, wars, diseases, shipwreck, so that you may not be a novice to any misfortune.
—Seneca

(See *Adversity*)

Mistakes

Remember your past mistakes just long enough to profit by them.
—Dan McKinnon

The Athenians, alarmed at the internal decay of their Republic, asked Demosthenes what to do. His reply: "Do not do what you are doing now."

—Joseph Ray

Do not look where you fell, but where you slipped.
—African proverb

We should deal with our life as we deal with our writings: bring the beginning, middle, and end into agreement and harmony. To do this, we must make many erasures.
—Joseph Joubert

No matter how far you have gone on a wrong road, turn back.
—Turkish proverb

Be not too rigidly censorious,
A string may jar in the best master's hand,
And the most skillful archer miss his aim;
I would not quarrel with a slight mistake.
—Earl of Roscommon

"Aim for success, NOT perfection." Never give up your right to be wrong, because then you will lose the ability to learn new things and to move forward with your life. Remember that fear always lurks behind perfectionism. . . . Confronting your fears and allowing yourself the right to be human can, paradoxically, make you a far happier and more productive person.
—Dr. David M. Burns

Remember, even monkeys fall out of trees.
—Korean proverb

Moderation

Well observe
The rule of Not Too Much, by temperance taught
In what thou eat'st and drink'st.
—John Milton

Love moderately; long love doth so.
—Friar Laurence in Shakespeare's
Romeo and Juliet

Do not cry havoc where you should but hunt with modest warrant.
—Menenius in Shakespeare's
Coriolanus

Those prone to overdo, would do well to make familiar the maxims,— "The world was not made in one day"; "Moderation is the life of business"; and try to forget the maxim,—"'Tis better to wear out, than to rust out."
—Author unknown

Don't overdo it. . . . This is the pace that kills.
—N. Marsh

Make not your sail too big for your ballast.
—English proverb

Don't pitch too high, or you won't get through the tune. Expenditure which begins at a great rate often comes to a sudden end by bankruptcy. Begin so that you can keep on, and even rise higher. Orators should beware of splendid openings, for it will never do to drop; and it will be hard to keep up the big style to the end.
—C. H. Spurgeon

Modesty

Be modest! It is the kind of pride least likely to offend.
          —Jules Renard

Make no display of your talents or attainments; for every one will clearly see, admire, and acknowledge them, so long as you cover them with the beautiful veil of modesty.
          —Nathaniel Emmons

          Pray thee, take pain
          To allay with some cold drops of modesty
          Thy skipping spirit.
                    —Bassanio in Shakespeare's
                    The Merchant of Venice

Modesty is the lowest of the virtues, and is a confession of the deficiency it indicates. He who undervalues himself, is justly undervalued by others.
          —William Hazlitt

Remember that with her clothes a woman puts off her modesty.
          —Herodotus

Money

Take the money and run.
          —American dictum

Put your money where your mouth is.
          —American dictum

If you have no money, be polite.
          —Danish proverb

How to have your cake and eat it: Lend it out at interest.
　　　　—Anonymous

Never esteem a man or thyself the more for money, nor condemn him for want of it.
　　　　—English proverb

Do not mistake a crowd of big wage-earners for the leisure class.
　　　　—Clive Bell

It's good to have money and the things that money can buy, but it's good, too, to check up once in a while and make sure you haven't lost the things that money can't buy.
　　　　—George Horace Lorimer

　　　If thou wouldst keep money, save money;
　　　If thou wouldst reap money, sow money.
　　　　—Thomas Fuller

Make money your god and it will plague you like the devil.
　　　　—Henry Fielding

A wise man should have money in his head, but not in his heart.
　　　　—Jonathan Swift

In your early twenties, adjust your spending to what you earn; in your late twenties and early thirties, prepare to have a bigger house; in your forties consider the problems of sending your kids to college (make your children pay as much as possible); in your fifties, get yourself ready for retirement; in your sixties consider whether you should sell your house (you may be losing money by staying in it); after your sixties don't scrimp to leave money to your children (you have left them a prosperous United States).
　　　　—Ben Stein

The best money advice ever given me was from my father. When I was a little girl, he told me, "Don't spend anything unless you have to."
　　　　—Dinah Shore

It is important for boy children, at least, to learn to count money at the age of four, since it is high time they were out selling papers. If small for his age, the child can sell tabloids.
—W. C. Fields

(See *Borrowing, Economy*)

Morality

If your morals make you dreary, depend upon it, they are wrong. I do not say give them up, for they may be all you have, but conceal them like a vice lest they should spoil the lives of better and simpler people.
—Robert Louis Stevenson

Beware of making your moral staples consist of the negative virtues. It is good to abstain, and to teach others to abstain, from all that is sinful and hurtful. But making a business of it leads to emaciation of character unless one feeds largely on the more nutritious diet of active benevolence.
—Oliver Wendell Holmes

Unattainable as pure rectitude is, and will long continue to be, we must keep an eye on the compass which tells us whereabout it lies; or we shall otherwise wander in the opposite direction.
—Herbert Spencer

Let us with caution indulge the supposition that morality can be maintained without religion. Reason and experience both forbid us to expect that national morality can prevail in exclusion of religious principle.
—George Washington

Whenever you are to do a thing, though it can never be known but to yourself, ask yourself how you would act were all the world looking at you, and act accordingly.
—Thomas Jefferson

To avert disaster, we have not only to teach men to make things, but to teach them to have complete moral control over the things they make.

—Charles, Prince of Wales

(See *Conscience, Honor, Uprightness, Virtue*)

Mortality

Remember: it is not given to man to take his goods with him.
No one goes away and then comes back.

—from the tomb of Egyptian King Inyotef,
2600 B.C.

Mark how fleeting and paltry is the estate of man—yesterday in embryo, tomorrow a mummy or ashes. So for the hair's-breadth of time assigned to thee live rationally, and part with life cheerfully, as drops the ripe olive, extolling the season that bore it and the tree that matured it.

—Marcus Aurelius

Forget not Death, O man! for thou
may'st be
Of one thing certain—he forgets not
thee.

—Persian saying

Every person ought daily to reflect upon the uncertainty of life, and the consequences of sudden death. And when he has reason to fear that his sudden death might occasion an undesirable distribution of his estate, he ought immediately to make a will, according to law, taking advice, if needful, in order to prevent the evils which are liable to follow the neglect of it. Reader, do what you ought, in this matter, without delay.

—Charles Simmons

Don't try to live forever. You will not succeed.
—George Bernard Shaw

Ah, if you want to live in peace on the face of the earth,
Then build your ship of death, in readiness
For the longest journey, over the last of seas.
—D. H. Lawrence

In a harbor, two ships sailed: one setting forth on a voyage, the other coming home to port. Everyone cheered the ship going out, but the ship sailing in was scarcely noticed. To this, a wise man said: "Do not rejoice over a ship setting out to sea, for you cannot know what terrible storms it may encounter and what fearful dangers it may have to endure. Rejoice rather over the ship that has safely reached port and brings its passengers home in peace."

And this is the way of the world: When a child is born, all rejoice; when someone dies, all weep. We should do the opposite. For no one can tell what trials and travails await a newborn child; but when a mortal dies in peace, we should rejoice, for he has completed a long journey, and there is no greater boon than to leave this world with the imperishable crown of a good name.
—The Talmud

(See *Death, Immortality*)

Mother's Advice

Put some color in your cheeks.

Sit up straight.

Never nap after a meal or you'll get fat.
—Michele Slung
quoting Mother's advice

Here's what I taught my daughters: Become women of substance. Work for yourselves if you can. That way you won't have to take any lip,

and you can work the hours you want. Never buy artificial fabric; always buy silk. If you can save any money, buy your own place, and keep it in your name. . . . And if you hate to save, or be tied down, put your money in jewelry. Even if it's only garnets or jade, it's yours, and it's wealth. And never, never do a job if it isn't fun.
> —Carolyn See
> University Professor

How to be a Jewish mother:
. . . Basic sacrifices to make for your child:
   Stay up all night to prepare him a big breakfast.
   Don't let him know you fainted twice in the supermarket from
      fatigue. (But make sure he knows you're not letting him know.)
   Open his bedroom window wider so he can have more fresh air,
      and close your own so you don't use up the supply.
> —Dan Greenburg

Advice to mothers: Take off your earrings, your ring, your precious family heirloom, and give it to [your daughter-in-law] along with your love and trust. Trust and love are wonderful, but don't forget the earrings.
> —Estée Lauder

(See *Children, Family, Parenthood*)

Mottoes

Take short views, hope for the best, and trust in God.
> —Sydney Smith

Love all, trust a few. Do wrong to none.
> —Countess in Shakespeare's
> *All's Well That Ends Well*

Look up and not down; look out and not in; look forward and not back, and lend a hand.

> —Edward Everett Hale
> (motto of young Theodore Roosevelt)

(See *Creeds*)

Movie Acting

I don't like showing the technique. I don't like people who say, "Here, I'm going to act, but first I have to bounce off this wall." If you have to bounce off the wall, do it by yourself. Don't feature the technique. My old drama coach used to say, "Don't just do something, stand there." Gary Cooper wasn't afraid to do nothing.

> —Clint Eastwood

It can be a simple sentence that makes one single point, and you build for that. You zero in on the one moment that gets that character, you go for it, that's it, man, and if you fail the whole thing is down the drain, but if you make it you hit the moon. In *China* [*Syndrome*] there was one line the guy says, "There was a vibration." That's all, the key to the whole thing.

> —Jack Lemmon

First rule of acting: Whatever happens, look as if it were intended.

> —Arthur Bloch

Live your character. It's like skiing. You can't be thinking too much. When you get on the hill, your skis are doing the work. You'd better just hang on. Acting is a bit the same way. You've got to submit to what's going on around you and be able to do that fully. You've got to behave as the character. A lot of what acting is is paying attention.

> —Robert Redford

The only line that's wrong in Shakespeare is "holding a mirror up to nature." You hold a magnifying glass up to nature. As an actor you

just enlarge it enough so that your audience can identify with a situation. If it were a mirror we would have no art.
—Montgomery Clift

(See *Acting/Actors, Applause, Show Business*)

Music

The man that hath no music in himself,
Nor is not moved with concord of sweet sounds,
Is fit for treasons, stratagems and spoils;
The motions of his spirit are dull as night,
And his affections dark as Erebus:
Let no such man be trusted.
—Lorenzo in Shakespeare's
The Merchant of Venice

The art of music is so deep and profound that to approach it very seriously *only* is not enough. One must approach music with a serious rigor and, at the same time, with a great, affectionate joy.
—Nadia Boulanger

Study for the love of music, not with the hope of glory. People can get tired of glory, but not of something they love.
—Ivan Galamian

My advice to all who want to attend a lecture on music is "Don't; go to a concert instead."
—Ralph Vaughan Williams

Cantate, cantate! (Sing, sing!)
—Arturo Toscanini, imploring his musicians

Music (Instrumental)

Played percussively, the piano is a bore. If I go to a concert and someone plays like that I have two choices: go home or to sleep. The goal is to make the piano sing, sing, sing.
—Vladimir Horowitz

As a young pianist, Vladimir Horowitz was shocked by the advice he was given by Artur Schnabel: "When a piece gets difficult, make faces."
—quoted by Clifton Fadiman

When you play, do not trouble yourself as to who is listening, yet always play as though a master listened to you.

If you have finished your daily musical work, and feel tired, do not force yourself to further labor. It is better to rest than to practice without pleasure or freshness.

You should never play bad compositions, and never listen to them when not absolutely forced to.
—Robert Schumann

The main thing is to be original—to play a way of your own.
—Coleman Hawkins

Years ago the biggest compliment was "You play just like a man." But then I started to worry about it. If I play like a man I must be loud, bombastic, and aggressive. I don't want to be all these things. You can still be forceful if you're a woman, you can still play with intelligence, and you can still be strong.
—Marian McPartland

(See *Art/Artists*)

Music (Singing)

Longevity is both physical and mental. How fast you develop depends on the individual voice, but if you sing with an uneasy technique at 22, then at 40 your career has troubles. At the beginning you should avoid straining the throat—sing things lighter than you think you are able to. Teachers say Mozart is good for young singers. The hell it is—it is very difficult. Be patient. The more delay, the better.
—Placido Domingo

Regard your voice as capital in the bank. When you go to sing, do not draw on your bank account. Sing on your interest and your voice will last.
—Lauritz Melchior

You have a beautiful voice. You should sing just as you are singing and don't listen to anybody. Do not push your voice to sound like someone else.
—Tito Schipa to the young tenor
Luciano Pavarotti

Joan Sutherland has one of the most remarkable voices of our age, perhaps of all time. . . . Basic to her method was the support she gave her voice from the diaphragm. If your body is not in shape to sing this way, she told me, you will push and push but keep falling back on your throat to make the sound. This will ruin your voice. She showed me a number of exercises that would strengthen the key muscles. I worked very hard at them. I also watched her constantly, often putting my hands on her rib cage to feel what was happening when she sang. (I did this only offstage.)
—Luciano Pavarotti

If you think you've hit a false note, sing loud. When in doubt, sing loud.
—Robert Merrill

(See *Art/Artists*)

N

Nature/Environment

Read nature; nature is a friend to truth.
—Edward Young

Live in each season as it passes; breathe the air, drink the drink, taste the fruit, and resign yourself to the influences of each.
—Henry David Thoreau

Wandering is one of the most sensible things in the world I do. I highly recommend the pursuit of happiness from east to west, bending and stooping, pausing, enjoying, not going anywhere in particular except down a beach or around a pond, always knowing that there is something wonderful just ahead. City street or country lane, for the naturalist there is always something to see: lichen puddled on the granite, a new fern frond uncurling like a mainspring, a pad of brilliant green moss studded with a scarlet mite. Ask why, and for every question you answer you'll have a bouquet of another dozen questions. And herein lies sanity.
—Ann H. Zwinger

Let us permit nature to have her way: she understands her business better than we do.
—Michel de Montaigne

Touch the earth, love the earth, honour the earth, her plains, her valleys, her hills, and her seas; rest your spirit in her solitary places.
—Henry Beston

People have got to understand that the commandment, "Do unto others as you would that they should do unto you" applies to animals, plants and things, as well as to people! and that if it is regarded as applying only to people . . . then the animals, plants and things will, in one way or another, do as badly by man as man has done by them. . . .
—Aldous Huxley

Negativism

You must watch negativism like a hawk. . . . I believe any normally healthy person can determine creatively his or her state of well-being and maintain it at a high level with a strongly held positive self-attitude. . . . See yourself declining and declining will inevitably set in. . . . Think health, eat sparingly, exercise regularly, walk a lot, think positively about yourself, keep your thoughts and your actions clean, ask God Who made you to keep on remaking you.
—Norman Vincent Peale

And, above all things, never think that you're not good enough yourself. A man should never think that. My belief is that in life people will take you very much at your own reckoning.
—Anthony Trollope

Never feel self-pity, the most destructive emotion there is. How awful to be caught up in the terrible squirrel cage of self.
—Millicent Fenwick

I remember one winter my dad needed firewood, and he found a dead tree and sawed it down. In the spring to his dismay new shoots sprouted around the trunk. He said, "I thought sure it was dead. The leaves had all dropped in the wintertime. It was so cold that twigs snapped as surely as if there were no life left in the old tree. But now I see that there was still life at the taproot." He looked at me and said, "Bob,

don't forget this important lesson. Never cut a tree down in the wintertime." Never make a negative decision in the low time.
—Robert H. Schuller

(See *Confidence, Despair, Disappointment, Discouragement, Positive Thinking, Self-Reliance, Self-Respect*)

Negotiation

Make your bargain before beginning to plough.
—Arab proverb

The Eleventh Commandment of a motion picture negotiation: Thou shalt not take less than thy last deal.
—John Gregory Dunne

When questioned on the West Bank situation, Shimon Peres responded: "No problem." He was then asked, "Does that mean you are ready to negotiate?" His answer: "Remember, where there is no solution, there is no problem."
—Lane Kirkland

(See *Argument, Diplomacy, Persuasion*)

Non-Violence

Select your purpose, selfless, without any thought of personal pleasure or personal profit, and then use selfless means to attain your goal. Do not resort to violence even if it seems at first to promise success; it can only contradict your purpose. Use the means of love and respect even if the result seems far off or uncertain. Then throw yourself heart and soul into the campaign, counting no price too high for working for the welfare of those around you, and every reverse, every defeat, will send you deeper into your own deepest resources. Violence can never bring an end to violence; all it can do is provoke more violence.

—Mohandas K. Gandhi

Some of you have knives, and I ask you to put them up. Some of you may have arms and I ask you to put them up. Get the weapon of non-violence, the breastplate of righteousness, the armor of truth, and just keep marching.

—Dr. Martin Luther King, Jr., addressing civil rights demonstrators in Alabama

I beg you, with pain in my heart, and at the same time with firmness and hope, that you reflect on the roads you have taken. In the name of God, change roads! . . . Evil is never the road to good. You cannot destroy the life of your brothers. You cannot continue sowing panic among mothers, wives and daughters. You cannot continue intimidating the elderly. The cruel logic of violence leads nowhere. No good is obtained by contributing to its growth. . . . Seek the roads of dialogue and not those of violence. Don't let your potential for generosity and altruism be exploited. Violence is not a medium of construction. It offends God, those who suffer and those who practice it.

—Pope John Paul II, urging non-violence in Peru's political struggle

O

Occupation

Beware of a misfit occupation. . . . Consider carefully your natural bent, whether for business or a profession.
—Marshall Field

Know thy work and do it. "Know thyself": long enough has that poor "self" of thine tormented thee, thou will never get to "know" it, I believe! Think it not thy business, this of knowing thy self; thou art an unknowable individual; know what thou canst work at; and work at it, like Hercules! That will be thy better plan.
—Thomas Carlyle

Go out into the world, find work that you love, learn from your mistakes, and work hard to make a difference.
—Maurice R. Greenberg

The secret of life is not to do what you like, but to like what you do.
—American proverb

The first thing to do in life is to do with purpose what one proposes to do.
—Pablo Casals

(See *Career, Job Hunting*)

Old Age

You have to know what you're going to do the next day.
> —Louis J. Lefkowitz, at age 79

Keep working as long as you can. Remember, you can't help getting older, but you don't have to get old. . . . There's an old saying, "Life begins at 40." That's silly—life begins every morning when you wake up. Open your mind to it; don't just sit there—do things.
> —George Burns

During your work years begin a small hobby, get in the habit of taking courses and joining organizations—find something that gives you satisfaction. Don't suddenly face 40 or 50 hours a week alone.
> —Judy Salwen

In old age most of all it is necessary to live every minute. Let death find us on horseback or planting cabbages—that is approximately what Montaigne said—"among games, festivals, jokes, common and popular amusements and music and amorous verses."
> —André Maurois

Brief is the space of life allotted to you; pass it as pleasantly as you can, not grieving from noon till eve.
> —Euripides

Take care that old age does not wrinkle your spirit even more than your face.
> —Michel de Montaigne

(See *The Elderly, Longevity, Retirement*)

Opinion

Despise not public opinion.
> —The Talmud

Accustom yourself to not knowing what your opinions are till you have blurted them out, and thus find out what they are.
　　　　—John Jay Chapman

We should always keep a corner of our heads open and free, that we may make room for the opinions of our friends. Let us have heart and head hospitality.
　　　　—Joseph Joubert

Don't try to fine-tune somebody else's view.
　　　　—George Bush

Examine carefully, and re-consider all your notions of things; analyze them, and discover their component parts, and see if habit and prejudice are not the principal ones; weigh the matter, upon which you are to form your opinion, in the equal and important scales of reason.
　　　　—Lord Chesterfield

Do not use power to suppress opinions you think pernicious, for if you do the opinions will suppress you.

Do not fear to be eccentric in opinion, for every opinion now accepted was once eccentric.
　　　　—Bertrand Russell

(See *Prejudice, Tolerance*)

Opportunity

Learn to listen. Opportunity could be knocking at your door very softly.
　　　　—Frank Tyger

　　　Do you wish to roam farther and farther?
　　　See! The Good lies so near.
　　　Only learn to seize good fortune,
　　　For good fortune's always here.
　　　　—Johann Wolfgang von Goethe

Do not wait to strike till the iron is hot; but make it hot by striking.
—William B. Sprague

Watch out for emergencies. They are your big chance!
—Fritz Reiner

Consider that people are like tea bags. They don't know their own strength until they get into hot water.
—Dan McKinnon

Let me say to you and to myself in one breath: Cultivate the tree which you have found to bear fruit in your soil. Regard not your past failures nor successes. All the past is equally a failure and a success; it is a success in as much as it offers you the present opportunity.
—Henry David Thoreau

Hit 'em from where you are. . . . There is nothing to be gained by wishing you were someplace else or waiting for a better situation. You see where you are and you do what you can with that.
—Jacob K. Javits

Oppression

Distrust all men in whom the impulse to punish is powerful.
—Friedrich Nietzsche

Do not hold the delusion that your advancement is accomplished by crushing others.
—Marcus Tullius Cicero

Do not expect justice where might is right.
—Phaedrus

(See *Force, Freedom, Warfare*)

Optimism/Pessimism

Open your eyes! The world is still intact; it is as pristine as it was on the first day, as fresh as milk!
—Paul Claudel

I don't believe in pessimism. If something doesn't come up the way you want, forge ahead. If you think it's going to rain, it will.
—Clint Eastwood

What shall be tomorrow, think not of asking. Each day that Fortune gives you, be it what it may, set down for gain.
—Horace

If you die in an elevator, be sure to push the UP button.
—Sam Levenson

Start every day off with a smile and get it over with.
—W. C. Fields

I think the best thing is always to put a good face upon a disagreeable state of affairs, and take that sensible view which may be taken even of the most distressing and adverse occurences, if you have a command over your temper and your head.
—Benjamin Disraeli
Beaconsfield's Maxims

(See *Cheerfulness, Good Humor*)

Originality

Don't worry about your originality. You could not get rid of it even if you wanted to. It will stick to you and show up for better or worse in spite of all you or anyone else can do.
—Robert Henri

Do not do what is already done.
　　　　　—Terence

Many have original minds who do not think it—they are led away by Custom. Now it appears to me that almost any Man may like the spider spin from his own inwards his own airy Citadel—the points of leaves and twigs on which the spider begins her works are few, and she fills the air with a beautiful circuitry. Man should be content with a few points to tip with the fine Web of his Soul, and weave a tapestry empyrean full of symbols for his spiritual eye, of softness for his spiritual touch, of space for his wandering, of distinctness for his luxury.
　　　　　—John Keats

Better to be good than to be original.
　　　　　—Ludwig Mies van der Rohe

If you want to be original, question all the truths that come down to you.
　　　　　—Niles Eldridge

(See *Creativity*)

P

Painting

Treat nature in terms of the cylinder, the sphere, and the cone; put the whole into the proper perspective so that each side of an object or a plane converges toward some central point.

Right now the moment of time is fleeting by! Capture its reality in paint! To do that we must put all else out of our minds. We must become that moment, make ourselves a sensitive recording plate . . . give the image of what we actually see, forgetting everything that has been seen before our time.
—Paul Cézanne

The painter should not paint what he sees, but what will be seen.
—Paul Valéry

It is well for young men to have a model, but let them draw the curtain over it when they are painting. It is better to paint from memory, for thus the work will be your own; your sensation, your intelligence, and your soul will triumph over the eye of the amateur.

Do not finish your work too much.
—Paul Gauguin

A picture is something which demands just as much knavery, malice, and vice as the perpetration of a crime; falsify and add a touch of nature.

—Edgar Degas

Keep painting and you'll develop your own style. . . . Remember, you paint forever. Think of that when you paint a picture.
—Andrew Lukach

(See *Art/Artists*)

Parenthood

And, ye fathers, provoke not your children to wrath.
—New Testament
Ephesians 6:4

It is better to bind your children to you by a feeling of respect, and by gentleness, than by fear.
—Terence

Don't demand respect, as a parent. Demand civility and insist on honesty. But respect is something you must earn—with kids as well as with adults.

—William Attwood

Don't make a baby if you can't be a father.
—National Urban League slogan

The most important thing a father can do for his children is to love their mother.
—Theodore Hesburgh

On naming children: Your last name should always be your first consideration. Always keep the first and middle names simple if you have a long last name. . . . Go ahead, give your child a middle name. Almost every President of America from Ulysses Simpson Grant to Ronald Wilson Reagan has had a middle name. . . . If you choose a trendy name, you run the risk of dating your child. For example, flower children favorites of the '60s—Chastity, Freedom and America—no longer seem as "meaningful" in the '80s.
—Dina Greenfield

The sooner you treat your son as a man, the sooner he will be one.
—John Dryden

The most important thing that parents can teach their children is how to get along without them.
—Frank Clark

To be a good parent, you have to put yourself second, to recognize that the child has feelings and needs separate from yours, and fulfill those needs without expecting anything in return.
—Howard Kogan

You need to analyze your career, how dedicated you are to it. You've got to face the issue of how ambivalent you are about motherhood and ask yourself how much your life would be enriched by children and how much you're willing to sacrifice.
—Marian Faux

Desire not a multitude of unprofitable children, neither delight in ungodly sons.
—Apocrypha

He that does not bring up his son to some honest calling and employment, brings him up to be a thief.
—Jewish maxim

Do all in your power to teach your children self-government. If a child is passionate, teach him, by gentle and patient means, to curb his temper. If he is greedy, cultivate liberality in him. If he is selfish, promote generosity. If he is sulky, charm him out of it, by encouraging frank good-humor. If he is indolent, accustom him to exertion, and train him to perform even onerous duties with alacrity. If pride comes in to make his obedience reluctant, subdue him, either by counsel or discipline. In short, give your children the habit of overcoming their besetting sins.
—William B. Sprague

All that we [old poets] can do is to keep our hearts as fresh as we may; to bear ever in mind that a father can guide a son but some distance

on the road, and the more wisely he guides the sooner (alas!) must he lose the fair companionship and watch the boy run on. It may sound a hard saying, but we can only keep him admiring the things we admire at the cost of pauperizing his mind.
—Sir Arthur Quiller-Couch

(See *Children, Family, Mother's Advice*)

Passions

Guard thy sail from passion's sudden blast.
—Charles Simmons

Govern your passions with absolute sway
And grow wiser and better as life wears away.
—Johann Lavater

No matter how you look at it, all the emotions connected with love are not really immortal; like all other passions in life, they are bound to fade at some point. The trick is to convert love into some lasting friendship that overcomes the fading of passion. But that requires effort and an honest attitude on all parts. . . .
—Harold Pinter

Let moderation on thy passions wait
Who loves too much, too much the lov'd will hate.
—Robert Herrick

To know your ruling passion, examine your castles in the air.
—Richard Whately

Jump out the window if you are the object of passion. Flee it if you feel it. . . . Passion goes, boredom remains.
—Gabrielle ("Coco") Chanel

(See *Desire*)

The Past

Never look for birds of this year in the nests of the last.
—Miguel de Cervantes

Don't let what happened yesterday inhibit what is happening today or will happen tomorrow. It's ancient history, and nothing you can do will change it. Stick to the present and the future; look to the past only when you can do it rationally and objectively as a way to improve on the other two. . . . The bottom line: Keep your eye on the road, and use your rearview mirror only to avoid trouble.
—Daniel Meacham

Respect the past in the full measure of its deserts, but do not make the mistake of confusing it with the present, nor seek in it the ideals of the future.
—José Ingenieros

As you look toward the future, always remember the treasures of our past. Every generation stands on the shoulders of the generation that came before. Jealously guard the values and principles of our heritage. They did not come easy.
—Ronald Reagan
Speech, Air Force Academy

(See *The Future, The Present*)

Patience

Upon the heat and flame of thy distemper
Sprinkle cool patience.
—The Queen in Shakespeare's
Hamlet, Prince of Denmark

Nothing great is created suddenly, any more than a bunch of grapes or a fig. If you tell me that you desire a fig, I answer you that there must be time. Let it first blossom, then bear fruit, then ripen.
— Epictetus

The secret of patience: do something else in the meantime.
— Anonymous

The most extraordinary thing about the oyster is this. Irritations get into his shell. He does not like them. But when he cannot get rid of them, he uses the irritation to do the loveliest thing an oyster ever has a chance to do. If there are irritations in our lives today, there is only one prescription: make a pearl. It may have to be a pearl of patience, but, anyhow, make a pearl. And it takes faith and love to do it.
— Harry Emerson Fosdick

> Wait till the sun shines, Nellie,
>   When the clouds go drifting by,
> We will be happy, Nellie,
>   Don't you sigh.
> — Andrew B. Sterling
>   Music by Harry von Tilzer

"Wait," says an Arab proverb, "and stay at your window; you will see your enemy's corpse pass by." I am not a man to harbour grudges and I prefer to say: "Wait, open your door and you will see an old enemy come in who has become your dear friend."
— André Maurois

Think of this doctrine—that reasoning beings were created for one another's sake; that to be patient is a branch of justice, and that men sin without intending it.
— Marcus Aurelius

(See *Endurance*)

Patriotism

On this Fourth of July, we do well to acknowledge the existence of heroes. They do not, as in ancient times, dwell on the mountaintops. Our heroes are those among us who, in putting aside all regard for themselves, act above and beyond the call of duty and in so doing give definition to patriotism and elevate all of us. Ideals such as peace, freedom, justice, opportunity and individualism are just dreams without someone to turn those ideals into reality. Let's never forget the debt we owe to our fellow citizens. America is the land of the free because we are the home of the brave.
—David Mahoney

I hope you will serve your country. The nation as a whole will profit from your private careers, but please give something of yourself back, something more than just tax dollars.
—Donald T. Regan

Don't spread patriotism too thin.
—Theodore Roosevelt

Peace

. . . we must seek, above all, a world of peace; a world in which peoples dwell together in mutual respect and work together in mutual regard; a world where peace is not a mere interlude between wars, but an incentive to the creative energies of humanity. We will not find such a peace today, or even tomorrow. The obstacles to hope are large and menacing. Yet the goal of a peaceful world must, today and tomorrow, shape our decisions and inspire our purposes.
—John F. Kennedy
Speech, Germany

If you want peace, understand war.
—B. H. Liddell Hart
quoted by Richard M. Nixon

It is in the years of peace that war is prevented and those foundations laid upon which the noble structures of the future can be built. That peace will not be preserved without the virtues which make victory possible in war. Peace will not be preserved by pious sentiments expressed in terms of platitudes, or by official grimaces and diplomatic correctitude, or by casting aside in dangerous times our panoply or war-like strength. There must be earnest thought. There must be faithful perseverance and foresight. Greatheart must have his sword and armor to guard the pilgrims on their way.
—Sir Winston Churchill

If they want peace, nations should avoid the pin-pricks that precede cannon-shots.
—Napoleon I

(See *Diplomacy, Force, Freedom, Military, Oppression, Preparedness—Military, Warfare*)

Peace of Mind

Do not let trifles disturb your tranquillity of mind. . . . Life is too precious to be sacrificed for the nonessential and transient. . . . Ignore the inconsequential.
—Grenville Kleiser

Do not seek to have everything that happens happen as you wish, but wish for everything to happen as it actually does happen, and your life will be serene.
—Epictetus

Sell all and purchase liberty.
—Patrick Henry

Thou shalt not be afraid of thy hidden impulses.

Thou shalt learn to respect thyself and then thou will love thy neighbor as thyself.

Thou shalt transcend inner anxiety, recognizing thy true competence and courage.

Thou shalt stand undismayed in the presence of grief. Thou shalt not deny the sadness of thy heart. Thou shalt make no detour around sorrow, but shall live through it, and by the aid of human togetherness and comradely sympathy thou shalt win dominion over sorrow.

Thou shalt eternally respect truth and tell it with kindness and also with firmness to all of thy associates.

—Joshua Loth Liebman

(See *Anxiety*)

Perfectionism

George Bernard Shaw warned [Jascha] Heifetz that the gods might envy his perfection and destroy him. Shaw advised the violinist to "play one wrong note every night before you go to bed."

—*U.S. News & World Report*

Perseverance

Life is not easy for any of us. But what of that? We must have perseverance and above all confidence in ourselves. We must believe that we are gifted for something, and that this thing, at whatever cost, must be attained.

—Marie Curie

When you come to the end of your rope, tie a knot and hang on.

—Attributed to Franklin D. Roosevelt

Boys, there ain't no free lunches in this country. And don't go spending your whole life commiserating that you got the raw deals. You've got to say, "I think that if I keep working at this and want it bad enough I can have it." It's called perseverance.
—Lee J. Iacocca

Ride on! Rough-shod if need be, smooth-shod if that will do, but ride on! Ride on over all obstacles, and win the race!
—Charles Dickens

Just don't give up trying to do what you really want to do. Where there's love and inspiration, I don't think you can go wrong.
—Ella Fitzgerald

When I was a cub in Milwaukee I had a city editor who'd stroll over and read across a guy's shoulder when he was writing a lead. Sometimes he would approve, sometimes he'd say gently, "Try again," and walk away. My best advice is, try again. And then again. If you're for this racket, and not many really are, then you've got an eternity of sweat and tears ahead. I don't just mean you. I mean anybody.
—Red Smith

You win some, you lose some, and some get rained out, but you gotta suit up for them all.
—J. Askenberg

(See *Resolution*)

Perspective

Ponder the life led by others long ago, the life that will be led after you, the life being led in uncivilized races; how many do not even know your name, how many will very soon forget it, and how many, who praise you perhaps now, will very soon blame you; and that neither memorial nor fame nor anything else at all is worth a thought.
—Marcus Aurelius

Resist your time—take a foothold outside it.
                            —Lord Acton

Maintain a sense of perspective and proportion in all your endeavors. . . . Don't let problems and setbacks block out the light of reason. The human mind is like a magnifying glass: It exaggerates. A simple rule of thumb: Whatever you're looking at is not as big a deal as you think it is.
                            —Daniel Meacham

May we never let the things we can't have, or don't have, or shouldn't have, spoil our enjoyment of the things we do have and can have. As we value our happiness let us not forget it, for one of the greatest lessons in life is learning to be happy without the things we cannot or should not have.
                            —Richard L. Evans

View your problems in perspective. Let me tell you a story about a college girl writing home to her parents.

"Dear Mom and Dad," she wrote. "I'm sorry I haven't written in a long time, but since our dormitory was burned down during the student demonstration, I haven't been able to see very well. But don't worry. The doctor says there is a good chance I'll get my sight back. While in the hospital I met a wonderful man who works as an orderly there. He is a Muslim and has convinced me to convert from Christianity. You'll soon have your wish of becoming grandparents. We are moving to Africa and expect to be married. Love, Mary.

"P.S. There was no demonstration or fire. I wasn't in the hospital. I'm not pregnant. I don't even have a boyfriend. But I did flunk chemistry and economics and I wanted you to view these problems in proper perspective."
                            —David Mahoney

(See *Society/The World*)

Persuasion

Whoever wants his judgment to be believed, should express it coolly and dispassionately; for all vehemence springs from the will. And so the judgment might be attributed to the will and not to knowledge, which by its nature is cold.
—Arthur Schopenhauer

Never hold any one by the button, or the hand, in order to be heard out; for if people are unwilling to hear you, you had better hold your tongue than them.
—Lord Chesterfield

We should dwell upon the arguments, and impress the motives of persuasion upon our own hearts, till we feel the love of them.
—Isaac Watts

Be true, if you would be believed. Let a man but speak forth with genuine earnestness the thought, the emotion, the actual condition of his own heart; and other men, so strangely are we all knit together by the tie of sympathy, must and will give heed to him.
—Thomas Carlyle

When met with opposition, even if it should be from your husband or your children, endeavour to overcome it by argument and not by authority, for a victory dependent on authority is unreal and illusory.
—Bertrand Russell

Before you try to convince anyone else, be sure you are convinced, and if you cannot convince yourself, drop the subject.
—John H. Patterson

The only way to convert the heathen is to travel into the jungle.
—Lane Kirkland
on working with capitalists

(See *Argument, Diplomacy, Negotiation*)

Pets

A *few observations from animal therapists:*
  Don't think your pet is a person in a fur coat.
  Don't overcorrect your pet.
  Don't praise your dog unless he *earns* it.
  Do get down on the floor and communicate on an animal's level.
                        —*New York Times* article
                        "Behavior Therapy for Troubled Pets"

On hot days;
Avoid walking your dog on hot pavements or beaches. The pads on
its paws are sensitive and can burn easily.

Keep birds away from the drafts from air conditioners and open windows. They can easily catch colds or even pneumonia.
                        —Maureen Early

Never tie up an animal outside a store or restaurant.
Don't leave a pet in a car parked at a shopping mall.
Don't leave an animal unattended in a yard.
If you live in a ground-floor apartment, don't let cats or small dogs sit
  on window sills—with or without gratings.
Don't walk animals in city parks without a leash. A dog that runs out
  of your view may never come back.
                        —Dave Lindorff

If a dog does have an accident, do not rub his nose in it. He won't
make the connection. The punishment—a stern "NO"—must be
made at the time of the "crime."
                        —*Glamour* magazine

Pettiness

One resolution I have made, and try always to keep, is this: "To rise above little things."
—John Burroughs

My favorite quotation is "Life is too short to be little," written by Disraeli. . . . Often we allow ourselves to be upset by small things we should despise and forget. Perhaps some man we helped has proved ungrateful . . . some woman we believed to be a friend has spoken ill of us . . . some reward we thought we deserved has been denied us. . . . We lose many irreplaceable hours brooding over grievances that, in a year's time, will be forgotten by us and by everybody. No, let us devote our life to worthwhile actions and feelings, to great thoughts, real affections and enduring undertakings.
—André Maurois

Don't stop the plough to kill a mouse. Do not hinder important business for the discussion of a trifle.
—C. H. Spurgeon

(See *Trifles*)

Physicians/Medicine

If it's working, keep doing it.
If it's not working, stop doing it.
If you don't know what to do, don't do anything.
—Medical school advice given to
Melvin Konner, M.D.

First of all, do no harm.
—Ancient medical proverb

There is a vast difference between curing and healing. There are also many times when a physician can help a patient to heal, even though he cannot cure him. . . . We must begin to nurture the needs, hopes and sensitivities of the promising young men and women who have elected this unique, stressful, beautiful, and challenging career [medicine]. We must spawn a generation of doctors who are not afraid to love.
—Dr. David E. Reiser and
Dr. David H. Rosen

One cardinal rule: One must always *listen* to the patient.
—Dr. Oliver Sacks
British neurologist

Say not too much, speak it gently, and guard it cautiously. Always remember that words used before patients are like coppers given to children; you think little of them but the children count them over and over, making all conceivable imaginary uses of them.
—Dr. Oliver Wendell Holmes

Never argue with a doctor; he has inside information.
—Bob Elliott and Ray Goulding

(See *Health, Illness*)

Planning

Determine on some course
More than a wild exposture to each chance
That starts i' th' way before thee.
—Volumnia in Shakespeare's
Coriolanus

As a regimen, as a discipline for a group of people, planning is very valuable. My position is, go ahead and plan, but once you've done your planning, put it on the shelf. Don't be bound by it. Don't use

it as a major input to the decision-making process. Use it mainly to recognize change as it takes place.
—Fletcher Byrom

If you fail to plan, you are planning to fail.
—Anonymous

It is best to lay our plans widely in youth, for then land is cheap, and it is but too easy to contract our views afterwards. Youths so laid out, with broad avenues and parks, that they may make handsome and liberal old men!
—Henry David Thoreau

Take charge of your life! . . . To act intelligently and effectively, we still must have a plan. To the proverb which says, "a journey of a thousand miles begins with a single step," I would add the words "and a road map."
—Cecile M. Springer

(See *Preparedness*)

Pleasing

If you mean to profit, learn to please.
—Charles Churchill

Don't try to please everybody. It's like that fable about the man, the boy, and the donkey walking down the street. People pointed and said isn't it terrible that the strong man is riding the donkey and making the small boy walk. So they changed places and people pointed and said, isn't that terrible that strong young boy is riding the donkey and making that poor man walk. So they both got on the donkey, the donkey came to the bridge, exhausted, fell into the river and drowned. And of course the moral of the story is if you try to please everybody, you'll lose your donkey.
—Donald Rumsfeld

If you have a voice, sing; if your limbs are supple, dance. In fact, do not neglect any means of giving pleasure.
—Ovid

Observe carefully what pleases you in others, and probably the same things in you will please others.

Remember, that to please, is almost to prevail, or at least a necessary step to it. You, who have your fortune to make, should more particularly study this art.
—Lord Chesterfield

Pick a day, any day. Choose a person. . . . Then say something unexpected, or nice, or flattering. Something like: "Everyone is secretly in love with you." Other nice things to say to people are:
You have my favorite name.
You keep a great secret.
You're childlike in the nicest way possible.
You should have your own show!
You have winner written all over your face.
You're nobody's fool.
Your phone has a wonderful ring.
You take corners very smoothly.
—Marcia Jacobs

Pleasure

Most of us miss out on life's big prizes. The Pulitzer. The Nobel. Oscars. Emmys. But we're all eligible for life's small pleasures. A pat on the back. A kiss behind the ear. A four-pound bass. A full moon. An empty parking space. A crackling fire. A great meal. A glorious sunset. Don't fret about copping life's grand awards. Enjoy its tiny delights. There are plenty for all of us.
—United Technologies message

Drink and sing, an inch before us is black night.
—Japanese proverb

Let not the enjoyment of pleasures now within your grasp, be carried to such excess as to incapacitate you from future repetition.
—Seneca

The rule of my life is to make business a pleasure, and pleasure my business.
—Aaron Burr

The secret of the enjoyment of pleasure is to know when to stop. Man does not learn this secret easily, but to shun pleasure altogether is cowardly avoidance of a difficult job. For we have to learn the art of enjoying things *because* they are impermanent.
—Alan W. Watts

(See *Hedonism, Leisure*)

Poets/Poetry

Any poet, if he is to survive as a writer beyond his twenty-fifth year, must alter; he must seek new literary influences; he will have different emotions to express.
—T. S. Eliot

Let us extract it [poetry/beauty] from everything, for it exists in everything and everywhere; there isn't a single atom but that contains thought; and let us grow accustomed to considering the world as a work of art, of which we must reproduce the methods in our works.
—Gustave Flaubert

Fainthearted animals move about in herds. The lion walks alone in the desert. Let the poet always walk thus.
—Alfred de Vigny

A poet ought not to pick nature's pocket; let him borrow, and so borrow as to repay by the very act of borrowing. Examine nature accurately,

but write from recollection, and trust more to your imagination than
to your memory.
—Samuel Taylor Coleridge

It is necessary to be a seer, to make oneself a seer. The poet makes
himself a seer by a long, immense and reasoned unruliness of the
senses. . . . He attains the unknown.
—Arthur Rimbaud

Political Pundits

In estimating the accuracy of a political opinion, one should take into
consideration the standing of the opinionist.
—Benjamin Disraeli

Politics

Don't write anything you can phone, don't phone anything you can
talk face to face, don't talk anything you can smile, don't smile anything
you can wink and don't wink anything you can nod.
—Earl Long

It is necessary for a Senator to be thoroughly acquainted with the
constitution; and this is a knowledge of the most extensive nature; a
matter of science, of diligence, of reflection, without which no Senator
can possibly be fit for office.
—Marcus Tullius Cicero

Sometimes in politics one must duel with skunks, but no one should
be fool enough to allow the skunks to choose the weapons.
—Joe Cannon

You don't shoot Santa Claus.
—Alfred E. Smith

Advice for lobbyists: Don't ask for too much. . . . Mentioning campaign contributions is tacky. . . . Don't cry wolf and say the world is coming to an end unless it is. . . . Don't think a bill will pass because of its moral value. . . .
>—from a typed list found in the
>Rayburn Office Building

Never, never, you must never . . . remind a man at work on a political job that he may be president. It almost always kills him politically. He loses his nerve; he can't do his work; he gives up the very traits that are making him a possibility.
>—Theodore Roosevelt to Lincoln Steffens

My dad was a Methodist minister and he once told me, "Son, be skeptical of deathbed conversions." I asked why. And he said, "Because sometimes they get well on you."
>—Walter F. Mondale

There are only three rules of sound administration, pick good men, tell them not to cut corners, and back them to the limit; and picking good men is the most important.
>—Adlai E. Stevenson

A President should never say never.
>—Ronald Reagan

When you are in a minority, talk; when you are in a majority, vote.
>—Roger Sherman
>A Founding Father

When in politics, it does not behoove you to have an interest in a newspaper. But when you are in a town, drop in on the local editors. They like it.
>—Calvin Coolidge

There are three ways in Washington to deal with embarrassing political situations. The best way is to admit them. "When I make a mistake, it's a beaut!" Fiorello La Guardia, former mayor of New York, once

said, disarming his critics. The next best way is to proclaim that your blunders were really triumphs. That wonderful old former Republican Senator from Vermont, George Aiken, advised President Johnson during the Vietnam War, "Say you won and get out!" Mr. Johnson ignored him and regretted it till the end of his days. The worst way is to pretend and blame everything that goes wrong on somebody else.
—James Reston

In any assembly the simplest way to stop the transacting of business and split the ranks is to appeal to a principle.
—Jacques Barzun

I have learned that one of the most important rules in politics is poise—which means looking like an owl after you have behaved like a jackass.
—Ronald Reagan

A politician would do well to remember that he has to live with his conscience longer than he does with his constituents.
—Melvin R. Laird

If you want to get on the front page of a newspaper you should attack someone, especially when you're in politics.
—Harry S Truman

Decide exactly what you have to achieve. Do you want to help people, or do you want to be powerful?
—Mario Cuomo

You've got to know when to keep your mouth shut. The Senate's the cruelest judge in the world. A man's a fool to talk to other fellows about any subject unless he knows more about that subject than they do.
—Lyndon B. Johnson

If the other guy is out there saying unfair things about you, you've got to respond or people will start to think they're right. When you're being attacked by the other guy, you better say something.
—Richard Thornburgh

Never lose your temper with the Press or the public is a major rule of
political life.
 —Christabel Pankhurst

Follow the first law of holes: If you are in one, stop digging.
 —Dennis Healey

Turn the rascals out!
 —Charles A. Dana
 In the *New York Sun*, 1871 (referring to the
 Tweed ring)

I would highly recommend the 11th Commandment that we gave
birth to in California. Thou shalt not speak ill of another Republican.
 —Ronald Reagan

Don't tax you, don't tax me; tax that fellow behind the tree.
 —Russell B. Long

Don't throw away your conscience.
 —George McGovern

Old prayer for politicians: Teach us to utter words that are tender and
gentle. Tomorrow we may have to eat them.
 —Morris Udall

If you don't create a pithy little description of yourself, then the press
will do it for you.
 —Senator Albert Gore

Rumsfeld's Rules: (for Administration officials):
 If you foul up, tell the President and others fast, and correct it.
 Know that it is easier to get into something than it is to get out of
 it.
 Never say "The White House wants"—buildings don't "want."
 Don't speak ill of your predecessors (or successors)—you did not
 walk in their shoes.
 Keep your sense of humor about your position. Remember the
 observation attributed to General Joe Stilwell that "the higher the

monkey climbs, the more you see of his behind":—you will find it has a touch of truth.
—Donald Rumsfeld

Do not run a campaign that would embarrass your mother.
—Senator Robert C. Byrd
Advice to Democratic candidates

If it's going to come out eventually, better have it come out immediately.
—Henry A. Kissinger

Advice on campaign behavior for first ladies: Always be on time. Do as little talking as humanly possible. Remember to lean back in the parade car so everybody can see the president. Be sure not to get too fat, because you'll have to sit three in the back seat.
—Eleanor Roosevelt

Trust, but verify.
—Old Russian proverb
quoted by President Ronald Reagan
at summit, December 1987

(See *Diplomacy, Government, Tact*)

Positive Thinking

Be not afraid of life. Believe that life *is* worth living and your belief will help create the fact.
—William James

Never mention the worst. Never think of it. Drop it out of your consciousness. At least ten times every day affirm, "I expect the best and with God's help will attain the best." In so doing your thoughts will turn toward the best and become conditioned to its realization.

This practice will bring all of your powers to focus on the attainment of the best. It will bring the best to you.
— Norman Vincent Peale

Here's one thing I've said many times to the people I've encouraged along and I hope you will remember it. If you *want* to make it, you can. You *can* move up the level system. You *can* become confident in yourself. You *can* graduate, if you *want* to.
— Annabel Victoria Safire

You have to believe in happiness or happiness never comes.
— Douglas Malloch

Now if you are going to win any battle you have to do one thing. You have to make the mind run the body. Never let the body tell the mind what to do. The body will always give up. It is always tired morning, noon, and night. But the body is never tired if the mind is not tired. When you were younger the mind could make you dance all night, and the body was never tired. . . . You've always got to make the mind take over and keep going.
— George S. Patton

(See *Confidence, Despair, Discouragement, Disappointment, Negativism, Self-Respect, Self-Reliance*)

Practicality

Don't fish for strawberries in the bottom of the sea. Never venture anything upon a mere possibility of success; a good probability should always be in view, before we enter upon expense or expose our reputation for any attempt.
— Samuel Palmer

Dream in a pragmatic way.
— Aldous Huxley

The best things are nearest—breath in your nostrils, light in your eyes, flowers at your feet, duties at your hand, the path of Right just before you. Do not grasp at the stars, but do life's plain common work as it comes, certain that daily duties and daily bread are the sweetest things in life.
—Robert Louis Stevenson

Use human means as if there were no divine ones, and divine means as if there were no human ones.
—Baltasar Gracián

(See *Illusion, Reality, Reason, Truth*)

Praise

Be quick to praise people. People like to praise those who praise them.
—Bernard M. Baruch

There's good in everybody. Boost—don't knock.
—Warren G. Harding

Commend a fool for his wit, or a knave for his honesty, and they will receive you into their bosom.
—Henry Fielding

Whenever you commend, add your reasons for doing so; it is this which distinguishes the approbation of a man of sense from the flattery of sycophants and admiration of fools.
—Sir Richard Steele

Beware of fishing for compliments—you might come up with a boot.
—Carol Weston

The only way to escape the personal corruption of praise is to go on working. One is tempted to stop and listen to it. The only thing is to turn away and go on working. Work. There is nothing else.
—Albert Einstein

Ye, who would in aught excel,
Ponder this simple maxim well.
A wise man's censure may appall
But a fool's praise is worst of all.
—Henry G. Bohn

(See *Applause, Fame, Greatness*)

Prayer

When you pray, think. Think well what you're saying, and make your thoughts into things that are solid. In that way, your prayer will have strength, and that strength will become a part of you in body, mind and spirit.
—Walter Pidgeon instructing
Roddy McDowall in *How Green Was My Valley*, screenplay by Philip Dunne, based on the novel by Richard Llewellyn

Pray to God only for those things which you cannot obtain from man.
—Pope Xystus I

We should pray with as much earnestness as those who expect everything from God: we should act with as much energy as those who expect everything from themselves.
—Charles Caleb Colton

Do not make long prayers; always remember that the Lord knows something.
—Joseph H. Choate

Our prayers should be for blessings in general, for God knows best what is good for us.
—Socrates

We should not permit prayer to be taken out of the schools; that's the only way most of us got through.
—Sam Levenson

We must not conceive of prayer as an overcoming of God's reluctance, but as a laying hold of His highest willingness.
—Richard Chenevix Trench
Archbishop of Dublin

Q. What counsel do you give to the young men who are fighting a losing battle with their lower selves and come to you for advice?
A. Simply prayer. One must humble oneself utterly and look beyond oneself for strength.
Q. But what if the young men complain that their prayer is not heard?
A. To want an answer to one's prayer is to tempt God. If prayer fails to bring relief, it is only lip-prayer. If prayer does not help, nothing else will. One must go on ceaselessly. This, then, is my message to the youth. In spite of themselves, the youth must believe in the all-conquering power of Love and Truth.
—Mohandas K. Gandhi

All prayers are answered. We need to distinguish between a prayer unanswered and one not answered how or when we would like it to be.
—Lloyd Ogilvie

Centering prayer (a simplified approach to forms of prayer that had previously been confined largely to monasteries) . . . consists of . . . simple rules: "(1) Relax. Realize that God is calling you to prayer and that you wish to give yourself to Him completely in love. To begin, express this. To end, pray the 'Our Father'—'The Lord's Prayer'—very slowly. (2) Pray inwardly your chosen word, expressive of your faith and love, of your desire for union with God. . . . " Father Basil [Pennington] recommends two daily sessions of at least 10 minutes each, morning and night.
—Kenneth A. Briggs

Pray devoutly and hammer stoutly.
—English proverb

I like to speak of prayer as listening. We live in a culture that is terribly afraid to listen. We'd prefer to remain deaf. The Latin root word of the word "deaf" is "absurd." Prayer means moving from absurdity to obedience. Let the words descend from your head to your heart so you can begin to know God. In prayer, you become who you are meant to be.

—Henri Nouwen

People who pray for miracles usually don't get miracles. . . . But people who pray for courage, for strength to bear the unbearable, for the grace to remember what they have left instead of what they have lost, very often find their prayers answered. . . . Their prayers helped them tap hidden reserves of faith and courage which were not available to them before.

—Harold S. Kushner

Let me not pray to be sheltered from dangers but to be fearless in facing them.

Let me not beg for the stilling of my pain but for the heart to conquer it.

Let me not look for allies in life's battlefield but to my own strength.

Let me not crave in anxious fear to be saved but hope for the patience to win my freedom.

Grant me that I may not be a coward, feeling your mercy in my success alone; but let me find the grasp of your hand in my failure.

—Rabindranath Tagore

Pray for our country—quietly and silently—each in his own way.

Where there is hate, let me sow love;
Where there is injury, pardon;
Where there is doubt, faith;
Where there is despair, hope;
Where there is darkness, light.

—Hubert H. Humphrey, quoting the prayer of Saint Francis of Assisi, in a speech

(See *God, Faith*)

Prejudice

Learn never to conceive a prejudice against others, because you know nothing of them. It is bad reasoning, and makes enemies of half the world.
—William Hazlitt

I don't think you should strip people of their prejudice—that's all they have, some of them. We should just leave them alone until they mature.
—Butterfly McQueen

Never suffer the prejudice of the eye to determine the heart.
—English proverb

Do not teach the child many things, but never to let him form inaccurate or confused ideas. I care not if he knows nothing provided he is not mistaken, and I only acquaint him with truths to guard him against the errors he might put in their place. Reason and judgment come slowly, prejudices flock to us in crowds, and from these he must be protected.
—Jean-Jacques Rousseau

Shake off all the fears of servile prejudices, under which weak minds are servilely crouched. Fix reason firmly in her seat, and call on her tribunal for every fact, every opinion. Question with boldness even the existence of God, because, if there be one, he must more approve of the homage of reason than that of blind faith.
—Thomas Jefferson

(See *Opinion, Tolerance*)

Preparedness

Always keep your spurs on, you never know when you'll meet a horse.
—Maureen Malarkey's mother

We can't cross a bridge until we come to it, but I always like to lay down a pontoon ahead of time.
—Bernard M. Baruch

Distrust yourself, and sleep before you fight.
—Dr. John Armstrong

In all negotiations of difficulties, a man may not look to sow and reap at once; but must prepare business, and so ripen it by degrees.
—Sir Francis Bacon

Dig a well before you are thirsty.
—Chinese proverb

It is important when you haven't got any ammunition to have a butt on your rifle.
—Sir Winston Churchill

Hope for the best, but prepare for the worst.
—English proverb

Never wait for trouble.
—Charles "Chuck" Yeager

Never bring the car home without gas in the tank.
—Ron Shelton

(See *Planning*)

Preparedness (Military)

Let him who desires peace prepare for war.
                —Flavius Vegetius Renatus

If we desire to avoid insult we must be able to repel it; if we desire to secure peace, one of the powerful instruments of our rising prosperity, it must be known that we are at all times ready for war.
                —George Washington
                Address to Congress

We must not be innocents abroad in a world that is not innocent.
                —Ronald Reagan

To you who call yourselves men of peace, I say: You are not safe unless you have men of action at your side.
                —Thucydides

(See *Diplomacy, Force, Freedom, Military, Oppression, Peace, Warfare*)

The Present

Try to be happy in this very present Moment; and put not off being so to a Time to come: as though that Time should be of another make from this, which is already come, and is ours.
                —Thomas Fuller

Write it in your heart that every day is the best day in the year. No man has learned anything rightly, until he knows that every day is Doomsday.
                —Ralph Waldo Emerson

Use thy best vase to-day, for to-morrow it may, perchance be broken.
—The Talmud

Hope for the moment. There are times when it is hard to believe in the future, when we are temporarily just not brave enough. When this happens, concentrate on the present. . . . Cultivate *le petit bonheur* ("the little happiness") until courage returns. Look forward to the beauty of the next moment, the next hour, the promise of a good meal, sleep, a book, a movie, the immediate likelihood that tonight the stars will shine and tomorrow the sun will rise. Sink roots into the present until the strength grows to think about tomorrow.
—Ardis Whitman

Always hold fast to the present. Every situation, indeed every moment, is of infinite value, for it is the representative of a whole eternity.
—Johann Wolfgang von Goethe

Use your best pitcher today. Tomorrow it may rain.
—Leo Durocher
Quoted by Henry Kissinger

(See *The Future, The Past*)

Pride

He who would climb and soar aloft
Must needs keep ever at his side
The tonic of a wholesome pride.
—Arthur Hugh Clough

If you want to succeed in the world it is necessary, when entering a salon, that your vanity should bow to that of others.
—Madame de Genlis

Be not proud because thou art learned, but discourse with the ignorant man as with the sage.
—Ptahhotep
24th century B.C.

I call on your pride. Remember what you've done, what you dream of doing, and rise up, great Heavens, consider yourself with more respect! and don't lack respect for me at the bottom of your mind, by having doubts of an intelligence which is undisputed.
—Gustave Flaubert
Advice to a depressed friend

(See *Arrogance, Humility*)

Principles

It's important to let people know what you stand for. It's equally important that they know what you won't stand for.
—B. Bader

Learn from the earliest days to insure your principles against the perils of ridicule. If you think it right to differ from the times, and to make a stand for any valuable point of morals, do it, however rustic, however antiquated, however pedantic it may appear; do it, not for insolence, but seriously, and grandly, as a man who wears a soul of his own in his bosom, and does not wait till it shall be breathed into him by the breath of fashion.
—Sydney Smith

Never "for the sake of peace and quiet" deny your convictions.
—Dag Hammarskjöld

Suggest what is right, oppose what is wrong; what you think, speak; try to satisfy yourself, and not others; and if you are not popular, you will at least be respected; popularity lasts but a day, respect will descend as a heritage to your children.
—T. C. Halliburton

There are still things worth fighting *against*. . . . It is better to be narrow-minded than to have no mind, to hold limited and rigid principles than none at all.
—Evelyn Waugh

Don't sacrifice your political convictions for the convenience of the hour.
—Edward M. Kennedy

Be as beneficent as the sun or the sea, but if your rights as a rational being are trenched on, die on the first inch of your territory.
—Ralph Waldo Emerson

(See *Beliefs, Dreams, Ideals, Vision*)

Proficiency

Let a man practice the profession which he best knows.
—Marcus Tullius Cicero

Handle your tools without mittens; remember that the cat in gloves catches no mice.
—Benjamin Franklin

It is not lonely at the top. It's better to be competent than well liked.
—Martha Friedman

If it ain't broke, improve it.
—Golden Rule of "yuppies"
(young urban professionals)

Better be proficient in one art than a smatterer in a thousand.
—Japanese proverb

If your project doesn't work, look for the part you didn't think was important.
—Arthur Bloch

(See *Ability, Ancestry, Favor, Merit*)

Promises

Let your promises be sincere, and so prudently confided as not to exceed the reach of your ability: He who promises more than he is able to perform, is false to himself; and he who does not perform what he has promised, is a traitor to his friend.
—George Shelley

Better break your word than do worse in keeping it.
—Thomas Fuller

Better a friendly refusal than an unwilling promise.
—German proverb

If asked when you can deliver something, ask for time to think. Build in a margin of safety. Name a date. Then deliver it earlier than you promised. The world is divided into two classes of people: the few people who make good on their promises (even if they don't promise as much), and the many who don't. Get in Column A and stay there. You'll be very valuable wherever you are.
—Robert Townsend

(See *Commitment*)

Protest

Do not begin to quarrel with the world too soon: for, bad as it may be, it is the best we have to live in—here. If railing would have made it better, it would have been reformed long ago: but as this is not to be hoped for at present, the best way is to slide through it as contentedly and innocently as we may. . . . Do not, however, mistake what I have here said. I would not have you, when you grow up, adopt the low and sordid fashion of palliating existing abuses or of putting the best

face upon the worst things. I only mean that indiscriminate, unqualified satire can do little good, and that those who indulge in the most revolting speculations on human nature, do not themselves always set the fairest examples, or strive to prevent its lower degradation.
—William Hazlitt
Letter to his son

Let people talk, let them blame you, condemn you, imprison you, even hang you, but publish what you think. It is not a right, but a duty, a strict obligation laid upon anyone who thinks, to express what he thinks in public for the common good . . . to speak is a good thing, to write is better, to print is an excellent thing.
—Paul-Louis Courier

I want you to get damn mad about the current state of affairs. I want you to get so mad that you use your new degree and your common sense to kick America off dead center. A little righteous anger really brings out the best in the American personality. Our nation was born when 56 patriots got mad enough to sign the Declaration of Independence. We put a man on the moon because Sputnik made us mad at being No. 2 in space. Getting mad in a constructive way is good for the soul—and the country.
—Lee J. Iacocca
Commencement Address

Prudence

If you don't throw it, they can't hit it.
—Lefty Gomez

Do right and fear no man; don't write and fear no woman.
—Adage favored by Basil Samuel

Admire a little ship, but put your cargo in a big one.
—Hesiod

Be careful of what you ask for; you just might get it.
                    —Anonymous

If you live in Rome, don't quarrel with the Pope.
                    —French proverb

Choose your neighbor before your house and your companion before
the road.
                    —Arab proverb

The envious Charles Lee denounced his superior, Washington, as
gifted too much with that "rascally virtue prudence." Exert it and
deserve his fame.
                    —Francis P. Blair to
                    General George McClellan

It is part of a wise man to keep himself today for tomorrow, and not
to venture all his eggs in one basket.
                    —Cervantes

Try the ice before you venture on it.
                    —American proverb

Never leave hold of what you've got until you've got hold of something
else.
                    —Donald Hertzberg

If you can't tie good knots, tie plenty of them.
                    —Yachtsman's credo

When you go to buy, don't show your silver.
                    —Chinese proverb

Always put off till tomorrow what you shouldn't do at all.
                    —Author unknown

(See *Caution, Discretion, Restraint*)

Public Relations

Always live better than your clients, so that they won't object to the fees you demand.
—Ben Sonnenberg

Six precepts for effective communication:
1. Think.
2. Discard bias.
3. Adapt for preconceptions.
4. Choose the words.
5. Select the messenger.
6. Then communicate.
—Andrew Heiskell

When I started, everyone was using hunch and insight, but that didn't go far enough. You have to use feedback. Today, you don't take a chance with public opinion when modern polling techniques can tell you within three percentage points why you're wearing that particular tie or color shirt.
—Edward L. Bernays

Do your damndest in an ostentatious manner all the time.
—George S. Patton

Punctuality

When you have a dinner date, be prepared so that you can dress without delay. Be ready on time. Even if you should appear a dream personified, and he has waited hours to take the dream to dinner, you've spoiled the evening. His over-hungry stomach won't let his eyes see all your beauty, his mood is bad, and by the time he's had his coffee and his mood is fine, you are quite angry and not beautiful.
—Marlene Dietrich

A Man consumes the Time you make him Wait
In thinking of your Faults—so don't be late!
　　　　—Arthur Guiterman

Never wait until the last minute. The last minute shall invariably
cometh and goeth quicker than you thought it would.
　　　　—Daniel Meacham

Punctuality is one of the cardinal business virtues: always insist on it
in your subordinates.

　　　　—Don Marquis

Punishment

How to tar and feather someone: First, strip a person naked, then heat
the tar until it is thin, and pour upon the naked flesh, or rub it over
with a tar brush. After which, sprinkle decently upon the tar, whilst
it is yet warm, as many feathers as will stick to it.
　　　　—Treatise, 1770
　　　　　quoted in the *Wall Street Journal*

Purpose

All men should strive to learn before they die
What they are running from, and to, and why.
　　　　—James Thurber

Having chosen our course, without guile and with pure purpose, let
us renew our faith in God, and go forward without fear with manly
hearts.

　　　　—Abraham Lincoln
　　　　Message to Congress, July 4, 1861

Since it is not granted us to live long, let us transmit to posterity some memorial that we have at least lived.
—Pliny the Younger

We live very close together. So, our prime purpose in this life is to *help* others. And if you can't help them at least don't hurt them.
—The Dalai Lama

I cannot believe that the purpose of life is to be "happy." I think the purpose of life is to be useful, to be responsible, to be honorable, to be compassionate. It is, above all, to matter: to count, to stand for something, to have made some difference that you lived at all.
—Leo C. Rosten

A life without a purpose is a languid, drifting thing; every day we ought to review our purpose, saying to ourselves: This day let me make a sound beginning, for what we have hitherto done is naught!
—Thomas à Kempis

Your task it is, amid confusion, rush, and noise, to grasp the lasting, calm and meaningful, and finding it anew, to hold and treasure it.
—Paul Hindemith

(See *Fulfillment, Happiness*)

Pursuits

Pursue some path, however narrow and crooked, in which you can walk with love and reverence.
—Henry David Thoreau

Take heed you do not find what you do not seek.
—English proverb

Learn to feel the supreme interest of the discipline of the mind; study the remarkable power which you can exercise over the habits of at-

tention and its trains of thought; and cultivate a sense of the deep importance of exercising this power according to the principle of wisdom and virtue. . . . Judging upon these principles, we are taught to feel that life has a value beyond the mere acquirement of knowledge and the mere prosecution of our own happiness. This value is found in those nobler pursuits which qualify us for promoting the good of others and . . . to become masters of ourselves.
—Dr. John Abercrombie

Do not expect to arrive at certainty in every subject which you pursue. There are a hundred things wherein we mortals in the dark and imperfect state must be content with probability, where our best light and reasonings will reach no farther.
—Isaac Watts

If the joys of youth and the vision of perfect love have faded from your world, will you allow any baser thing to fetter you there? Let your heart rather follow its true object where that object is gone, into eternity.
—George Santayana

(See *Interests*)

Q

Quality

Read first the best books. The important thing for you is not how much you know, but the quality of what you know.
—Desiderius Erasmus

Get the confidence of the public and you will have no difficulty getting their patronage. . . . Remember always that the recollection of quality remains long after the price is forgotten.
—H. George Selfridge

If you refuse to accept anything but the best, you'll get the best. Begin to live as you wish to live.
—Anonymous

If you can't afford the expensive one, don't buy it.
—Andrew A. Rooney

Father used to say, "Never give away your work. People don't value what they don't have to pay for."
—Nancy Hale

Quality of Life

1. Realize that each human being has a built-in capacity for recuperation and repair.
2. Recognize that the quality of life is all-important.
3. Assume responsibility for the quality of your own life.
4. Nurture the regenerative and restorative forces within you.
5. Utilize laughter to create a mood in which the other positive emotions can be put to work for yourself and those around you.
6. Develop confidence and the ability to feel love, hope and faith, and acquire a strong will to live.
   —Norman Cousins

Discover day-to-day excitement.
   —Charles Baudelaire

Never cease to be convinced that life might be better—your own and others'.
   —André Gide

We must learn to reawaken and keep ourselves awake, not by mechanical aids, but by an infinite expectation of the dawn, which does not forsake us in our soundest sleep. I know of no more encouraging fact than the unquestionable ability of man to elevate his life by a conscious endeavor. It is something to be able to paint a particular picture, or to carve a statue, and so to make a few objects beautiful; but it is far more glorious to carve and paint the very atmosphere and medium through which we look, which morally we can do. To affect the quality of the day, that is the highest of arts.
   —Henry David Thoreau

I who am blind can give one hint to those who see—one admonition to those who would make full use of the gift of sight: Use your eyes as if tomorrow you would be stricken blind. And the same method can be applied to the other senses. Hear the music of voices, the song of a bird, the mighty strains of an orchestra, as if you would be stricken

deaf tomorrow. Touch each object you want to touch as if tomorrow your tactile sense would fail. Smell the perfume of flowers, taste with relish each morsel, as if tomorrow you could never smell and taste again. Make the most of every sense.
—Helen Keller

The happiness of your life depends upon the quality of your thoughts; therefore, guard accordingly.
—Marcus Antoninus

(See *Life, Living*)

Questionable Advice

When taking a country the conqueror must be careful to commit all his cruelties at once, to avoid being obliged to be cruel every day.
—Niccolò Machiavelli

Be a scribe! Your body will be sleek, your hand will be soft. . . . You are one who sits grandly in your house; your servants answer speedily; beer is poured copiously; all who see you rejoice in good cheer.
—Ptahhotep
24th century B.C.

When on a trip, throw away shame.
—Japanese proverb

It is better to be unfaithful than faithful without wanting to be.
—Brigitte Bardot

Never settle with words what you can accomplish with a flamethrower.
—Bruce Feirstein

If you can't convince 'em, confuse 'em.
—Harry S. Truman

. . . when the heart wilts from boredom, it is necessary to awaken it by the needle of jealousy. Give your mistress cause to worry a little so that her heart may become warm again. Let her grow pale at the proof of your infidelity.
—Ovid

Quit while you're behind.
—Laurence J. Peter

Above all, we must abolish hope in the heart of man. A calm despair, without angry convulsions, without reproaches to Heaven, is the essence of wisdom.
—Alfred de Vigny

You should make a woman angry if you wish her to love.
—Publilius Syrus

You have to dissemble, you have to recognize that you can't say what you think about [an] individual because you may have to use him sometime in the future. There's a lot of hypocrisy and so forth in political life. It's necessary in order to get into office and in order to retain office.
—Richard M. Nixon

If one person tell thee that thou hast ass's ears, do not mind it; but if two persons make this assertion, at once place a pack-saddle upon thy back.
—The Talmud

The way to get on in the world is to be neither more nor less wise, neither better nor worse than your neighbor.
—William Hazlitt

Always believe the expert.
—Virgil

Etiquette for children: If you use the wrong fork, lick it clean and slip it back onto the table cloth when no one is looking.
—Judith Martin
"Miss Manners"

Never be a pioneer. It's the early Christian that gets the fattest lion.
—"Saki" (H. H. Munro)

What you need is religion. What you should do is go to Uttar Pradesh in India—the ground is so holy that the vibes coming up from the ground will clear up your head.
—A psychiatrist's advice to writer Robert Stone

Success Techniques for the Ambitious Woman:
Develop a steely uncompromising gaze.
If you can learn to keep your eyes steadily on target and to let one or two teardrops appear at the corners of your eyes at the crucial moment in a negotiation, you have it made. . . . Needless to say, this technique should not be attempted on another woman, where it would be useless and self-defeating. Remember: there is no such thing as humiliation if you want to win.
Avoid any hint of prissy, nagging, schoolmarmish tone in your voice.
Take a hard line on every occasion. If a man suggests that the situation calls for a stiff letter, say "Stiff letter, hell, let's sue." Go for the jugular, and at least you'll never be accused of feminine weakness.
—Michael Korda

Never get a reputation for a small perfection, if you are trying for fame in a loftier area. The world can only judge by generals, and it sees that those who pay considerable attention to the minutiae, seldom have the minds occupied with great things.
—Edward Bulwer-Lytton

A man should have any number of little aims about which he should be conscious and for which he should have names, but he should have neither name for, nor consciousness concerning, the main aim of his life.
—Samuel Butler

Love and you shall be loved. All love is mathematically just, as much as the two sides of an algebraic equation.
—Ralph Waldo Emerson
"Compensation"

To do a great right, do a little wrong.
> —Bassanio in Shakespeare's
> *The Merchant of Venice*

You can't use tact with a Congressman. A Congressman is a hog. You must take a stick and hit him on the snout.
> —Henry Adams

> Some for the Glories of This World: and some
> Sigh for the Prophet's Paradise to come;
> Ah, take the Cash and let the Credit go,
> Nor heed the rumble of a distant Drum!
> —Omar Khayyám

What good are vitamins? Eat four lobsters, eat a pound of caviar—live! If you are in love with a beautiful blonde with an empty face and no brain at all, don't be afraid, marry her—live!
> —Artur Rubinstein

Have no truck with first impulses as they are always generous ones.
> —Casimir, Comte de Montrond

Be, as many now are, luxurious to yourself, parsimonious to your friends.
> —Juvenal

If you have the moon, ignore the stars.
> —Moorish proverb

Submit to your own nature; if it means you to be mediocre, be mediocre. Yield to those wiser than you, adopt their opinions, and do not trouble the world, since you cannot govern it.
> —Joseph Joubert

A woman should have a prosaic husband and take a romantic lover.
> —Stendhal (Marie-Henri Beyle)

If your dreams never come true, stop dreaming.
> —Elizabeth Fuller

Never say no when the world says aye.
> —Elizabeth Barrett Browning

On taxation: Ask the impossible so as to receive as much as possible.
> —Peter the Great

To journalists: Remember, son, many a good story has been ruined by over-verification.
> —James Gordon Bennett

Strive not with your superiors in argument, but always submit your judgment to others with modesty.
> —George Washington

Do not live by fixed principles, live by opportunity and circumstance.
> —Baltasar Gracián

A famous handbook on how to play *scopa*, the most common Italian card game, written in Naples by a Monsignor Chitarella, begins: "Rule Number One: always try to see your opponent's cards." A good concrete practical rule.
> —Luigi Barzini

(See *Advice, Bad Advice, Counsel, Facetious Advice*)

Questions

Be ever questioning. Ignorance is not bliss. It is oblivion. You don't go to heaven if you die dumb.
Become better informed. Learn from others' mistakes. You could not live long enough to make them all yourself.
> —Admiral Hyman Rickover

You do not need to justify asking questions. But if you think you have found answers, you do not have the right to remain silent.
> —Jacob Neusner

Don't ask questions of fairy tales.
                    —Jewish proverb

Be patient toward all that is unsolved in your heart and try to love the
questions themselves like locked rooms and like books that are written
in a very foreign tongue. Do not now seek the answers, which cannot
be given you because you would not be able to live them. And the
point is, to live everything. Live the questions now. Perhaps you will
then gradually, without noticing it, live along some distant day into
the answer.

                    —Rainer Maria Rilke

(See *Curiosity, Inquiry*)

R

Reading

If you would understand your own age, read the works of fiction produced in it. People in disguise speak freely.
—Arthur Helps

No one is supposed to tell others what is good. I tell you what is good. You can't live, you can't mesh with this world, unless you *read*. . . . We are not only a body and a bowel. People who bring children into the world and are not prepared to feed their brains are, in my philosophy, ignoble. . . . The idiots who run TV, and look at the ratings, think people are pleased at the low, hypnotic and opiate level. . . . You're in for trouble. . . . You're vulnerable. For God's sake, take Hamlet's advice—"Readiness is all."
—Dr. Frank Baxter

Let not the authority of the writer offend thee whether he be of great or small learning; but let the love of pure truth draw thee to read.
—Thomas à Kempis

Do not dictate to your author; try to become him. Be his fellow-worker and accomplice. If you hang back, and reserve and criticise at first, you are preventing yourself from getting the fullest possible value from what you read. But if you open your mind as widely as possible, then signs and hints of almost imperceptible fineness, from the twist and turn of the first sentences, will bring you into the presence of a human being unlike any other. Steep yourself in this . . . and soon you will find that your author is giving you, or attempting to give you, something far more definite.

—Virginia Woolf

Make it a rule, never to read at meal-times, nor in company when there is any (even the most trivial) conversation going on, nor ever to let your eagerness to learn encroach upon your play-hours. Books are but one inlet of knowledge; and the pores of the mind, like those of the body, should be left open to all impressions.

—William Hazlitt

(See *Authorship, Books, Literary Composition, Writing*)

Reality

Beware that you do not lose the substance by grasping at the shadow.

—Aesop

Let us take things as we find them: let us not attempt to distort them into what they are not. True philosophy deals with facts. We cannot make facts. All our wishing cannot change them. We must use them.

—John Henry Cardinal Newman

We must always think about things, and we must think about things as they are, not as they are said to be.

—George Bernard Shaw

Let us try to see things as they are, and not wish to be wiser than God.

—Gustave Flaubert

Lest men suspect your tale untrue
Keep probability in view.

—John Gay

Fearful as reality is, it is less fearful than evasions of reality. . . . Look steadfastly into the slit, pin-pointed malignant eyes of reality as an old hand trainer dominates his wild beasts.
      —Caitlin Thomas

(See *Illusion, Practicality, Reason, Truth*)

Reason

Come now, and let us reason together, saith the Lord: though your sins be as scarlet, they shall be as white as snow; though they be red like crimson, they shall be as wool.
      —Old Testament
      Isaiah 1:18

Be led by reason.
      —Greek proverb

We must convince by reason, not prescribe by tradition.
      —Cyprian

Do not govern your life by fancy, but by reason.

One ought always to side with reason and duty; so that neither vulgar passion, nor tyrannical violence may be able to make one abandon them. The crafty often stand neuter; and by a plausible and metaphysical subtilty endeavour to reconcile their consciences to their passions with reasons of state. But an upright man looks upon that way of trimming as a kind of treason, thinking it more honour to be *good* than to be *great*.
      —George Shelley

Fancy is always to act in subordination to Reason. We may take Fancy for a companion, but must follow Reason as our guide. We may allow Fancy to suggest certain ideas in certain places; but Reason must always

be heard when she tells us that those ideas and those places have not natural or necessary relation.
                    —Samuel Johnson

Do not reason coldly with youth. Clothe your reason with a body, if you would make it felt. Let the mind speak the language of the heart, that it may be understood.
                    —Jean-Jacques Rousseau

(See *Illusion, Practicality, Reality, Truth*)

Reciprocity

Give, and it shall be given unto you; good measure, pressed down, and shaken together, and running over, shall men give into your bosom. For with the same measure that ye mete withal it shall be measured to you again.
                    —New Testament
                    Luke 6:38

Moral Support: Try to give her as much as she needs, for tomorrow you may need it back.
                    —Ad slogan contributed by Ann Elise Rubin

Always go to other people's funerals, otherwise they won't come to yours.
                    —Yogi Berra
                    quoted by Herb Schmertz

Regret

"Undress," as George Herbert says, "your soul at night," not by self-examination, but by shedding, as you do your garments, the daily sins whether of omission or commission, and you will wake a free man, with a new life. To look back, except on rare occasions for stock-taking, is to risk the fate of Lot's wife. Many a man is handicapped in his course by a cursed combination of retro- and introspection, the mistakes of yesterday paralysing the efforts of to-day, the worries of the past hugged to his destruction, and the worm Regret allowed to canker the very heart of his life. To die daily, after the manner of St. Paul, ensures the resurrection of a new man, who makes each day the epitome of a life.

—William Osler

Assimilate every mistake without dwelling on it. By all means, you should do whatever you can to get off your own back.

—Dr. Richard M. Suinn

Beware of starting what you may later regret.

—Publilius Syrus

Relationships

You have to work constantly at rejuvenating a relationship. You can't just count on its being O.K.; or it will tend toward a hollow commitment, devoid of passion and intimacy. People need to put the kind of energy into it that they put into their children or career.

—Dr. Robert Sternberg
Yale University psychologist

You shouldn't go into a relationship expecting that he or she will change. If you pick your mate wisely, you will both make adjustments, but it's unfair to expect your future mate to make basic changes. Put yourself in his or her shoes. Would you want to be overhauled or would you expect your mate to love you as you are?

—Dr. Zev Wanderer and Erika Fabian

Never idealize others. They will never live up to your expectations. Don't over-analyze your relationships. Stop playing games. A growing relationship can only be nurtured by genuineness.

—Leo Buscaglia

Beware of the danger signals that flag problems: silence, secretiveness, or sudden outburst.
—Sylvia Porter

If you want to gather honey, don't kick over the beehive.
—Dale Carnegie

On going to bars to meet first-rate men: If you want to catch trout, don't fish in a herring barrel.
—Ann Landers

"How to hold a man":
1. Never put makeup on at the table.
2. Never ask a man where he has been.
3. Never keep him waiting.
4. Never baby him when he is disconsolate.
5. Never fail to baby him when he is sick or has a hangover.
6. Never let him see you when you are not at your best.
7. Never talk about your other dates or boyfriends of the past.
—Mae West

You know how I end relationships in New York now? I don't say, "This isn't working out." Or, "I don't want to see you anymore." This is a tip to remember, girls. If I never want to see a man again, I just say, "You know, I love you. . . . I want to marry you. . . . I want to have your children. . . ." Sometimes they make skid marks.
—Rita Rudner

What can you say when someone says he loves you but the feeling is not mutual?
Point out to him that he is lucky, for if he loves you that much, he has the capacity to love others as well, whereas you may never feel so passionately about someone. Try to restrain the envy in your voice.
—Patricia Marx

If you are 48 and you have not seen people in 30 years, do not do it. They're 48. They look like parents.
—Bill Cosby

(See *Couples, Dating, Husbands/Wives, Marriage, Wooing*)

Religion

Avoid, as you would the plague, a clergyman who is also a man of business.
— Saint Jerome

Remembrance

Remember the days of old, consider the years of many generations: ask thy father, and he will shew thee; thy elders, and they will tell thee.
— Old Testament
Deuteronomy 32:7

Remember them that are in bonds, as bound with them; and them which suffer adversity, as being yourselves also in the body.
— New Testament
Hebrews 13:3

There is one popular view now, best expressed by the poet Christina Rossetti: "Better far that you should forget and smile than that you should remember and be sad." But presumably all these monuments in Washington weren't built to remind us to forget. . . . There is plenty to remember that has all but been forgotten. Not only the carnage of the two world wars . . . but so many other atrocities that few people dare to recall them. . . . Only the old folks can't help but remember.
— James Reston

All of us, whether guilty or not, whether old or young, must accept the past. . . . It is not a case of coming to terms with the past. That is not possible. It cannot be subsequently modified or undone. However, anyone who closes his eyes to the past is blind to the present.

Whoever refuses to remember the inhumanity is prone to new risks of infection. . . . Seeking to forget makes exile all the longer; the secret of redemption lies in remembrance.

—Richard von Weizsäcker
President of Federal Republic of Germany

Reporting

How to Be a Better Reporter:

One: See a thing clearly and describe it simply.

Two: Keep in mind the great crowd that cannot afford to hire a corporation lawyer, but can afford a three-cent newspaper. Every newspaper man owes to his poorest reader the loyalty that a great lawyer owes to his richest client. Some newspaper owners forget that, especially after they become rich, and no longer remember how it feels to be poor.

Three: Write so that the reader will say, "I feel as though I had actually SEEN what the newspaper describes."

Four: In reporting, don't forget to bring back PICTURES. One good picture tells more than a thousand words, and this is the picture age.

Five: Write plain, simple English, avoiding "newspaper English." Don't be afraid to use the same word twice. Don't write "horse," then "equine," or "dog," then "canine," or "rat," then "rodent."

Avoid fancy writing. The most powerful words are simplest. "To be or not to be, that is the question," "In the beginning was the word," "We are such stuff as dreams are made on, and our little life is rounded with a sleep," "Out, out, brief candle," "The rest is silence." Nothing fancy in those quotations. A natural style is the only style.

Make your writing striking, and musical, if you can. Don't try for onomatopoeia. English, unlike German, Greek and some other languages, does not lend itself to it. Never overdo "apt alliteration's artful aid."

Six: Feed your mind as you feed your body, EVERY day. Feed your body less, and your mind more, if you want to be a good newspaper man. A prizefighter can't fight on the beef-steak he ate ten years ago. Newspaper men can't do good work on the THINKING of twenty years ago. READ AND THINK. Keep your mind open to new ideas.

Write with difficulty. "Work, as nature works, in fire," was Dante's advice quoted by D'Annunzio. If you do not burn as you work, readers will be cold as they read.

Seven: Read as much as you can of the best writers, and read Shakespeare all through life. Compared to the rest of literature, he is like the Pacific Ocean compared to the chain of Great Lakes. The lakes are respectable, but they are NOT the Pacific Ocean. Read five or six books at a time. . . .

Eight: Read books that tell you what your predecessors on the earth have believed and done, and how they escaped their superstitions. Read also some of the old classics. Plato's description of the men in a cave and of the trial and death of Socrates; more, if you can stand it. Read enough of Sophocles, Euripides, Aeschylus, to let you know how those powerful minds of antiquity expressed themselves.

Nine: Read a history of philosophy. . . . Read enough of Goethe, Schiller, Heine, Villon, Molière, Racine, Corneille, to know a little about the French and German mind. Read Dante and Cervantes. Not to know both is harmful ignorance. Read all you can of Homer—enough to know just why Homer, Dante, Goethe, Cervantes and Shakespeare are the world's most famous writers. In short, READ, always coming back to Shakespeare. And keep yourself to yourself, at least part of the time, remembering Goethe's true saying: "Talent is built in the silence, character in the stream of the world."

Ten: Learn to edit your copy. Strike out "very" always. Strike out most of your adjectives, remembering the wise Frenchmen's remark: "The adjective is the enemy of the noun."

—Arthur Brisbane
Advice posted in the office of
John Reagan ("Tex") McCrary

Checklist for writing a story:
   Stick to the facts. Never *wish* facts.
   When in doubt, attribute.*
   Never insert your personal opinion.
   Be discreet in the use of adjectives.
   Avoid cheap shots.
   Remember you are an observer, not a protagonist.
   Listen to your editors—they will fire you if you don't.
   Remember the children. Even thieves can have families. Try to put
    yourself in the place of the people you are writing about.

*Attributes, such as "police said," "investigators charge," "witnesses responded" can clutter good writing but they can also save you from litigation.
      —Leonard Ray Teel and Rod Taylor

"One sacred rule of journalism": The writer must not invent. The legend on the license must read: None of This Was Made Up. The ethics of journalism, if we can be allowed such a boon, must be based on the simple truth that every journalist knows the difference between the distortion that comes from subtracting observed data and the distortion that comes from adding invented data.
      —John Hersey

Let there be a fresh breeze of new honesty, new idealism, new integrity. And there, gentlemen, is where you come in. You have typewriters, presses and a huge audience. How about raising hell?
      —Jenkin Lloyd Jones

(See *Communication, Journalism, Media, Television*)

Reputation

The short and true way to reputation is to take care to be in truth what we would have others think us to be. A good reputation is a second, or half an estate.
      —Spanish saying

Let it never be forgotten by you that the reputation established by a boy at school and college, whether it be of merit or demerit, will follow him through life.
—Martha Wilson, 1811

Don't worry about people knowing you, son, just make yourself worth knowing.
—Fiorello H. La Guardia
to a young Joey Adams

Always conduct yourself so you will be welcome to return to your hometown.
—James V. Forrestal
to Annapolis graduates
(favorite saying of
Admiral William J. Crowe,
chairman of Joint Chiefs of Staff)

(See *Applause, Fame, Greatness, Praise*)

Resignation/Acceptance

If you can alter things, alter them. If you cannot, put up with them.
—English proverb

Accustom yourself to submit on all and every occasion, and on the most minute, no less than on the most important circumstances of life, to a small present evil, to obtain a greater distant good. This will give decision, tone and energy to the mind, which, thus disciplined, will often reap victory from defeat, and honour from repulse.
—Charles Caleb Colton

Accept things as they are, not as you wish them to be.
—Napoleon I

. . . hope takes work. No matter how negative the situation, you seek the positive elements and build on them. . . . Hope is especially important when there is nothing you can do. . . . In American culture, there is a powerful equation that says to lose control is to lose everything. But the most serious problems—a terrible accident, a major disease—are those in which we are objectively helpless. Then the best way to cope is to find out how to live with it. It's fine to keep fighting when you can change your situation. But when you can't change the facts, accept them. That's the key to health—and to wisdom.

—Shlomo Breznitz
Director of the Ray D. Wolfe Centre for the Study of Psychological Stress, University of Haifa, Israel

(See *Limitations, Restraint*)

Resolution

Resolve, and thou art free.
—Henry Wadsworth Longfellow

Resolve, and keep your resolution; choose, and pursue your choice. If you spend this day in study, you will find yourself still more able to study to-morrow; not that you are to expect that you shall at once obtain a complete victory. Depravity is not very easily overcome. Resolution will sometimes relax, and diligence will sometimes be interrupted; but let no accidental surprise or deviation, whether short or long, dispose you to despondency. Consider these failings as incident to all mankind. Begin again where you left off, and endeavor to avoid the seducements that prevailed over you before.
—Samuel Johnson
Advice to James Boswell

If you cannot win, you *must* win.
—Maxim of Reb Menshim Mendl of Kotsk

Hast thou attempted greatnesses?
    Then go on;
Back-turning slackens resolution.
    —Thomas Herrick

Never tell your resolution beforehand.
    —John Selden

(See *Dedication, Perseverance*)

Restraint

Rule lust, temper the tongue and bridle the belly.
    —English proverb

Before buying anything, it is well to ask if one could do without it.
    —John Lubbock

Sacrifice not thy heart upon every altar.
    —Thomas Fuller

Judges ought to remember that their office is *jus dicere*, and not *jus dare*; to interpret law, and not to make law, or give law.
    —Sir Francis Bacon

Should you happen to notice that another person is extremely tall or overweight, eats too much or declines convivial drinks, has red hair or goes about in a wheelchair, ought to get married or ought not to be pregnant—see if you can refrain from bringing these astonishing observations to that person's attention.
    —Judith Martin
    "Miss Manners"

It is not always good to utter one's inmost thoughts; but we must try to have nothing in our hearts that we cannot tell.
    —Paul Janet

He that is without sin among you, let him first cast a stone at her.
—New Testament
John 8:7

Don't shake hands too eagerly.
—Greek proverb

Put the words on me, but don't touch or spit at me.*
—Nestor Chylak
Baseball Umpire

*NOTE: One afternoon, when veteran American League baseball umpire Bill Guthrie was working behind the plate, the catcher for the visiting team repeatedly protested his calls. Guthrie endured this for three innings. In the fourth inning, Guthrie stopped him.

"Son," he said gently, "you've been a big help to me in calling balls and strikes, and I appreciate it. But I think I've got the hang of it now. So I'm going to ask you to go to the clubhouse and show whoever's there how to take a shower."
—Quoted by Dan McKinnon

(See *Caution, Discretion, Limitations, Prudence*)

Retirement

You must keep busy. Continue working if you can, or develop an interest that you can pursue as though it were a livelihood. Too many people look on retirement as a permanent vacation. They find that the vacation ends after a few weeks or months, leaving an empty future. Activity is the only antidote.
—B. F. Skinner

Don't halt before you are lame.
—English proverb

I learned a lesson about retirement that was certainly true for me, and might be a help to many other people. When you finish with a job it is wiser to make the break completely. Cut off the old life, clean and sharp. If your mind is tired, that is the only way. If your mind is lively you will soon find other interests.

—Caroline Lejeune

I don't think you should quit working, ever. If you do have to retire, find something else to do. You've got to keep your mind busy or you'll spend too much time dwelling on unpleasant things.

—Milton Berle

This notion of tapering off is just crazy. That's the way you die. Retire and die. I'll never forget an article I read by a heart specialist. "We Don't Wear Out, We Rust Out," it was called. Put a car upon the block for six months and it's no good. Put a *man* up on the block for six months, *he's* no good. It's as simple as that.

—Mortimer Adler

(See *The Elderly, Longevity, Old Age*)

Right and Wrong

Let the truth and right by which you are apparently the loser be preferable to you to the falsehood and wrong by which you are apparently the gainer.

—Moses Maimonides

Pray let no quibbles of lawyers, no refinements of Casuists, break into the plain notions of right and wrong, which every man's right reason and plain common-sense suggests to him. To do as you would be done by, is the plain, sure and undisputed rule of morality and justice. Stick to that.

—Lord Chesterfield

There is only one duty, only one safe course, and that is to try to be right.

—Sir Winston Churchill

There's right and there's wrong. You got to do one or the other. You do the one, and you're living. You do the other, and you may be walking around but you're dead as a beaver hat.
                                    —John Wayne

Be advised that every time you avoid doing right, you increase your disposition to do wrong.
                                    —Anonymous

Be not righteous overmuch.
                                    —Old Testament
                                    Ecclesiastes 7:16

Risk

Remember, you can't steal second if you don't take your foot off first.
                                    —Mike Todd

. . . about risk-taking—either you do or you don't; there is no middle ground, for you cannot compromise risk any more than you can compromise pregnancy.

                                    —A. E. Hotchner

When fog prevents a small-boat sailor from seeing the buoy marking the course he wants, he turns his boat rapidly in small circles, knowing that the waves he makes will rock the buoy in the vicinity. Then he stops, listens and repeats the procedure until he hears the buoy clang. By making waves, he finds where his course lies . . . Often the price of finding these guides is a willingness to take a few risks, to "make a few waves." A boat that stays in the harbor never encounters danger— but it also never gets anywhere.

"Put out into deep water." (New Testament, Luke 5:4).
                                    —Richard Armstrong

You can't expect to hit the jackpot if you don't put a few nickels in the machine.
                                    —Flip Wilson

Take risks . . . be willing to put your mind and your spirit, your time and your energy, your stomach and your emotions on the line. To search for a safe place, to search for an end to a rainbow, is to search for a place that you will hate once you find it. The soul must be nourished along with the bank account and the resume. The best nourishment for any soul is to create your own risks.
—Jim Lehrer

Love your country. Don't be afraid to stick your neck out. And take a chance on the young.
—Jacob K. Javits

. . . take a chance on people. Somebody took a hell of a chance on me.
—Walter Wriston

(See *Boldness, Courage, Daring, Fortitude, Prudence, Spirit*)

S

Safety

Damn the lights. Watch the cars. The lights ain't never killed nobody.
— Jackie ("Moms") Mabley

On the highway, beware of rolling stoned.
— Anonymous

Every time you pass on a blind curve, every time you hit up on a slippery road, every time you step on it harder than your reflexes will safely take, every time you drive with your reactions slowed down by a drink or two, every time you follow the man ahead too closely, you're gambling a few seconds against . . . blood and agony and sudden death.
— J. C. Furnas (with Ernest A. Smith)

Carry nothing worth fighting for, because you could get seriously hurt trying to resist a robber.
— Detective Lucille Barrascano

Try breaking into your own home. Most people find several ways to get inside in just a few minutes.
— Ray Johnson
Security consultant (former burglar)

Never bolt your door with a boiled carrot.
— Irish proverb

How to cope with terrorism abroad:

PERSONAL SECURITY
Don't wear flashy jewelry.
Don't face attackers; give up valuables.
Do drive a locally made car.
Do watch for surveillance.

VEHICLE SECURITY
Don't drive your car with the windows open; bombs can be thrown through them.
Don't ignore loose wires on or near your car; they could lead to a bomb.
Do check the back seat for strange boxes or hidden attacker.

HOME SECURITY/OFFICE SECURITY
Don't accept unmarked packages.
Don't go to windows if you hear gunfire or bombings; take cover.
> —From "Terrorism: Avoidance and Survival,"
> instructions to U.S. Government personnel
> from U.S. Department of State

(See *Crime, Danger*)

Science

Keep your early enthusiasm . . . but let it ever be regulated by rigorous examinations and tests. Never advance anything which cannot be proved in a simple and decisive fashion. . . . Worship the spirit of criticism. If reduced to itself, it is not an awakener of ideas or a stimulant to great things, but without it, everything is fallible; it always has the last word.
> —Louis Pasteur

The secret of science is to ask the right question, and it is the choice of problem more than anything else that marks the man of genius in the scientific world.
> —Sir Henry Tizard

The artist would be well advised to keep his work to himself till it is completed, because no one can readily help him or advise him with it . . . but the scientist is wiser not to withhold a single finding or a single conjecture from publicity.

—Johann Wolfgang von Goethe

I cannot give any scientist of any age better advice than this: the intensity of a conviction that a hypothesis is true has no bearing over whether it is true or not.

—Sir Peter Medawar

Regarding research: There's an old saying in research: it's okay to sleep with a hypothesis, but you should never marry one. Always be ready to follow a new lead and shift techniques, even if it means giving up a favorite idea. One thing I remember about Picasso was that he was always changing, always trying something new. That's just as important in science.

—J. William Langston

Teach at the outset, before any of the fundamentals, the still imponderable puzzles of cosmology. Let it be known, as clearly as possible, by the youngest minds, that there are some things going on in the universe that lie beyond comprehension, and make it plain how little is known. . . . Teach ecology early on.

—Dr. Lewis Thomas

Anybody who has been seriously engaged in scientific work of any kind realizes that over the entrance to the gates of the temple of science are written the words: *Ye must have faith.* It is a quality which the scientist cannot dispense with.

—Max Planck

Sculpture

If a young person came to me and said he wanted to be a sculptor and asked what advice I'd give him, I'd tell him to see as much of past sculpture as he could, from primitive times to the present day.

Perhaps more important, I would tell him to spend years and years learning to draw. You learn to draw because drawing makes you look. You may do a very bad drawing, but if you try to draw something, you *look* much more intensely than if you just look. And this is its value. I would make drawing a part of general education for everybody.
—Henry Moore

The art of the sculptor is made of strength, exactitude, and will. In order to express life, to render nature, one must will and will and will with all the strength of heart and brain; nature exceeds—and greatly—human genius; she is superior in everything; to believe that you can equal her, to believe that you can create outside her is as stupid as wanting to measure the stars with your hands. . . . There are unknown forces in nature; when we give ourselves wholly to her, without reserve, she lends them to us; she shows us these forms, which our watching eyes do not see, which our intelligence does not understand or suspect. In art, to admit only what one understands leads to impotence.
—Auguste Rodin

(See *Art/Artists*)

Secrets

And whatsoever else shall hap tonight,
Give it an understanding, but no tongue.
—Hamlet in Shakespeare's
Hamlet, Prince of Denmark

Tell no tales about friend or foe; unless silence makes you an accomplice, never betray a man's secret. Suppose he has heard you and learned to distrust you, he will seize the first chance to show his hatred.
—Ben Sira

Never participate in the secrets of those above you: you think you share the fruit, and you share the stones . . . the confidence of a prince is not a grant, but a tax.
—Baltasar Gracián

As long as a secret is secure in your heart, you are its master, and you can ride on it. As soon as you disclose it, it becomes your master and rides on you.
                    —Anonymous

Wash your soiled linen in private.
                    —Napoleon I

Be this your wall of brass, to have no guilty secrets, no wrong-doing that makes you turn pale.
                    —Horace

Don't tell secrets to the children of your own relations.
                    —Irish proverb

Think twice before burdening a friend with a secret.
                    —Marlene Dietrich

Self-Expression

Do not try to imitate the lark or the nightingale, if you can't do it. If it's your destiny to croak like a toad, then go ahead! And with all your might! Make them hear you!
                    —Louis-Ferdinand Céline

A man should dress by instinct. His wardrobe should match his life, looks and personality. For me, shirts are the basis of everything. I love them very well made and perfectly pressed.
                    —Karl Lagerfeld

Dressing for lunch: If the top of what you wear does not match the bottom of what you wear and you do not work in any of the "creative" fields, it is best to remain seated all through lunch.
                    —Louise Bernikow

Develop your eccentricities while you're young. That way, when you are old, people won't think you're going gaga.
—David Ogilvy

Self-Improvement

Keep company with those who may make you better.
—English saying

To remain whole, be twisted!
To become straight, let yourself be bent.
To become full, be hollow.
Be tattered, that you may be renewed.
—Lao Tzu

Do your work for six years; but in the seventh, go into solitude or among strangers, so that the memory of your friends does not hinder you from being what you have become.
—Leo Szilard

No matter how well you are doing, do better. There is an old Spanish proverb which says, "Enjoy the little you have while the fool is hunting for more." The energetic American ought to turn this proverb upside down and make it read, "While the fool is enjoying the little he has, I will hunt for more." The way to hunt for more is to utilize your odd moments. . . . The man who is always killing time is really killing his own chances in life; while the man who is destined to success is the man who makes time live by making it useful.
—Arthur Brisbane

Next to being what we ought to be, the most desirable thing is that we should become what we ought to be as fast as possible.
—Herbert Spencer

Above all, challenge yourself. You may well surprise yourself at what strengths you have, what you can accomplish.
—Cecile M. Springer

Be willing to shed parts of your previous life. For example, in our 20s we wear a mask; we pretend to know more than we do. We must be willing, as we get older, to shed cocktail party phoniness and admit, "I am who I am."
—Gail Sheehy

You learn in life that the only person you can really correct and change is yourself. You can't do that with anyone else. But you can do it with yourself, if you want to sufficiently. Now we are taught you must blame your father, your sisters, your brothers, the school, the teacher— you can blame anyone, but never blame yourself. It's never your fault. But it's ALWAYS your fault, because if you wanted to change, you're the one who has got to change. It's as simple as that, isn't it?
—Katharine Hepburn

What you dislike in another take care to correct in yourself.
—Thomas Sprat

Be not indifferent to contempt, even from very ordinary people, but rather look well to the cause of it.
—Charles Simmons

Confront the dark parts of yourself, and work to banish them with illumination and forgiveness. Your willingness to wrestle with your demons will cause your angels to sing. Use the pain as fuel, as a reminder of your strength.
—August Wilson

(See *Identity, Introspection, Meditation*)

Self-Knowledge

Consider what thou wert, and make it thy business to know thy self, which is the most difficult lesson in the world. Yet from this lesson thou will learn to avoid the frog's foolish ambition of swelling to rival the bigness of the ox.
—Miguel de Cervantes

Self-Preservation

It's important to run not on the fast track, but on *your* track. Pretend you have only six months to live. Make three lists: the things you have to do, want to do, and neither have to do nor want to do. Then, for the rest of your life, forget everything in the third category.
—Robert S. Eliot and Dennis L. Breo

Rule of survival: Pack your own parachute.
—T. L. Hakala

You've got to decide on an inner discipline to protect yourself. Step out of the interesting, dynamic rhythm every so often and focus on your internal life. Say "Stop the world, I want to get off" for a while at least.
—Naomi Rosenblatt

Notice the world, sense it, react to it, change it. If you work in a room with harsh fluorescent lighting and windows that can't be opened . . . sense how these things present themselves, how they affect you. Don't fall prey to the therapist's fantasy that the problem is always in you, when you're suffering because of the room. Do what you can to change it, make it as personal as you can, fit it to you. Be eccentric; put a lampshade over the light.
—Dr. James Hillman

If you are losing a tug-of-war with a tiger, give him the rope before he gets to your arm. You can always buy a new rope.
—Max Gunther

If you don't get the better of yourself, someone else will.
—Anonymous

(See *Stress, Survival*)

Self-Reliance

It was on my fifth birthday that Papa put his hand on my shoulder and said, "Remember, my son, if you ever need a helping hand, you'll find one at the end of your arm."
—Sam Levenson

If you would have a faithful servant, and one that you like, serve yourself.
—Benjamin Franklin

If you want a thing done well, do it yourself.
—Napoleon I

When the job is important, and it's something you do well, do it yourself. Depending on others has a surface attractiveness, providing a ready scapegoat if things go wrong; but the bottom line is that you've only yourself to blame.
—James C. Freund

One should respect public opinion insofar as it is necessary to avoid starvation and keep out of prison, but anything that goes beyond this is voluntary submission to an unnecessary tyranny.
—Bertrand Russell

Do not rely completely on any other human being, however dear. We meet all life's greatest tests alone.
—Agnes Macphail

Work out your own salvation.
—New Testament
Philippians 2:12

(See *Independence, Individuality*)

Self-Respect

Consider well the seed from which you grew;
You were not formed to live like animals
But rather to pursue virtue and knowledge.
  —Dante Alighieri

Have respect for your species. . . . You are a man; do not dishonour mankind.
  —Jean-Jacques Rousseau

If you want to be respected by others the great thing is to respect yourself. Only by that, only by self-respect will you compel others to respect you.
  —Fyodor Dostoevsky

. . . *you must have a self you respect.* . . . Winston Churchill ex-emplified integrity and respect in the face of opposition. Churchill was attending an official ceremony. Several rows behind him two gentle-men began whispering "That's Winston Churchill." "They say he is getting senile." "They say he should step aside and leave the running of the nation to younger, more dynamic, and capable men." Churchill sat facing forward, but when the ceremony was over, he stopped by the row where the men were seated. He leaned forward and said, "Gentlemen, they also say he is deaf!"
  —Barbara Hatcher

I have an everyday religion that works for me. Love yourself first and everything else falls into line. You really have to love yourself to get anything done in this world.
  —Lucille Ball

Do not make yourself low; people will tread on your head.
  —Yiddish proverb

Learn to value yourself, which means: to fight for your happiness.
  —Ayn Rand

Do thyself no harm.
                    —New Testament
                    Acts 16:28

(See *Confidence*, *Negativism*, *Positive Thinking*, *Self-Reliance*)

Selling

To sell something, tell a woman it's a bargain; tell a man it's deductible.
—Earl Wilson

Of the importance of things not said: If you're selling someone a transistor clock/radio, I don't think you're obligated to point out that the battery will run down in twenty-one months or that a year from now there will be a better digital model on the market for less money. State the positives and omit irrelevant or semi-irrelevant negatives. Be ethical, be moral—and be aware of the joys of silence.
—Mark H. McCormack

Murray's Law: Never ask a salesman if his is a good price.
—Arthur Bloch

Basic steps in a sales call: "When in doubt, probe." You probe to uncover a sales opportunity and then probe further to convert that opportunity into a need for your product. For example, if you are selling a pen that writes in the water and upside down, you might ask, "Do your employees ever have to write under unusual conditions?" If the client replies that his West Coast people do a lot of their work in hot tubs and some of their best ideas get washed away, you have uncovered an opportunity.
—Jeremy Main

Rules for shopgirls . . . commandments of boutique behavior:
  Do not pretend that your name is Monique and that you are just killing time before the release of the major motion picture which you have written, directed, and star in.
  Here are a few sentences it is best not to utter: "Everyone loves this

one." "We're selling a lot of these." "This is a very big look right now." But if you want to, you can say, "It's you. It's really *you*." This is an amusing concept.
—Cynthia Heimel

Sensitivity

Never touch a butterfly's wing with your finger.
—Colette

Serendipity

Never think that God's delays are God's denials.*
—Author unknown

*A lone shipwreck survivor on an uninhabited island managed to build a rude hut in which he placed all that he had saved from the sinking ship. He prayed to God for deliverance, and anxiously scanned the horizon each day to hail any passing ship.

One day he was horrified to find his hut in flames. All that he had was gone. To the man's limited vision, it was the worst that could happen and he cursed God. Yet the very next day a ship arrived. "We saw your smoke signal," the captain said.
—Adapted from *Guideposts*, quoted by
Walter A. Heiby

Servants *

Make thy face to shine upon thy servant.
—Old Testament
Psalms 31:16

Expect more from thy servants than is just;
Reward them well, if they observe thy trust,
Nor with them cruelty or pride invade;
Since God and nature them our brothers made.
              —Sir John Denham

Rebuke your servant without passion, with soft words and strong arguments, lest he see a fault in you, while you are reproving one in him. If he is ingenuous, this may reform him; if not, he is stupid, and so not fit for your service.
              —George Shelley

Let your maidservant be faithful, strong—and homely.
              —Benjamin Franklin

(See *House/Home*)

Service to Others

Live for another if you wish to live for yourself.
              —Seneca

Do whatever comes your way to do as well as you can. Think as little as possible about yourself and as much as possible about other people and about things that are interesting. Put a good deal of thought into the happiness that you are able to give.
              —Eleanor Roosevelt

Giving to others heals me, as the Indians healed themselves with herbs. They did not understand what the herbs did, how they operated, they only knew their healing powers. So with me. I do not want to know what there is about the process of giving that heals me. It is my herb. I must not try to pick it apart. Just use it and know what it does and be grateful.
              —Catherine Deneuve

I think there should be an Eleventh Commandment: "Always make friends with people who do you a service."
—Alfred North Whitehead

. . . the mere resolve not to be useless, and the honest desire to help other people, will, in the quickest and delicatest ways, improve yourself.
—John Ruskin

Sex

Sex is like a small business; you gotta watch over it.
—Mae West

You must lay down the treasures of your body.
—Angelo in Shakespeare's
Measure for Measure

You vote for or against being slender. You vote for or against a sex life as you get older. . . . Either you just retire from sex entirely, or you make up your mind to be sexual for the rest of your life. You decide either to be slender or comfortable, you can't be both. It's a straight decision you make in your 40s, when statistically we need half the calories we needed at 20. It has to do with health and it has to do with vanity. . . . You can't be sexual at 60 if you're fat.
—Helen Gurley Brown

It is not enough to conquer; one must know how to seduce.
—Voltaire

Do not confuse sex, love and intimacy. One does not necessarily imply the other. Experiencing one does not necessarily satisfy our need for the other. While all three ideally come together at certain moments, each of them must be attended to and appreciated. And finally, do not forsake one for the other. You can have them all.
—Dr. Aaron Hass

Do not exploit. Do not be exploited. Remember that sex is not out there, but in here, in the deepest layer of your own being. There is not only a morning after—there are also lots of days and years afterward.

—Jacob Neusner

Be advised by me, do not come too soon to the climax of your pleasure, but by skilful holding back, reach it gently. . . . Do not, by setting too much sail, leave your mistress behind you; nor let her get too much in front of you. Row together towards the port. Voluptuousness reaches its greatest height when, overcome by it, lover and mistress are overcome at the same time. This ought to be your rule when there is no hurry and you are not compelled by fear of discovery to hasten your furtive pleasures. But if there is any danger in your taking your time, then, bent over the oars, row with all your strength, and press your spurs into the thighs of your steed.

Women, let pleasure penetrate even to the marrow of your bones, and let the enjoyment be equally divided between you and your lover. Whisper tender words, murmur softly, and let licentious suggestions sharpen your sweet sport.

Do not let too strong a light come into your bedroom. There are in a Beauty a great many things which are enhanced by being seen only in a half-light.

—Ovid

Be romantic! A good meal or a stroll in the park can set the stage for great sex.
Don't stint on foreplay—or afterplay. Be inventive!
Don't share your fantasies unless you're sure your partner really wants to hear them.
Don't criticize in the sack. Discuss constructively later.
Satisfy your partner even when you may not feel like sex.
Don't fake your pleasure. Try sex a different way.
Use contraceptives if you'd rather not be parents.

—Dr. Ruth Westheimer

The best cure for hypochondria is to forget about your own body and get interested in someone else's.
　　　　　—Goodman Ace

Make War, Not Love. It's Safer.
　　　　　—Lapel button worn by Henny Youngman

Never advertise what you don't have for sale.
　　　　　—Mother's advice quoted by Michele Slung

Do not have sex with people that you do not know and whose state you cannot attest to.
　　　　　—Surgeon General C. Everett Koop

When you finish having sex you should never say to your partner, "You were great," but "*We* are great."
　　　　　—R. Ron Edell

Sexist Advice

No man should marry until he has studied anatomy and dissected at least one woman.
　　　　　—Honoré de Balzac

Praise a woman's taste, and you may attack her judgment with impunity.
　　　　　—English proverb

If you don't think women are explosive, drop one.
　　　　　—Gerald F. Lieberman

Never praise a woman for having masculine traits.
　　　　　—English proverb

You may safely flatter any woman.
　　　　　—Lord Chesterfield

Therefore don't you be gentle to your wife either. Don't tell her everything you know, but tell her one thing and keep another thing hidden.
—Homer
The Odyssey

Success is feminine and like a woman; if you cringe before her, she will override you. So the way to treat her is to show her the back of your hand. Then maybe she will do the crawling.
—William Faulkner

Be to her virtues very kind;
Be to her faults a little blind.
Let all her ways be unconfin'd
And clap your padlock on her mind.
—Matthew Prior

Do not put such unlimited power into the hands of the husbands. Remember, all men would be tyrants if they could.
—Abigail Adams

Show Business

Always leave them wanting more.
—George M. Cohan

Never answer the phone on the first ring.

Never let them see you sweat.
—Axioms for Hollywood actors

Never tell the box-office man that you can't hear well or he will sell you a seat where you can't see either.
—Kin Hubbard

Advice on making crime-thriller films: Torture the heroine.
—Alfred Hitchcock, quoting the 19th-century
French dramatist Sardou

Diversify. Learn all you can about acting and singing, as well as dancing. Learn to trust and follow your own instincts. Keep working anywhere you can. And take risks—you don't move forward by staying still.
—Donna McKechnie

Re: Publicity: Never let yourself be seen in public unless they pay for it.
—David Belasco
quoted by Randolph Scott

I've never minded playing a mother. My own mother, who's 87, says: "Keep moving. Then you won't get bitter."
—Eva Marie Saint

On receiving Tony awards: I beg you to remember that acceptance speeches should be intelligent, witty, and brief. When you leave the stage, your award will be taken from you so that it can be engraved. If you take longer than 30 seconds to accept your award, it will be returned to you eventually, but your name will be misspelled.
—Alexander Cohen

On watching a play: One must let the play happen to one: one must let the mind loose to respond as it will, to receive impressions, to sense rather than know, to gather rather than immediately understand.
—Edward Albee

(See *Acting/Actors, Applause, Movie Acting*)

Sin

Use sin as it will use you; spare it not, for it will not spare you; it is your murderer, and the murderer of the world; use it, therefore, as a murderer should be used. Kill it before it kills you; and though it kill your bodies, it shall not be able to kill your souls. . . . You love not death; love not the cause of death.
—Richard Baxter

Do not blunt your sense of sin.
　　　　　　　—William Ewart Gladstone

Shun the least appearance of sin: For sometimes indifferent things are fatal in their consequences, and strike us at the rebound. He who will not keep his distance from the gulf, may be drawn in by the eddy.
　　　　　　　—George Shelley

If you sin, hide it.
　　　　　　　—Arab proverb

Make peace with man and war with your sins.
　　　　　　　—Russian proverb

You must pay for your sins. If you have already paid, please ignore this notice.
　　　　　　　—Sam Levenson

(See *Crime, Evil*)

Sincerity

Do not let your sincerity degenerate into simple-mindedness, nor your intelligence into trickery. Better be esteemed for your wisdom, than feared for your foxiness; the simple in heart are loved, even though they are cheated. Let your greatest cunning lie in covering up what looks like cunning.
　　　　　　　—Baltasar Gracián

Don't look over other people's shoulders. Look in their eyes. Don't talk *at* your children. Take their faces in your hands and talk *to* them. Don't make love to a body, make love to a person.
　　　　　　　—Leo Buscaglia

Do not let the artificial obliterate the natural . . . do not let virtue be sacrificed for fame.
　　　　　　　—Chuangtse

Let every man do according as he is disposed in his heart, not grudgingly, or of necessity.
　　　　　　　　　—Anonymous

When you are obliged to make a statement that you know in advance will cause displeasure, you must say it with every appearance of sincerity; this is the only way to make it palatable.
　　　　　　　　　—Paul De Conde

(See *Affectation, Honesty, Hypocrisy*)

Skepticism

Do not consider a thing as proof because you find it written in books; for just as a liar will deceive with his tongue, he will not be deterred from doing the same thing with his pen. They are utter fools who accept a thing as convincing proof simply because it is in writing.
　　　　　　　　　—Moses Maimonides

Distrust all those who love you extremely upon a very slight acquaintance and without any visible reason.
　　　　　　　　　—Lord Chesterfield

　　　　Never believe on faith,
　　　　see for yourself!
　　　　What you yourself don't learn
　　　　you don't know.
　　　　　　—Bertolt Brecht
　　　　　　The Mother

We have to distrust each other. It is our only defense against betrayal.
　　　　　　　　　—Tennessee Williams

To students: Your generation is subject to more information than any generation in history. Let me suggest one thing. Don't let me get away with it. Check me out, but check everybody else out. Don't just take it for granted because you read it someplace or because someone stood

up in a lecture course and told you from a lecture platform. Check it out. Don't be the sucker generation.
—Ronald Reagan

Never swallow anything whole. We live perforce by half-truths and get along fairly well as long as we do not mistake them for whole truths, but when we do mistake them, they raise the devil with us.
—Alfred North Whitehead

(See *Faith, Trust*)

Slander/Scandal

The best way to ride out scandal is to hang in, keep cool, and not protest too much. Concentrate on appearing happy, rich and fit. Men often doubt what they hear.
—Blythe Holbrooke

Whenever you deny a story that appears in the press, you reinforce your vulnerability. When you refute a libel, you give the newspaper and gossip-sheet editors license to publish your denial, but also to repeat the libel. It's counterproductive!
—Steve Hannigan

If anyone speak ill of thee, consider whether he hath truth on his side; and if so, reform thyself, that his censures may not affect thee.
—Epictetus

(See *Gossip, Rumor*)

Sleeping

No matter how big or soft or warm your bed is, you still have to get out of it.
—Grace Slick

Cultivate the habit of early rising. It is unwise to keep the head long on a level with the feet.
—Henry David Thoreau

Spill not the morning (the quintessence of the day!) in recreations.— For sleep is a recreation. Add not, therefore, sauce to sauce. . . . Pastime, like wine, is poison in the morning. It is then good husbandry to sow the head, which hath lain fallow all night, with some serious work.
—Thomas Fuller

Rid yourself of . . . "the Thomas Edison syndrome." That's the belief that people who accomplish a lot do so because they get by with little sleep.
—*Business Week*

Sleeping rules:
Go to bed and get up about the same time every day, weekends included. A regular routine keeps you in step with your biological rhythms.

We all have the capacity to fall asleep. It is built into us. If we don't sleep for a night or two, no harm will come unless we try too hard. So don't try to force sleep. If you cannot sleep, get out of bed. Do something boring. Don't watch TV.
—Earl Ubell

> Clay lies still, but blood's a rover
> Breath's a ware that will not keep.
> Up lad: when the journey's over
> There'll be time enough to sleep.
> —A. E. Housman

After a relaxing night of sleep, tense up to meet the day.
—Anonymous

Go to bed early, get up early—this is wise. Some authorities say get up with the sun; some others say get up with one thing, some with another. But a lark is really the best thing to get up with. It gives you a splendid reputation with everybody to know that you get up with the lark, and if you get the right kind of a lark, and work at him right,

you can easily train him to get up at half past nine, every time—it is no trick at all.
—Mark Twain
"Advice to Youth"

Socializing

"Steinbeck's Code for Social Survival": Never let a drunk catch your eye.
—John Steinbeck

When in the company of sensible men, we ought to be doubly cautious of talking too much, lest we lose two good things—their good opinion and our own improvement; for what we have to say we know, but what they have to say we know not.
—Charles Caleb Colton

If you want to meet new people, pick up the wrong golf ball.
—Anonymous

Carry with you into company all the gaiety and spirits, but as little of the giddiness of youth as you can. The former will charm; but the latter will often, though innocently, implacably offend.
—Lord Chesterfield

Do not carry a spirit of contradiction, for it is to be freighted with stupidity and with peevishness, and your intelligence should plot against it; though it may well be the mark of mental genius to see objection, a wrangler about everything cannot escape being marked a fool, for he makes guerrilla warfare of quiet conversation.
—Baltasar Gracián

Don't make a date for anything more than a month in advance.
—Andrew A. Rooney

Never floss with a stranger.
—Joan Rivers

Society/The World

Do not require too much of the universe; there are other demands made upon it which may conflict with yours. You are a part of a whole, and every other part will expect you to remember it. Ask too much and it shall not be given you; knock too loudly and it shall not be opened unto you; seek impatiently and you shall not find. Do not call the world names because it has other designs than yours; perhaps if you could see the entirety you would perceive, like Job, that the order of the plants is more important than your sores.

—Will Durant

I am afraid we must make the world honest before we can honestly say to our children that honesty is the best policy.

—George Bernard Shaw

If a society is to preserve stability and a degree of continuity, it must learn how to keep its adolescents from imposing their tastes, values and fantasies on everyday life.

—Eric Hoffer

We must not indulge in unfavourable views of mankind, since by doing it we make bad men believe that they are no worse than others, and we teach the good that they are good in vain.

—Walter Savage Landor

Do not let spacious plans for a new world divert your energies from saving what is left of the old.

—Sir Winston Churchill

(See *Perspective*)

Solitude

Be able to be alone. Lose not the advantage of solitude, and the society of thyself.

—Sir Thomas Browne

We should have wife, children, goods, and above all health if we can; but we must not so set our heart upon them that our happiness depends on them. We must reserve a back shop wholly our own, entirely free, wherein to establish our true liberty and our principal retreat and solitude. . . . We have a soul that can be turned upon itself; it can be its own company; it has the means to attack and to defend, to receive and to give; let us not fear that in this solitude we shall stagnate in tedious idleness,

> In solitude be to thyself a throng.
> —Michel de Montaigne

Cultivate solitude and quiet and a few sincere friends, rather than mob merriment, noise and thousands of nodding acquaintances.
> —William Powell

No man has earned the right to intellectual ambition until he has learned to lay his course by a star which he has never seen,—to dig by the divining rod for springs which he may never reach. . . . Only when you have worked alone,—when you have felt around you a black gulf of solitude more isolating than that which surrounds the dying man, and in hope and in despair have trusted to your own unshaken will,—then only will you have achieved. Thus only you gain the secret isolated joy of the thinker. . . .
> —Oliver Wendell Holmes, Jr.

(See *Loneliness*)

Soul

> Dress and undress thy soul: mark the decay
> And growth of it; if, with thy watch, that too
> Be down, then wind up both; since we shall be
> Most surely judged, make the accounts agree.
> —George Herbert

Call the world if you please "The vale of soul-making."
—John Keats

Let your soul stand cool and composed before a million universes.
—Walt Whitman

Try to keep your soul young and quivering right up to old age, and to imagine right up to the brink of death that life is only beginning. I think that is the only way to keep adding to one's talent, to one's affections, and one's inner happiness.
—George Sand

Every human being has been brought into the world according to the will of God. And God created us in such a way that every human being can either save his own soul or destroy it. Man's task in life is to save his soul. In order to save our souls, we must live according to the ways of God, and in order to live according to the ways of God, we must renounce the sensual pleasures of life; we must labor, suffer and be kind and humble.
—Leo Tolstoy

Sources of Strength

Think of a big color—who cares if people call you Rothko. Release your childhood. Release it.
—Larry Rivers and Frank O'Hara

Specialization

As you emphasize your life, you must localize and define it. The more truly and earnestly you come to do anything, the more clearly you will see that you cannot do everything. He who is truly good must be good for something. To be good for everything is to be good for nothing.
—Phillips Brooks

Never do what a specialist can do better. Discover your own specialty. Do not despair if your specialty appears to be more delicate, a lesser thing. Make up in finesse what you lose in force.
——Jean Cocteau

The sooner one tries to master a certain profession and a certain handicraft and adopt a fairly independent way of thinking and acting, and the more one keeps to strict rules, the firmer the character one will acquire, and for all that one need not become narrow-minded. It is wise to do so, for life is but short, and time passes quickly; if one is master of one thing and understands one thing well, one has at the same time insight into and understanding of so many things into the bargain. . . . One must never trust the occasion when one is without difficulties, or some care or trouble, and one must not take things too easily.
——Vincent van Gogh

Spirit

Let us keep open the connections whereby the human spirit may freely move between the arts and the sciences and thus make more of each. May we thus become better violinists, scientists, artists, writers, and above all, better human beings, by enlarging and enriching our personal needs to include each other's.
——Yehudi Menuhin

It is better to be high-spirited even though one makes more mistakes, than to be narrow-minded and all too prudent.
——Vincent van Gogh

Your prayer must be that you may have a sound mind in a sound body. Pray for a bold spirit, free from all dread of death; that reckons the closing scene of life among Nature's kindly boons.
——Juvenal

There is no greater satisfaction than standing up to your own humanity and giving confidence and courage to those who love you and will even love you more if you show a flaming, indomitable human spirit. . . . Families must not write off the person, but show confidence in their ability to carry on. Families help if they live by the attitude that all is not lost so long as the brain is ticking.
—Jacob K. Javits

(See *Courage, Daring, Fortitude, Risk, Self-Preservation, Survival*)

Sports

[To a young boxer]: Some night you'll catch a punch between the eyes and all of a sudden you'll see three guys in the ring against you. Pick out the one in the middle and hit him, because he's the one who hit you.
—Jack Dempsey

Kill the body and the head will die.
—Smokin' Joe Frazier

The way to get Johannsson is to make him miss. Then step inside.
—Joe Louis's advice to Floyd Patterson, who knocked out Johannsson

You could tell a grade school or high school student—as I tell my daughter, Theresa Ann, who's 6—"Go out and play and do something just as well as you possibly can, as well as your ability will allow, and then be satisfied with your performance, regardless of whether you won or lost." But not in professional sports, because the nature of it, the reason you're playing, is to win.
—Bill Bradley

Drive for show. But putt for dough.
—Bobby Locke

Take heed to avoid all those games and sports that are apt to take up much of thy time, or engage thy affections. He that spends all his life in sports, is like one who wears nothing but fringes, and eats nothing but sauces.

—Thomas Fuller

You know what Rogers Hornsby told me forty-five years ago? It was the best batting advice I ever got. "Get a good ball to hit." What does that mean? It means a ball that does not fool you, a ball that is not in a tough spot for you. Think of trying to hit it back up the middle. Try not to pull it every time.

—Ted Williams

Hit 'em where they ain't.

—Willie Keeler

Cardinal rule for all hitters with two strikes on them: Never trust the umpire!

—Robert Smith

How to hit home runs: I swing as hard as I can, and I try to swing right through the ball. In boxing, your fist usually stops when you hit a man, but it's possible to hit so hard that your fist doesn't stop. I try to follow through in the same way. The harder you grip the bat, the more you can swing it through the ball, and the farther the ball will go. I swing big, with everything I've got. I hit big or I miss big. I like to live as big as I can.

—George Herman ("Babe") Ruth

When the ball is over the middle of the plate, the batter is hitting it with the sweet part of the bat. When it's inside, he's hitting it with the part of the bat from the handle to the trademark; when it's outside, he's hitting it with the end of the bat. You've got to keep the ball away from the sweet part of the bat. To do that the pitcher has to move the hitter off the plate.

—Don Drysdale

Strength

Let us roll all our strength and all
Our sweetness up into one ball,
And tear our pleasures with rough strife
Through the iron gates of life.
　　　　—Andrew Marvell

Only be thou strong, and very courageous. . . . then thou shalt make
thy way prosperous, and then thou shalt have good success.
　　　　—Old Testament
　　　　Joshua 1:7–8

Luck and strength go together. When you get lucky, you have to have
the strength to follow through. You also have to have the strength to
wait for the luck.
　　　　—Mario Puzo

When strong, be merciful, if you would have the respect, not the fear,
of your neighbors.
　　　　—Chilon, 6th century B.C.

Place a guard over your strong points! Thrift may run into niggardli-
ness, generosity into prodigality or shiftlessness. Gentleness may become pusillanimity, tact become insincerity, power become
oppression. Characters need sentries at their points of weakness, true
enough, but often the points of greatest strength, are, paradoxically,
really points of weakness.
　　　　—Constance M. Wishaw

Give spiritual strength to people and they will give genuine affection
to you.
　　　　—Anonymous

Stress

You must always remember that irritations influence your mind and your mind influences your muscles. All the irritations of daily life subject your mind and nerves and then your muscles, to repeated tension. You can work out most of this tension with your exercise program, but if you are smart, you will try to avoid most of the tension to begin with.
> —Dr. Leon Root

Learn not to sweat the small stuff.
> —Dr. Kenneth Greenspan

The rule is, jam tomorrow and jam yesterday—but never jam today.
> —Lewis Carroll

There are ways we can all stay well during stress. Here are some of the most important: *Experience your feelings. . . . Talk out bad feelings. . . . Avoid making too many changes at once. . . . Learn how to take it easy. . . . Turn to your friends. . . . Exercise adequately. . . . Decide to live.* When Dr. Victor Frankl studied survivors of Nazi concentration camps to learn why they had lived while others had not, he found that the difference was in their having strong reasons for wishing to live. Perhaps what is most important in avoiding stress-related disease is to have enough reason for wanting to stay healthy.
> —Catherine Houck

Regular exercise is a good way to reduce stress. In some cases doctors prescribe medications to keep stress down to tolerable levels. But the experts agree that the best stress medicine is preventive—avoiding high stress situations when you can, thinking about upcoming events optimistically without being too optimistic, and making them less stressful through decisive planning. The holiday season is an ideal time to try out the technique.
> —Bradley Hitchings
> *Business Week*

(See *Anxiety, Depression, Despair, Disappointment, Melancholy/
Blues, Worry*)

Style

When I was twelve, people told me that if I want to be successful, I must change my grip, give up this two-handed backhand. I said I would change, but I knew I wouldn't. The truth is I am a very stubborn person. I was hitting the ball and it felt good to me, so I said to myself, why change? It is important to find your own personality in the game, your own style. You have to find it, no one else can find it for you.
—Bjorn Borg

Strunk and White have pointed out one element of style which may very well be common among all writers, and which I suspect to be associated with the intoxication and sound of one's own words. They express it in the form of a brief injunction: "Kill your darlings." . . . The point is simple enough. Words, sentences, paragraphs that call much attention to themselves are not doing the job they are intended to do. While the reader is paying them due reverence, he is likely to ignore the message they were meant to convey.
—Stephen White

I envision a style: a style that would be beautiful, that someone will invent some day, ten years or ten centuries from now, one that would be rhythmic as verse, precise as the language of the sciences, undulant, deep-voiced as a cello, tipped with flame: a style that would pierce your idea like a dagger, and on which your thought would sail easily ahead over a smooth surface, like a skiff before a good tail wind. Prose was born yesterday: keep that in mind.
—Gustave Flaubert

Yeats once wrote that man is forced to choose between perfecting his life or his work. Yeats was wrong. It is only a matter of which comes first—your life or your work. If you are a stylist, the choice is as easy as it is obvious. Your life comes first. Then you inject it into your work. You bring what you are to what you do. Your job should bear the imprint of your personality, not vice versa.
—Quentin Crisp and Donald Carroll

Suffering

To scale great heights, we must come out of the lowermost depths.
The way to heaven is through hell.
>—Herman Melville

Don't look forward to the day when you stop suffering. Because when
it comes, you'll *know* you are dead.
>—Tennessee Williams

Man was born to live, to suffer, and to die, and what befalls him is a
tragic lot. There is no denying this in the final end. *But we must,
dear Fox, deny it all along the way.*
>—Thomas Wolfe
>Last letter to Fox in
>*You Can't Go Home Again*

I have always believed that God never gives a cross to bear larger than
we can carry. No matter what, he wants us to be happy, not sad. Birds
sing after a storm. Why shouldn't we?
>—Rose Kennedy

If we must suffer, let us suffer nobly.
>—Victor Hugo

You may regret calamities if you can thereby help the sufferer, but if
you cannot, mind your own business.
>—Ralph Waldo Emerson

Survival

It is too late to save yesterday's victims. . . . But it is not too late to
save ourselves. The next time we truly hear the word Holocaust, it

will be preceded by the word atomic. We had better learn from whom we can, while we can.
　　　　　—Elie Wiesel

If one comes to kill you, make haste and kill him first.
　　　　　—The Talmud
　　　　　　　quoted by George Shultz, citing the
　　　　　　　Talmud as supporting the "universal law of
　　　　　　　self-defense," in a speech against terrorism

Put fear out of your heart. This nation will survive, this state will prosper, the orderly business of life will go forward if only men can speak in whatever way given them to utter what their hearts hold— by voice, by posted card, by letters or by press. Reason never has failed them. Only force and oppression have made the wrecks in the world.
　　　　　—William Allen White

Our tragedy today is a general and universal physical fear so long sustained by now that we can even bear it. There are no longer problems of the spirit. There is only the question: When will I be blown up? . . . [A young man or woman] must teach himself that the basest of all things is to be afraid; and, teaching himself that, forget it forever, leaving no room in his workshop for anything but the old verities and truths of the heart, the old universal truths lacking which any story is ephemeral and doomed—love and honor and pity and pride and compassion and sacrifice. Until he does so, he labors under a curse. . . .
　　　　　—William Faulkner
　　　　　Stockholm Address
　　　　　Accepting Nobel Prize

(See *Courage, Daring, Self-Preservation, Spirit*)

Suspicion

Convince if you can by your acts
Him that has suspicion of thee.
　　　　　—Joaquin Setanti

It was a maxim with Foxey—our revered father, gentlemen—"Always suspect everybody."
—Charles Dickens

Always suspect a man who affects great softness of manner, an unruffled evenness of temper, and an enunciation studied, slow, and deliberate. These things are all unnatural, and bespeak a degree of mental discipline into which he that has no purpose of craft or design to answer cannot submit to drill himself. The most successful knaves are usually of this description, as smooth as razors dipped in oil, and as sharp. They affect the innocence of the dove, which they have not, in order to hide the cunning of the serpent, which they have.
—Charles Caleb Colton

Suspect everybody, and keep your suspicions to yourself.
—Charles Simmons

We learn from Othello this very useful moral, not to make an unequal match; in the second place, we learn not to yield too readily to suspicion.
—Samuel Johnson

Sympathy

When you see a man in distress, recognize him as a fellow man.
—Seneca

Being unwanted, unloved, uncared for, forgotten by everybody, I think that is a much greater hunger, a much greater poverty than the person who has nothing to eat. . . . We must find each other.
—Mother Teresa

Help the man who is down today
Give him a lift in his sorrow

Life has a very strange way
No one knows what may happen tomorrow.
—Doggerel favored by H. Ross Perot

If thou art something, bring thy soul and interchange it with mine.
—Friedrich von Schiller

Do not believe that he who seeks to comfort you lives untroubled among the simple and quiet words that sometimes do you good. His life has much difficulty and sadness and remains far behind yours. Were it otherwise he would never have been able to find those words.
—Rainer Maria Rilke

We should spread joy, but cut down sadness as much as we can. He who asks for pity without reason is a man not to be pitied when there is reason. . . . By continually putting on a pitiful act, we become pitiable to no one.
—Michel de Montaigne

(See *Charity, Compassion, Generosity, Kindness*)

T

Tact

The nearer you come in relation with a person, the more necessary do tact and courtesy become.
— Oliver Wendell Holmes

If you can't be kind, at least be vague.
— Judith Martin
"Miss Manners"

Before you are frank with another, ask yourself: *why?* Is it to diminish the other, to make yourself feel better at his expense? The ethical question is to ask: will this foster the relationship? There is always a way to be honest without being brutal.
— Arthur Dobrin

A never-failing way to get rid of a fellow is to tell him something for his own good.
— Kin Hubbard

Never tell a lie, but the truth you don't have to tell.
— George Safir

When you shoot an arrow of truth, dip its point in honey.
— Arab proverb

Here is my favorite story about tact, as told by John Steinbeck.

Two men were meeting in a bar when the subject of Green Bay, Wisconsin, came up. The first man said, "it's a real nice place." The second responded, "What's nice about it? Only things ever come out of Green Bay are the Packers and ugly whores." "Now, wait just one minute, you sonofabitch," said the first man. "My wife is from Green Bay." "Oh," the other replied. "She is? What position does she play?"
— Dr. Wayne W. Dyer

Keep the other person's well being in mind when you feel an attack of soul-purging truth coming on.
— Betty White

(See *Diplomacy, Government, Politics*)

Talent

"Ethel," Gershwin asked her during intermission, "do you know what you're doing?" "No," she said. "Well," he replied, "never go near a singing teacher."
— George Gershwin to Ethel Merman
Quoted by Edward Rothstein

When I first looked at Yaz [Carl Yastrzemski] as a rookie, it was obvious that he had so much talent that I told him what Lefty O'Doul told me—"Don't change a thing."
— Ted Williams

To make good you must have some talent other than determination.
— William Feather

Let us not overstrain our talents, lest we do nothing gracefully; a clown whatever he may do, will never pass for a gentleman.
— Jean de La Fontaine

You know Lenin's old line, "Walk at the head of the parade but not too far ahead," because, you know, you'll go straight and they'll turn the corner.

—Artie Shaw

Talking

Let not your tongue say what your head may pay for.
—Italian proverb

Never fail to know that if you are doing all the talking, you are boring somebody.

—Helen Gurley Brown

For one word a man is often deemed to be wise, and for one word he is often deemed to be foolish. We should be careful indeed of what we say.

—Confucius

Put your mind in gear before you put your tongue in action.
—Sydney H. Schanberg's teacher

Never talk for more than half a minute without pausing and giving others an opportunity to strike in.

—Sydney Smith

Be straightforward in the way you dodge issues.
—Anonymous

(See *Conversation*)

Television

I maintain that there is now more good television available than there is time to watch. But, if you looked at it all, you'd be a passive spectator

of life, not a participant . . . the trick is to be selective. Choose carefully from among what is available. Good television does what a good
book does—spurs the imagination and creates images in your mind
that compel you, the individual, to cross boundaries that have psychological "no trespassing" signs on them. That happens when you
have good television.
—Bill Moyers

On success in TV: It's in the preparation—in those dreary pedestrian
virtues they taught you in seventh grade and you didn't believe. It's
making the extra call and caring a lot.
—Diane Sawyer

Don't be quick to want to get on the air and anchor. Learn to write.
If you write well, you can do anything in this business.
—Connie Chung

On TV entertaining: If you want to last, you have to grow. That little
screen is merciless and if you aren't constantly more interesting and
intriguing, they—the public—will drop you, ruthlessly.
—Arthur Godfrey

Look . . . ours is a business of appearances, and it's terribly important
to appear to be self-confident. The minute you give evidence of doubt,
people are going to eat you alive.
—Ted Koppel

On breaking into television: Get a job doing anything, and do it as
well as you possibly can. I have very little patience with young people
who say they want to write, direct, or act but who complain, "It's a
closed world." Television isn't just three networks; it's thousands of
stations across the country. In fact, working at a station in your hometown is a very lucrative and happy way to spend your life—beats
running the local lumber business, which is what my father did for a
living.
—Grant Tinker

(See *Communications, Journalism, Media, Reporting*)

Thanksgiving

Let never day nor night unhallowed pass,
But still remember what the Lord hath done.
—King Henry in Shakespeare's
King Henry VI, Part II

Be satisfied, and pleased with what thou art,
Act cheerfully and well th' allotted part;
Enjoy the present hour, be thankful for the past,
And neither fear, nor wish, th' approaches of the last.
—Martial

Stand up, on this Thanksgiving Day, stand upon your feet. Believe in man! Soberly and with clear eyes, believe in your own time and place.
—Phillips Brooks

Thoroughness

Whatever you do, do it to the purpose; do it thoroughly, not superficially. Go to the bottom of things. Any thing half done, or half known, is, in my mind, neither done nor known at all. Nay, worse, for it often misleads.
—Lord Chesterfield

Never let well enough alone. A stockbroker follows the advice that her father gave her the day she started her first job. "Make one more call, my daddy told me," she said. "And I always do. I never leave my office at night without making one more call, doing one more thing. . . . It pays off."
—Dr. Joyce Brothers

Do not hover always on the surface of things, nor take up suddenly, with mere appearances; but penetrate into the depth of matters, as far

as your time and circumstances allow, especially in those things which relate to your own profession.
—Isaac Watts

If thou hast commenced a good action, leave it not incomplete.
—The Talmud

It is not right to know only one thing—one gets stultified by that; one should not rest before one knows the opposite too.
—Vincent van Gogh

Be thorough in all you do; and remember that although ignorance often may be innocent, pretension is always despicable.
—William Ewart Gladstone

Thought

Give yourself more to thinking than to reading, for reading without thinking will make you vain, rather than knowing. . . . Learn to think steadily, closely, and acutely, upon every subject to which your instructors direct your attention.
—Charles Simmons

Think—or be damned!
—Bryan Penton

Think for yourself. Whatever is happening at the moment, try to think for yourself.
—Jean Riboud

Do not craze yourself with thinking, but go about your business anywhere. Life is not intellectual and critical, but sturdy.
—Ralph Waldo Emerson

To think is not enough; you must think of something.
—Jules Renard

As long as you're going to be thinking anyway, think big.
—Donald Trump

Time

Think not thy time short in this world, since the world itself is not long. The created world is but a small parenthesis in eternity and a short interposition, for a time, between such a state of duration as was before it and may be after it.
—Sir Thomas Browne

William Saroyan wrote a great play on this theme,—that purity of heart is the one success worth having. "In the time of your life—live." That time is short and it doesn't return again. It is slipping away while I write this and while you read it, and the monosyllable of the clock is loss, loss, loss unless you devote your heart to its opposition.
—Tennessee Williams

Do not manage as if you had ten thousand years before you. Look you, death stands at your elbow; make the most of your minute, and be good for something while it is in your power.
—Charles Palmer

> The span of life is waning fast;
> Beware, unthinking youth, beware!
> Thy soul's *eternity* depends
> Upon the record *moments* bear!
> —Eliza Cook

If you want to kill time, why not try working it to death.
—Sam Levenson

The great rule of moral conduct is, next to God, to respect Time.
—Johann Kaspar Lavater

Tolerance

Be of them that are persecuted, not of them that persecute.
—The Talmud

Have I done a neighborly act? I am therefore benefited. Let this be always ready to your mind, and never stop. . . . Men have come into the world for the sake of one another. Either instruct them, then, or bear with them. . . . Whoever does wrong, wrongs himself; whoever does injustice, does it to himself, making himself evil.
—Marcus Aurelius

Truth resides in every human heart, and one has to search for it there, and to be guided by truth as one sees it. But no one has a right to coerce others to act according to his own view of truth.
—Mohandas K. Gandhi

Everything has two handles, by one of which it ought to be carried and by the other not. If your brother wrongs you, do not lay hold of the matter by the handle of the wrong that he is doing, because this is the handle by which the matter ought to be carried; but rather by the other handle—that he is your brother, that you were brought up together, and then you will be laying hold of the matter by the handle by which it ought to be carried.
—Epictetus

(See *Opinion, Prejudice*)

Travel

On my first trip abroad, years ago, a wise Englishman gave me a few rules, to my life-long profit. "In a foreign restaurant," he said, "never ask for a dish which you can get anywhere at home." What's the use of travel if you avoid new experiences? Learn the cuisine of the country. Wherever you eat, ask for the spécialité de la maison, the dish on

which that restaurant prides itself. In fact, when you're in a new land never order the meal, least of all the wine; ask the waiter what he would recommend. Such a request is a great compliment, as from one connoisseur to another.
—John Erskine

Never eat Chinese food in Oklahoma.
—Bryan Miller

If you want to know a man, travel with him.
—English proverb

Before he sets out, the traveller must possess fixed interests and faculties, to be served by travel. If he drifted aimlessly from country to country he would not travel but only wander, ramble or tramp. . . . He must not go nosing about like a pedlar for profit or like an emigrant for a vacant lot. Everywhere he should show the discretion and maintain the dignity of a guest. Everywhere he should remain a stranger no matter how benevolent, and a critic no matter how appreciative.
—George Santayana

Drink lots of plain fluids on the plane, since dehydration (the atmosphere aloft can be as dry as a terrestrial desert) aggravates the distress of jet lag. Caffeine, sweetened soft drinks and alcohol compound the problem because they are dehydrating. Avoid smoking and eating big meals on the plane; these add to the stress on the body. As often as possible, move around while on the plane. Try some relaxing isometric exercises while seated.
—Jane E. Brody

Best way to combat traveler's diarrhea: If you can't peel it, cook it or boil it, forget it.
—Peace Corps saying (attributed)

Don't wear perfume in areas where malaria is common because the mosquitoes that transmit the disease are attracted by the fragrance.

Watch out for mixed drinks on return flights—they may contain ice cubes made from contaminated water obtained before the plane took off from a country with poor sanitation.
—Dr. Martin Gordon

On packing: Lay out all your clothes and all your money. Then, take half the clothes and twice the money.
—Susan Butler Anderson

Trifles

Think naught a trifle, though it small appear;
Sands make the mountain, moments make the year,
And trifles, life. Your care to trifles give,
Else you may die ere you have learned to live.
—Edward Young

Only with prudence and foresight can we achieve great ends. It is but a step from victory to defeat. I have learned that, in the last resort, everything invariably turns upon a trifle.
—Napoleon I

Fall not out with a friend for a trifle.
—American proverb

Never dispute upon mere trifles, things that are utterly useless to be known, under a vain pretense of sharpening the wit.
—Isaac Watts

You should treat all disasters as if they were trivialities but never treat a triviality as if it were a disaster.
—Quentin Crisp

(See *Pettiness*)

Trust

Trust in Allah, but tie up your camel.
—Turkish proverb

In God we trust
All others pay cash.
—Sign used in retail stores
during the Depression

Never trust a sentimentalist. They are all alike, pretenders to virtue,
at heart selfish frauds and sensualists.
—J. B. Yeats in letter to his son,
William Butler Yeats

Trust not those cunning waters of his eyes,
For villainy is not without such rheum;
And he, long traded in it, makes it seem
Like rivers of remorse and innocency.
—The Earl of Salisbury in
Shakespeare's *King John*

Just trust yourself, then you will know how to live.
—Johann Wolfgang von Goethe

Never trust a woman who mentions her virtue.
—French proverb

(See *Faith, God, Skepticism*)

Truth

Accustom your children to a strict attention to Truth, even in the most
minute particulars. If a thing happened at one window, and they,
when relating it, say that it happened at another, do not let it pass,
but instantly check them: you do not know where deviations from
Truth will end.
—Samuel Johnson

If you add to the truth, you subtract from it.
　　　　　—The Talmud

Though all the winds of doctrine were let loose to play upon the earth,
so Truth be in the field, we do ingloriously, by licensing and prohib-
iting, to misdoubt her strength. Let her and Falsehood grapple: who
ever knew Truth put to the worse in a free and open encounter?
　　　　　—John Milton

As best you can, stare the truth in the face.
　　　　　—Richard von Weizsäcker
　　　　　President of Federal Republic
　　　　　of Germany

Don't be afraid of being out of tune with your environment. The idea
which underlies this university—any university—is greater than any
of its physical manifestations; its classrooms, its laboratories, its clubs,
its athletic plant, even the particular groups of faculty and students
who make up its human element as of any given time. What is this
idea? It is that the highest condition of man in this mysterious universe
is the freedom of the spirit. And it is only truth that can set the spirit
free.

Your days are short here; this is the last of your springs. And now in
the serenity and quiet of this lovely place, touch the depths of truth,
feel the hem of heaven. You will go away with old, good friends.
Don't forget when you leave why you came.
　　　　　—Adlai E. Stevenson
　　　　　Speech at Princeton

Believe those who are seeking the truth; doubt those who find it.
　　　　　—André Gide

(See *Candor, Honesty, Illusion*)

T-Shirt Advice

Get even. Live long enough to be a problem to your kids.

Don't start with me. You know how I get.

Life is a bitch. Then you die. Have a nice day.
                    —T-Shirt worn by Willie Nelson

Don't tell me what kind of day to have.

If you don't like the way I drive, get off the sidewalk.

> If you love someone, set them free.
> If they don't come back
> Hunt them down and shoot them.

Don't drink and drive. You may hit a bump and spill your drink.

If all else fails, lower your standards.
                    —Words stitched on a pillow

Trust me, I'm a doctor.

Support your local bloodhound. Get lost.

U

Understanding

I know nothing—I have read nothing—and I mean to follow Solomon's directions, "Get learning—get understanding."
—John Keats

Do everything you can to understand the other person's point of view—it takes the wind out of the sails of a blustering Manipulator. If you can demonstrate that you're trying to understand their needs, eventually they will run down and you will be able to assert your point of view.
—Robert E. Decker

Do naught thou dost not understand.
—Pythagoras

(See *Education, Knowledge, Learning, Wisdom*)

Uprightness

Recommend thy self to the Divine Providence, and be sure never to depart from uprightness of intention; I mean, have still a firm purpose and design to be thoroughly inform'd in all the business that shall come before thee, and act upon just grounds, for heaven always favours good desires.

—Miguel de Cervantes

(See *Conscience, Goodness, Honor, Morality, Virtue*)

V

Virtue

It is not enough merely to possess virtue, as if it were an art; it should be practiced.
> —Marcus Tullius Cicero

Sell not virtue to purchase wealth.
> —English proverb

Search others for their virtues, thyself for thy vices.
> —English proverb

(See *Conscience, Goodness, Honor, Morality*)

Vision

The task of the leader is to get his people from where they are to where they have not been. The public does not fully understand the world into which it is going. Leaders must invoke an alchemy of great vision. Those leaders who do not are ultimately judged failures, even though they may be popular at the moment.
> —Henry Kissinger

You have to set double goals, but you still have to have a very lofty vision. You need a well-articulated vision that people can follow.
        —Stephen P. Jobs

I see that my steadfast *desire* was alone responsible for whatever progress or mastery I have made. The reality is always there, and is preceded by vision. And if one keeps looking steadily the vision crystallizes into fact or deed. . . . One should not be worrying about the degree of "success" obtained by each and every effort, but only concentrate on maintaining the vision, keep it pure and steady.
        —Henry Miller

We must not think our world is the only one. There are worlds outside our experience. "Call that a sunset?" said the lady to Turner as she stood before the artist's picture. "I never saw a sunset like that." "No, madam," said Turner. "Don't you wish you had?" Perhaps your world and mine is only mean because we are near-sighted. Perhaps we miss the vision not because the vision is not there, but because we darken the window.
        —Anonymous, under the pseudonym
        "Alpha of the Plough"

(See *Beliefs, Dreams, Ideals, Principles*)

Visiting

To the house of a friend if you're pleased to retire,
You must all things admit, you must all things admire;
You must pay with observance the price of your treat,
You must eat what is praised, and must praise what you eat.
        —George Crabbe

If you want to become the perfect guest, then try to make your host feel at home.
        —W. A. ("Dub") Nance

Withdraw thy foot from thy neighbour's house; lest he be weary of thee, and so hate thee.
—Old Testament
Proverbs 25:17

Visits should be short, like a winter's day.
Lest you're too troublesome, hasten away.
—Benjamin Franklin

Don't go to visit your friend in the hour of his disgrace.
—Simeon Ben Eleazer

(See *Entertaining, Hospitality*)

Vulnerability

He who has a head of butter must not come near the oven.
—Dutch proverb

Don't make yourself a mouse or the cat will eat you.
—A. B. Cheales

Conceal your weakness from your child, lest he despise your instruction, and be hardened in his folly; for he who sees your folly, will scarce be ashamed of his own.
—George Shelley

To grow, a lobster must shed its old shell numerous times. Each shedding renders the creature totally defenseless until the new shell forms. . . . When risk becomes frightening, think of the lobster: vulnerability is often the price of growth. "Be fearless then, be confident, for go where you will, the Lord your God is with you." (Joshua 1:9)
—Richard Armstrong

Do not show your wounded finger, for everything will knock up against it.
—Baltasar Gracián

W

Warfare

To fight out a war, you must believe something and want something with all your might. More than that, you must be willing to commit yourself to a course, perhaps a long and hard one, without being able to foresee exactly where you will come out. All that is required of you is that you should go somewhither as hard as ever you can. The rest belongs to fate.
> —Oliver Wendell Holmes, Jr.

Don't get small units caught in between the forces of history.
> —General John W. Vesey, Jr.

The United States has broken the second rule of war. That is, don't go fighting with your land army on the mainland of Asia. Rule number one is, don't march on Moscow. I developed these two rules myself.
> —Viscount Montgomery of Alamein
> (Sir Bernard Law)

Rely not on the likelihood of the enemy's not coming, but on our own readiness to receive him; not on the chance of his not attacking, but rather on the fact that we have made our position unassailable.

Keep your plans dark and impenetrable as night and when you move, fall like a thunderbolt.

What is of supreme importance in war is to attack the enemy's strategy. To win 100 victories in 100 battles is not the acme of skill. To subdue

the enemy without fighting is the acme of skill. . . . All warfare is based on deception. Therefore, when capable, feign incapacity; when active, inactivity. When near, make it appear that you are far away; when far away, that you are near. . . . Those skilled in war subdue the enemy's army without a battle.
—Sun Tzu, 300 B.C.

Thunder on! Stride on! Democracy. Strike
with vengeful stroke!
—Walt Whitman

Establish the eternal truth that acquiescence under insult is not the way to escape war.
—Thomas Jefferson

(See *Peace, Force, Military, Preparedness—Military*)

Will

Be master of your will and a slave to your conscience.
—Lieb Lazerow

Remember this lesson. History does not teach fatalism. There are moments when the will of a handful of free men breaks through determinism and opens up new roads. People get the history they deserve.
—Charles de Gaulle

If we cannot do what we will, we must will what we can.
—Yiddish proverb

No mind should submit their mind to another mind: He that complies against his will is of his own opinion still—that's *my* motto. I won't be brainwashed.
—M. Spark

Don't let your will roar when your power only whispers.
—Thomas Fuller

Wisdom

Dare to be wise! Energy of spirit is needed to overcome the obstacles which indolence of nature as well as cowardice of heart oppose to our instruction.
—Friedrich von Schiller

Cultivate the habit of attention and try to gain opportunities to hear wise men and women talk. Indifference and inattention are the two most dangerous monsters that you ever meet. Interest and attention will insure to you an education.
—Robert A. Millikan

Mingle a little folly with your wisdom; a little nonsense now and then is pleasant.
—Horace

[King] Solomon has made it clear that the need for preliminary studies is a necessity and that it is impossible to attain true wisdom except after having been trained. For he says: *If the iron be blunt, and he do not whet the edge, then must he put to more strength; but even more preparation is needed for wisdom.* [Ecclesiastes 10:10] And he also says: Hear counsel and receive instruction that thou mayest be wise in thy latter end. [Proverbs 19:20].
—Moses Maimonides

Wisdom is the principal thing; therefore get wisdom; and with all thy getting get understanding.
—Old Testament
Proverbs 4:7

You must not expect old heads upon young shoulders.
—English proverb

(See *Education, Knowledge, Learning, Understanding*)

Women (Advice to Men About Women)

If thou wouldst please the ladies, thou must endeavor to make them pleased with themselves.
—Thomas Fuller

Be intellectual with pretty women, frivolous with intellectual women, serious with young girls, and flippant with old ladies.
—Gelett Burgess

Be careful not to make a woman weep. God counts her tears.
—The Talmud

Never paw a woman. A woman does not like to be pawed. She likes to be—ah, liked.
—Porfirio Rubirosa

What I learned constructive about women is that no matter how old they get, always think of them the way they were on the best day they ever had.
—Ernest Hemingway

Advice to young men: Talk to women, talk to women as much as you can. This is the best school. This is the way to gain fluency, because you need not care what you say, and had better not be sensible. They, too, will rally you on many points, and as they are women you will not be offended. Nothing is of so much importance and of so much use to a young man entering life as to be well criticized by women.
—Benjamin Disraeli

Prince Vasili seized Pierre's hand and said to Anna Pavlovna: "Educate this bear for me. He has been staying with me a whole month and

this is the first time I have seen him in society. Nothing is so necessary for a young man as the society of clever women."
—Leo Tolstoy

Women's Rights

Never forget that your girl or your wife is every damn bit as much a person as you are. . . . She thinks the world revolves around her just as you do around yourself, just as anyone does. She has a vote in life as well as in politics, she eats and sleeps and suffers and loves and thinks (regardless of how badly you or I may think she thinks) like you and me. She was born, she lives, she's got to die; and for you to attempt to dominate her, to pinch her personality, is some kind of sin.
—John O'Hara to his younger brother,
Thomas

What a woman should demand of a man in courtship, or after it, is first—respect for her as she is a woman; and next to that—to be respected by him above all other women. Let her first lesson be . . . *reverence for her sex.*
—Charles Lamb

We have come a long way, but we are not there yet. . . . The missionary work must continue. As union leader Lane Kirkland put it, "The only way to convert the heathen is to travel into the jungle." . . . Don't let yourself be pegged as a staff person, for staff people are perceived as paper pushers and rarely rise to top management jobs. . . . Try to develop . . . a "special sensing system" that helps you anticipate problems in time to solve them before they erupt publicly.
—Carole Howard

Let woman then go on—not asking as favour, but claiming as right, the removal of all the hindrances to her elevation in the scale of being—

let her receive encouragement for the proper cultivation of all her powers, so that she may enter profitably into the active business of life.

—Lucretia Mott, 1850

Wooing

Do proper homage to thine idol's eyes,
But not too humbly, or she will despise
Thee and thy suit though told in moving tropes;
Disguise even tenderness, if thou art wise.
—Lord Byron

He that would the daughter win
Must with the mother first begin.
—English saying

Brevity may be the soul of wit, but not when someone's saying "I love you." When someone's saying "I love you," he always ought to give a lot of details: Like, Why does he love you? And, How much does he love you? And, When and where did he first begin to love you? Favorable comparisons with all the other women he ever loved are also welcome. And even though he insists it would take forever to count the ways in which he loves you, let him start counting.
—Judith Viorst

An elderly man should not fall in love. He should walk into it. He should survey the ground carefully as Mr. Barkis did [in Charles Dickens' *David Copperfield*]. That admirable man took the business of falling in love seriously:

" 'So she makes,' said Mr. Barkis, after a long interval of reflection, 'all the apple parsties, and does all the cooking, do she?'
"I replied that such was the fact.
" 'Well, I'll tell you what,' said Mr. Barkis. 'P'raps you might be writin' to her?'

" 'I shall certainly write to her,' I rejoined.

" 'Ah!' he said, slowly turning his eyes towards me. 'Well! if you was writin' to her, p'raps you'd recollect to say that Barkis was willin', would you?' "

This is a model of caution in the art of middle-age love-making.
—Anonymous, under the pen name of
"Alpha of the Plough"

(See *Couples, Courtship, Marriage—Contemplation of, Relationships*)

Words

Whatever the thing you wish to say, there is but one word to express it, but one verb to give it movement, but one adjective to qualify it; you must seek until you find this noun, this verb, this adjective. . . . When you pass a grocer sitting in his doorway, a porter smoking a pipe, or a cab stand, show me that grocer and that porter . . . in such a way that I could never mistake them for any other grocer or porter, and by a single word give me to understand wherein the cab horse differs from fifty others before or behind it.
—Gustave Flaubert

Use the active rather than the passive voice. Avoid wordiness. Keep sentences lean and short. Do not use nouns or adjectives as verbs, such as *to impact, to interface, it obsoletes*. Use the precise word or phrase: *datum* (singular), *data* (plural); *think* is mental, *feel* is physical or emotional (to think thoughts; feel feelings).
—Malcolm Baldrige

In ordinary composition, use orthodox spelling. Do not write *nite* for *night, thru* for *through, pleez* for *please*, unless you plan to introduce a complete system of simplified spelling and are prepared to take the consequences.

Avoid the elaborate, the pretentious, the coy and the cute. . . . Never call a stomach a tummy without good reason.
—William Strunk, Jr., and E. B. White

(See *Language/Writing*)

Work Psychology

Never say you don't know—nod wisely, leave calmly, then run like hell to find the nearest expert.
—S. M. Oddo

Who would wish to be valued must make himself scarce.
—Thomas Lynch

In seeking to save another, beware of drowning yourself.
—Sir Francis Osborne to his son, 1646

Avoid victories over superiors.
—Baltasar Gracián

From a bad paymaster get what you can.
—English proverb

Make yourself all honey and the flies will devour you.
—English proverb

Beware of him who has nothing to lose.
—Italian proverb

Don't depend on a big wheel to do you a good turn.
—Joan I. Welsh

Don't let your superiors know you are better than they are.
—Arthur Bloch

Affect rather to be useful than popular.
                    —Anonymous

Be aware, a favorite has no friend.
                    —English proverb

Next to knowing when to seize an opportunity, the most important
thing in life is to know when to forego an advantage.
                    —Benjamin Disraeli

Look for a tough wedge for a tough log.
                    —Publilius Syrus

Most people have ears, but few have judgment; tickle those ears, and,
depend upon it, you will catch their judgments, such as they are.
                    —Lord Chesterfield

It is sometimes necessary to play the fool to avoid being deceived by
clever men.
                    —François de La Rochefoucauld

Be careful you don't get yourself into an unneeded adversary relationship.
                    —Mortimer Feinberg

Never make two bites of a cherry. If a job can be done in one short
spell of work, don't break off and come back to it later.
                    —Ronald Rideout and Clifford Whitting

Don't watch the clock; do what it does. Keep going.
                    —Sam Levenson

Do your job and demand your compensation—but in that order.
                    —Cary Grant
                    quoted by David Mahoney

Worry

This is the chief thing: Be not perturbed: for all things are according to the nature of the universal.
> —Marcus Aurelius

If only the people who worry about their liabilities would think about the riches they do possess, they would stop worrying. Would you sell both your eyes for a million dollars . . . or your two legs . . . or your hands . . . or your hearing? Add up what you do have, and you'll find that you won't sell them for all the gold in the world. The best things in life are yours, if you can appreciate yourself. That's the way to stop worrying—and start living!
> —Dale Carnegie
> in an interview with Leonard Safir

I highly recommend worrying. It is much more effective than dieting.
> —William Powell

I am reminded of the advice of my neighbor. "Never worry about your heart till it stops beating."
> —E. B. White

How to worry:

IF YOU DON'T KNOW HOW TO WORRY:
1. Overeat. 2. Get into an uncomfortable position near the telephone.

THEN THINK ABOUT:
1. The rat race. 2. Getting fat and/or old. 3. Where did it all go?

IF YOU DO NOT LIKE TO WORRY ALONE:
1. Go to a doctor (any doctor) and sit in his waiting room. 2. Ask people about their problems and then switch the conversation to yours.
> —Robert Benton and Harvey Schmidt

Don't hurry, don't worry. You're only here for a short visit. So be sure to stop and smell the flowers.
　　　　　　　—Walter Hagen

(See *Anxiety, Depression, Despair, Disappointment, Melancholy/ Blues*)

Writing

To overcome writer's block, get something—anything—down on paper. Don't wait for perfection to issue forth. Since the key to good lawyerly writing is re-writing, give yourself something to edit.
　　　　　　　—James C. Freund

The only way to find out if you can write is to set aside a certain period every day and *try*. Save enough money to give yourself six months to be a full-time writer. Work every day and the pages will pile up.
　　　　　　　—Judith Krantz

It is wise to write on many subjects, to try many themes, that so you may find the right and inspiring one. You must try a thousand themes before you find the right one, as nature makes a thousand acorns to get one oak.
　　　　　　　—Henry David Thoreau

Before employing a fine phrase, make a place for it.

Do not let your phrase hamper your thought; it should be to it like a body that does not cramp the soul. Nothing too exact!—this is the great rule of grace, in literature as well as conduct.

In writing, we ought to fancy ourselves in the presence of the lettered few; but it is not to them that we should speak.
　　　　　　　—Joseph Joubert

Write what you like; there is no other rule.
　　　　　　　—O. Henry

To be accurate, write; to remember, write; to know thine own mind, write.
      —Martin Farquhar Tupper

Find out what gave you the emotion, what the action was that gave you the excitement. Then write it down making it so clear that . . . it can become a part of the experience of the person who reads it.
      —Ernest Hemingway

Everybody is different—even writers. You have to learn how to use your energy and not squander it. In the writing process, the more a story cooks, the better. The brain works for you even when you are at rest. I find dreams particularly useful. . . . You can only learn to be a better writer by actually writing. I don't know much about creative writing programs. But they're not telling the truth if they don't teach, one, that writing is hard work, and, two, that you have to give up a great deal of life, your *personal* life, to be a writer.
      —Doris Lessing

Write regularly, day in and day out, at whatever times of day you find that you write best. Don't wait till you feel that you are in the mood.
      —Arnold J. Toynbee

The artist ought not to judge his characters or what they say, but be only an unbiased witness. . . . My business is to be talented, that is, to be able to distinguish important testimony from trivia, to illuminate the figures and speak their language. . . . When I write, I rely fully on the reader, on the assumption that he himself will add the subjective elements that are lacking in the story.
      —Anton Chekhov

Read every sentence aloud to yourself. Nothing which your own ear is dissatisfied with should stand.

Never let the craze for realistic writing run away with you. Any fool can take down commonplace talk verbatim. The highest art demands that while you are true to the spirit of the speaker, you should sift his language in your own mind before committing it to paper. Then bring

the speech out as forcibly as it went in, but so far as your education
permits, put it in better form.
                                        —Robert Louis Stevenson

Writing (Humor)

Take the utmost trouble to find the right thing to say, and then say it
with the utmost levity.
                                        —George Bernard Shaw

When you endeavor to be funny in every line, you place an intolerable
burden not only on yourself but on the reader. You have to allow the
reader to breathe. Whenever George S. Kaufman saw three straight
funny lines in a play that he was directing, he cut the first two.
                                        —William Zinsser

On writing humor: There must be courage; there must be no awe.
There must be criticism, for humor, to my mind, is encapsulated in
criticism. There must be a disciplined eye and a wild mind. There
must be a magnificent disregard of your reader, for if he cannot follow
you, there is nothing you can do about it.
                                        —Dorothy Parker

The playwright Charles MacArthur . . . was finding it difficult to write
visual jokes.
   "What's the problem?" asked Charlie Chaplin.
   "How could I make a fat lady, walking down Fifth Avenue, slip on
a banana peel and still get a laugh?" said MacArthur. "Do I show first
the banana peel, then the fat lady approaching; then she slips? Or do
I show the fat lady first, then the banana peel, and *then* she slips?"
   "Neither," said Chaplin. "You show the fat lady approaching; then
you show the banana peel; then you show the fat lady and the banana
peel together; then she steps *over* the banana peel and disappears down
a manhole."
                                        —Clifton Fadiman

Writing/Playwriting

Say nothing now but what you now should say:
The rest cut out—or use another day.
—Horace

Dramatic writing is to book writing as a telegram is to a letter. The ideal dialogue is that in which each line advances the story at least a fraction of an inch. No line should let it stand still.
—Nunnally Johnson

Every playwright should try acting, just as every judge should spend some weeks in jail to find out what he is handing out to others.
—Erich Maria Remarque

On writing musicals:

GREEN: The most important thing is conflict of characters, their yearning.
COMDEN: Also, what does it mean to you? Don't work on something if you're not inspired by it.
GREEN: A little moment between two people can be worth 20 pages.
—Adolph Green and Betty Comden

Writing (for Novices)

To a novice writer: Write from experience and experience only. Try to be one of the people on whom nothing is lost.
—Henry James

If you want to become a writer it is very necessary to expose yourself to the vicissitudes of life, and it isn't enough to wait for experience to

come to you, you must go out after it. Even if you bark your shins now and then, that again will be grist for your mill. . . . The more highly cultured you can make yourself, the richer your work will be. Few people know how much industry and how much patience are needed to achieve anything worth doing. I speak exactly like Polonius.
          —W. Somerset Maugham

My advice to younger writers is to get a job of some kind—part-time if possible—so that the monthly nut is covered. Trying to write is extremely difficult all by itself. If you add financial pressure to the artistic pressure, it may become impossible. Young writers should be realistic about these matters and not expect too much, not expect that someone is going to carry them.
          —Frank Conroy

"The great thing about writing": Stay with it . . . ultimately you teach yourself something very important about yourself.
          —Bernard Malamud

Advice to young writers: Be lucky.
          —E. B. White

(See *Authorship, Books, Language/Writing, Literary Composition, Reading, Words*)

Y

Youth

Rejoice, O young man, in thy youth; and let thy heart cheer thee in the days of thy youth, and walk in the ways of thine heart, and in the sight of thine eyes: but know thou, that for all these *things* God will bring thee into judgment. Therefore remove sorrow from thy heart, and put away evil from thy flesh: for childhood and youth *are* vanity.

    —Old Testament
    Ecclesiastes 11:9–10

You will make all kinds of mistakes, but as long as you are generous and true, and also fierce, you cannot hurt the world or even seriously distress her. She was made to be wooed and won by youth.

    —Sir Winston Churchill

What old people tell you you cannot do, you try and find you can. . . . I am convinced that to maintain ourself on this earth is not a hardship, but a pastime, if we may live simply and wisely.

    —Henry David Thoreau

Advice for school: Treat your playmates as Hamlet advises Polonius to treat the players, "according to your own dignity rather than their deserts." If you fly out at everything in them that you disapprove or think done on purpose to annoy you, you lie constantly at the mercy

of their caprice, rudeness or ill-nature. You should be more your own master.
                              —William Hazlitt

Woe to the man whose heart has not learned while young to hope, to live, to love—and to put its trust in life!
                              —Joseph Conrad

INDEX